Ending Auschwitz

Ending Auschwitz

*The Future of Jewish
and Christian Life*

Marc H. Ellis

Westminster/John Knox Press
Louisville, Kentucky

© 1994 Marc H. Ellis

All rights reserved. No part of this book may be reproduced or transmitted in any form or by any means, electronic or mechanical, including photocopying, recording, or by any information storage or retrieval system, without permission in writing from the publisher. For information, address Westminster/John Knox Press, 100 Witherspoon Street, Louisville, Kentucky 40202-1396.

Book and cover design by Drew Stevens

Cover illustration: Auschwitz, *acrylic by Martin Rollins*

First edition

Published by Westminster/John Knox Press
Louisville, Kentucky

This book is printed on acid-free paper that meets the American National Standards Institute Z39.48 standard. ∞

PRINTED IN THE UNITED STATES OF AMERICA
9 8 7 6 5 4 3 2 1

Library of Congress Cataloging-in-Publication Data

Ellis, Marc H.
   Ending Auschwitz : the future of Jewish and Christian life / Marc
H. Ellis. — 1st ed.
      p.   cm.
   Includes bibliographical references.
   ISBN 0-664-25501-9 (alk. paper)

   1. Holocaust, Jewish (1939–1945)—Influence. 2. Judaism—
Relations—Christianity—1945–   3. Christianity and other
religions—Judaism—1945–   I. Title.
D804.3.E48 1994
940.53'18—dc20
                                                     93-34040

To Richard Rubenstein
On the Occasion of His Seventieth Birthday

And to my teachers
at Florida State University:
Leo Sandon
Lawrence Cunningham
Charles Wellborn
Walter Moore
Charles Swain
Paul Piccard
William Miller

[postmarked September 15, 1943]

Christine,

Opening the Bible at random I find this: "The Lord is my high tower." I am sitting on my rucksack in the middle of a full freight car. Father, Mother and Mischa are a few cars away. In the end, the departure came without warning. On sudden special orders from the Hague. We left the camp singing, Father and Mother firmly and calmly, Mischa too. We shall be traveling for three days. Thank you for all your kindness and care. Friends left behind will still be writing to Amsterdam; perhaps you will hear something from them. Or from my last letter from camp.

Good-bye for now from the four of us,

Etty

This postcard, thrown out of the train by Etty Hillesum, a young Dutch Jew, on September 7, was found by farmers outside Westerbork camp and posted by them. Etty Hillesum died in Auschwitz on November 30, 1943.

July 18, 1991

And now, as the screams grow weaker, as they change to a kind of sob-bing, wailing, you know that from this moment on nothing will ever again be as it was. Because a person who has heard the screams of an-other person being tortured is already a different person. . . . A person who has heard the screams of another person being tortured incurs an obligation.

Ari Shavit, Israeli Army Reserve, Gaza Beach Detention Camp for Palestinian Political Prisoners

Contents

Preface

This book signals a completion of what has become in retrospect a trilogy, beginning in 1987 with *Toward a Jewish Theology of Liberation*, and continued in 1990 with *Beyond Innocence and Redemption: Confronting the Holocaust and Israeli Power*. In this trilogy, I wrestle with some of the critical issues of contemporary Jewish and Christian life, in particular the issues of Jewish and Christian religiosity after Auschwitz and 1492, two events that are historical and contemporary in their relevance. Perhaps the term relevance is inadequate to the events and their consequences, for both events carry the burden of mass dislocation and death, historically and into the present. Both mark Jewish and Christian religiosity in deep and compelling ways.

I do not attempt to offer an exhaustive account of either the Holocaust or 1492, or their political, cultural, and religious consequences. Rather, I attempt to share with my readers a point of view that comes from my own experience of these two events as a Jew born in the first generation after the Holocaust, one who has also experienced some aspects of contemporary Christian life. As part of an ongoing conversation, this book developed from a trip to Auschwitz in the spring of 1992, when I was invited by the Oxford Centre for Postgraduate Hebrew Studies to join a delegation of Jewish scholars and intellectuals. Recorded here are some of my reflections that crystallized on and after what became for me a journey of endings and, as significant, new beginnings.

This book is dedicated to Professor Richard Rubenstein, my teacher, on the occasion of his seventieth birthday; he was with our delegation at Auschwitz. Because he initiated me into this journey years ago, my debt to him is enormous. This book is also dedicated to my other teachers in the Department of Religion at Florida State University who were equally instrumental in this journey: Professors Leo Sandon, Lawrence Cunningham, Charles Wellborn, Walter Moore, and Charles Swain. I am greatly indebted to this entire department for the model of learning and search they embodied and passed on to me. In this regard, I also want to thank Professors Paul Piccard and William Miller, who shared with me their knowledge and, of equal importance, their way of life.

As is noted in this book, my experience as a professor at the Maryknoll School of Theology has helped to expand my world beyond Judaism and America. During the past fourteen years at Maryknoll, a Catholic missionary community known for its concern for and involvement with struggling peoples around the world, I have met and traveled with so many people who have influenced my life that it is impossible to mention all of them. I am particularly grateful to the Superior Generals who have led Maryknoll during my tenure at the school: the Reverends James Noonan, William Boetler, and Kenneth Thessing. I am also grateful for the support and friendship of the Reverend John Halbert, president of the School of Theology, who, among many other acts of support, funded my travel to Auschwitz. The students in my course "The Future of Religious Resistance and Affirmation" first heard these ideas before and after my travel to Auschwitz; their solidarity with my journey was extremely important to me. I want to thank the students who have been part of my life over the past years: Patricia Martinez, Mark Chmiel, Agnes Ballesteros, Paul Hansen, Donald Steele, Karen Root, Mary Manning, Leo Kazeri, and Wangiri. Nancy Kennedy typed a portion of this manuscript.

Of special significance to me has been the witness and friendship of Rosemary Ruether and Herc Ruether. They have become my friends on the deepest level, standing by me in difficult moments, especially relating to the issue of Israel and Palestine. I am indebted to James Cone for encouraging my work and for his own work, which I have been reading for over two decades and which has influenced me tremendously.

I want to acknowledge Jeffries Hamilton and the staff of Westminster/John Knox Press for their early support of the possibilities of this book and for their encouragement throughout the publication process.

Finally, I want to thank Ann M. McDonald, first and final editor of this work, and my son Aaron, both of whom figure prominently in the journey this book reflects.

1

Preparing for Auschwitz

In the summer of 1991, I received an invitation to travel to Auschwitz as part of a delegation of Jewish scholars and intellectuals. The purpose of the delegation was to consult with the museum staff of Auschwitz about the narrative of Jewish suffering presented to the public. Over 700,000 people visit Auschwitz yearly, and the new democratic government in Poland was eager to update and expand the museum's scope and sensitivity, focusing for the first time on the fact that the vast majority of those killed at Auschwitz were Jews.[1]

Though the task seemed simple, past Jewish delegations and contemporary Polish national sympathies made this task arduous, one very nearly requiring the skills and sensitivity inherent to diplomacy. The Carmelite convent controversy in 1989–90, with the resulting Jewish protest and Polish Cardinal Glemp's sermonizing, fanned the flames of discord rather than mediated a difficult moment in Jewish-Polish relations. The conflict grew from a shared moment of suffering, with each group accusing the other of intrigue and using the sacred ground of suffering over against the other. For the Poles, Auschwitz is a symbol of national suffering and resistance; for the Jews, it is the quintessential symbol of the attempt to annihilate all of Jewish life. We, as Jewish scholars and intellectuals rather than representatives of Jewish organizations and religious bodies, were called together to discern and, in tandem with the museum staff, to suggest ways to mitigate the conflict, perhaps even to point a way out of the quagmire. Organized by

Jonathan Webber and the Oxford Centre for Postgraduate Hebrew Studies, the delegation gathered at Auschwitz in April 1992 under the title "The Future of Auschwitz." In the delegation were well-known and significant Holocaust historians and theologians such as David Roskies of Jewish Theological Seminary, Michael Marrus of the University of Toronto, and my former teacher, Richard Rubenstein of Florida State University. Also included were prominent rabbis such as David Rosen of Israel, Dow Marmur of Toronto, and Jonathan Magonet, principal of Leo Baeck Seminary in London, as well as the philosopher Gillian Rose of the University of Warwick.[2]

Frankly, I was surprised that I was invited. I am neither prominent nor established and my work is controversial in the Jewish world. During recent years in particular, I have been writing and speaking on the question of how the Holocaust and Holocaust theology impact the Palestinian people. In general, my view is that Jewish Israelis and their supporters in the West often use the memory of the Holocaust to further policies that oppress the Palestinian people. Thus one can understand my surprise at the invitation. If the delegation was to be low-key, even subdued, could I be trusted to concentrate simply on the history of the Holocaust, thereby burying the present use of that history? Of course, this concern raised the question of my own responsibility vis-à-vis our present history as Jews. Could I go to Auschwitz and remain silent? There were as well the potential difficulties in group dynamics. No doubt some of these scholars knew of my work and rejected it. How would they deal with me at Auschwitz, the factory of mass death? As I found out later, there was also the issue of my teaching position at the Maryknoll School of Theology. My theology and my affiliation would be for some at the conference simply too much.

These remained as questions to be pondered as I flew across the Atlantic en route to Auschwitz. Like other members of the delegation, I brought much with me to this place of horror. Traveling to Auschwitz was more a journey than a destination, and this journey was a rendezvous with Jewish history as well as my own.

In many ways, my physical journey to Auschwitz in April 1992 was a continuation of a journey that started in the year of my birth, 1952, just seven years after the Holocaust. Thus I was part of the first Jewish generation to be born after the Holocaust; and, though in North Miami Beach, Florida, it was difficult to understand the enormity of our suffering, my Hebrew school education, starting in 1958, initiated me into the complexities that emerged from this history. At the Orthodox synagogue Temple Young Israel and later at the Conservative synagogue Beth Torah, I was informed that I was part of a surviving generation, a generation that had endured the "mass slaughter" in Europe. This

"mass slaughter" had yet to be named, and it stood before our consciousness as something raw and undefined, but nonetheless tangible. Holocaust as a naming of the event did not emerge until the mid to late 1960s.
Yet even without a name, the devastation in Europe charged us with
the task of surviving and continuing the Jewish tradition, a task I recall
as being communicated by my Hebrew school teachers and my first
rabbi's gentle insistence. The background of slaughter and survival—
the teaching of the Jewish tradition itself—was, of course, sorely tested
by the surrounding secular American culture and by a generation of
Jewish adults, my family included, who struggled to make it in this culture and economy. What we were taught during the day in public
school by non-Jews was the dream of America and progress; during af-
ternoons and weekends we were initiated into a world of Hebrew and
prophets and mass suffering. Understandably, my Hebrew school
teachers were ill prepared to bridge these two profoundly different realities, as were we as mere youngsters.

And yet I remember those days with fondness, especially Temple
Young Israel. The synagogue was housed in a small wooden structure.
The teachers were so few and the finances so meager that we six-year-
olds often studied with those twice our age. The financial situation en-
sured that the rabbi was part-time, and though he worked another job
to support his family he made time to visit with us individually. I wonder now whether he was "properly" trained with a seminary certificate.
He was, as I recall, decidedly lacking in professional accommodations:
he had no separate office or study and no personal secretary. Instead,
he spent most of his time relating to us the stories of our tradition and
with a style that was unforgettable. The stories of Abraham and the destruction of the idols, of Moses and the journey of the Israelites through
the wilderness, came alive for us then and have remained with me into
my adult years.

Though the destruction of the Jewish people was there in the background, the tradition was handed down whole and intact, as if it was
too soon for my teachers to understand that the slaughter in Europe
had irreparably shattered it. That understanding came later. As a child I
experienced the synagogue only as small and unpretentious, with a
warmth that made it easy to embrace my heritage. By the time of my
bar mitzvah in 1965, the conservative synagogue to which I had transferred had grown to a thousand families; the properly accredited rabbi
was seen from a distance. Attendance at synagogue became a chore,
something from which to flee.

There was little mention of Israel in my early years at Hebrew
school, and some who did mention it referred to it as Palestine. Like the
Holocaust, Israel was present but as yet unnamed and unrecognized for

the central role it was to play for Jews. In the months before my bar mitzvah, we had a teacher who had arrived from Israel; we experienced her as foreign in look and accent. She was introduced as having smuggled weapons during the war for Israeli independence, an action we as a class thought quite intriguing. Yet looking back, I suspect that we marveled more at her participation in war than we identified with her struggle for Jewish independence. It is strange, in retrospect, that we were never told where she was born. Was she descended from a Jewish family who settled in Palestine during the early mandate period? Or, more likely, was she part of a family who had fled Europe during the Holocaust and arrived in Palestine as survivors of the Holocaust? Neither were we apprised of the journey that led her to our classroom. Was she part of the first wave of European Jews who immigrated to Israel and then left Israel for America? The questions I have now were hardly formed then. Mrs. Meir—her life, her past, her look, her accent, her very being—was unknown and, quite frankly, totally foreign to us.

Two years later, in June 1967, the Jewish world changed radically, and the Holocaust and Israel assumed such center stage that Mrs. Meir became to my memory the archetypal Jew, one not to be mistaken as to who she was in our experience. It was the Israeli-Arab war, or what later became known as the Six-Day War, that dramatically changed Jewish identity and in the coming years did the same for Jewish theology. I recall those days vividly. Away at a working class summer camp in Ocala, Florida, the only Jew, I listened at night to my transistor radio, following the details of this war, which was at once remote and near. To be sure, I hardly knew where Israel was geographically or the concrete history of its founding; I knew even less about the horrid quality of war, even one that lasted only six days. As a teenager, however, I recognized intuitively what others, older and wiser, argued symbolically and theologically—that the victory of 1967 was somehow a response to the Holocaust and that a deeply wounded people had triumphed. Far away from the battlefield I felt an inner strength, a pride about being Jewish. Paradoxically, it was in this triumph that the real tragedy of the Holocaust was named. It was as if a long-buried hurt, a devastating wound, burst open in a miraculous victory. I hardly realized it then that a new Judaism would form from these two events and that the next Jewish generation would experience a more certain, sometimes militant, identity than I knew as a child.[3]

Even then, however, a jarring note sounded. With the end of the war, Jewish tourism to Israel exploded. Many of the tours sponsored by Jewish organizations aimed at recruiting reluctant or passive supporters of the Jewish state or at least energizing them in their support of the state. One of these tourists was my former Hebrew school teacher who worked part-time at odd jobs to supplement his income. After return-ing from Israel, he was building bookshelves in our home and ap-proached me to discuss his recent trip. I listened attentively to the wonders he spoke of: the re-creation of Jewish political life, the revival of Hebrew, the rebuilding of the Jewish working class and Jewish cul-ture. Recently, I had read in *Time* magazine about the plight of Palestin-ian refugees, historically in the 1948 war and more recently in the 1967 war. I was unfamiliar with the term *Palestinian* and found it difficult to place "our" victory and their tragedy into a coherent picture. So I inno-cently inquired of my teacher if he had met any Palestinians and if he had, what he thought of them. I immediately became the object of his anger, an almost uncontrollable outburst. After a few moments he stalked away, leaving with the comment, "What could you possibly know? You have never been there."

Such a scolding and parting statement only served to whet my ap-petite for a visit to this unknown place, a visit I successfully achieved five years later in 1973. But that is to get ahead of the story, for then I was much more involved in finishing high school and preparing for col-lege. In those days, northern universities discriminated against students from southern high schools, so most of my applications were rejected. The school I wanted to attend, American University in Washington, D.C., which intrigued me because John F. Kennedy had given his fa-mous foreign policy lecture there after becoming president, accepted me. But the scholarship offered was too small, so I instead decided to at-tend Florida State University in Tallahassee, declining an acceptance at the University of Florida because too many of my friends were already in attendance there. I wanted to experience a different setting.

The adjustment to Florida State and to Tallahassee was difficult in many ways. Chief among these was Tallahassee's southern culture, something I had not experienced in my Jewish neighborhood in North Miami Beach, populated largely by transplanted northerners. At the same time I wondered whether I could do college work satisfactorily, and the panoply of courses offered made choosing difficult. Though boldly declaring myself a political science major, I also registered for an introductory course in religion. Here I was initiated into a diversity of religious persuasions, including Buddhism and Hinduism, and reli-gious thinkers such as Martin Buber and James Cone. It was also in this class that I learned of a lecture by a new member of the religious stud-ies department, Richard Rubenstein, who was to speak on the Holo-caust and contemporary Jewish life.

As a freshman, I was totally ignorant as to Rubenstein's status. Though he was a new faculty member, after hearing him speak I felt cer-tain that he had been at the university forever. Because of his self-assurance and eloquence, I could hardly fathom his difficult and exilic journey. What I did know was that he was speaking and naming the questions that had been in the background of my childhood. That night he named for me, as he named for countless others, the mass slaughter of Jews as the Holocaust. At the same time he pronounced the end of Jewish traditional belief in the God of history as unjustifiable after the Holocaust, a position hardly addressed in my Hebrew school education. More than the details of his theology, the importance of Rubenstein for me was that he had taken on these difficult questions as the essential task of the surviving generation. I was drawn to this task almost immediately, as something deeply my own. The following semester I registered for his class on the sociology of religion, where among other books we read Peter Berger's *Sacred Canopy*. Though not assigned as a text, I devoured Rubenstein's then recently published (now classic) *After Auschwitz: Radical Theology and Contemporary Judaism*. Unbeknownst to me, though certainly present in his lectures, Rubenstein was writing a book on Paul that would be equally important in my journey. Published in 1972, *My Brother Paul* represents, among other things, Rubenstein's break with normative Judaism. If *After Auschwitz* defined the inability to believe, *My Brother Paul* was for Rubenstein an encounter with another Jew who had little choice but to follow his own experience. For Paul, it was the risen Christ as the salvific event that brought him beyond Judaism; for Rubenstein, it was psychoanalysis that rescued him from despair and promised a healing after Auschwitz and a tormented religious and personal life.[4]

Yet despite this healing, one often experienced Rubenstein as raw and angry. His ideas were clear and incisive; his theology bleak, almost despairing. For me at the age of eighteen, being opened to the pain of Jewish history and the prospect of a godless world, it was difficult to accept the end point of Rubenstein's struggle with God. Was the universe devoid of God and compassion? Were justice and community illusory? In fact, Rubenstein did believe in a God from the Jewish mystical tradition, a God who contracted to allow human life to exist and then in the end consumed all into eternal nothingness. I can recall Rubenstein pronouncing belief in this divinity and the shudder that ran through me hearing him speak of it.[5]

It was at this point that I encountered Christianity for the first time in my life. After my introductory course in religion and my subsequent courses with Rubenstein, I decided to major in religion and was taken in by Leo Sandon, a Protestant theologian and then chaplain at the university, and Lawrence Cunningham, an ex-priest and expert on the Catholic tradition, who is now chair of the theology department at the University of Notre Dame. As I attended their courses and conversed with them after class, Sandon and Cunningham probably had little idea how profoundly ignorant I was of this important world religion and of theologians such as Reinhold Niebuhr and John Courtney Murray, whom they brought so vividly to life. I also attended a course on southern religion, co-taught with a neighboring African-American university, Florida A&M. Visiting such an institution was an enlightening experience for me, and it was in this milieu that I first read the works of the African-American theologian James Cone. Though Cone quoted Niebuhr and Tillich, I recognized even then a profound difference in tone and style; his view of white Christianity as demonic introduced a jarring note into my studies. At the same time, Cone's vision of a black Christ energized me, as did the ambiance at Florida A&M. I realized that this was another world, one that took me years to place in perspective or come to understand. Soon after, I heard Rosemary Radford Ruether lecture and later attended a small group discussion with her. The contemporary feminist movement was new and left unnoticed in my studies. What intrigued me about Ruether was her strength and insistence. Like Cone, Ruether was mapping out a territory I understood only years later, but to which I was drawn immediately. Finally, in my senior year, quite by chance I came to know William Miller, a southern historian who had recently written a book on Dorothy Day and the Catholic Worker movement, a woman and a movement that emphasized spirituality and social justice in the commitment to live and work with the poor. Though these movements presented a strange world to me, the force of their theologians and activists intrigued me.[6]

Toward the end of my senior year, in April 1974, I met Dorothy Day and like so many others was fascinated by her and drawn to the life she lived. I was neither attracted nor repulsed by her orthodox Catholicity, for I understood so little about it at the time. Rather, it was her presence and the sense that she had raised questions about God in the midst of suffering that drew me to her and to the Catholic Worker movement in New York City, where, after my graduation in 1974, I lived and worked for ten months.

My experience at the Catholic Worker was difficult, to say the least. To be among Catholics—that is, in a specifically Catholic environment—was a culture shock of greater proportion than my introduction to southern life. The symbolism of the cross and the Christian language used were reminders of the oppression of my own people. Could I trust Christians to shelter me (and my own people) if anti-Semitism took active political form now? Was Christianity always and forever an oppressor religion? Or was a transformation taking place, a renewal or retrieval of an essential message untainted by anti-Jewishness? After absorbing these views in my childhood and studying them at university, I wanted to find this out for myself.

Dealing with the internal questions of Christian oppression and renewal was one thing; dealing with the abject poverty and violence in New York City was quite another. The Catholic Worker is situated on the poverty-stricken Bowery; facing the homeless and the lost was my first genuine contact with human suffering. To see and tend to people who were hungry and homeless, who were bleeding and afflicted with mental illness was a street introduction to ideas presented abstractly in sociology texts. I can still recall the young mother with two children who came to us for shelter and the many others for whom we had no room. I had read about Auschwitz; at the Catholic Worker I experienced what Michael Harrington labeled "the other America."[7]

I further experienced this America in the St. Thomas Projects in New Orleans, Louisiana, in 1976, where, under the auspices of Hope House, I spent a year organizing and teaching poor African-American women. As an organizer I was a complete failure; yet the people received me into their homes, where I met their families and heard their stories. I was somewhat more successful in teaching a course on African-American history. Twice a week I joined ten women gathered at Hope House, where we spoke about the history of African-American people from their roots in Africa to their experience of the middle passage and slavery. It was a moving time for me as the women, some of whom were illiterate, came faithfully to share their stories, listen to the reading of slave narratives, and then for the first time speak of this history with their own children. I gave little; what I received in being with these women was a new feeling of the rhythms of my own history, including a deeper appreciation of the Exodus story and our own peoplehood. And I began to appreciate at a deeper level the suffering of African-Americans and their special place in American and world history.

The Catholic Worker and Hope House had a profound effect on my life and led me ultimately in 1980 to the Maryknoll School of Theology, where I teach today. Maryknoll transported me from the streets of New York City and New Orleans to the global dimensions of poverty and the struggles of the oppressed, as well as to theologies of liberation that seek to mitigate, if not eliminate, the misery often buried under the myth of twentieth-century progress. These experiences of Christianity at the Catholic Worker, Hope House, and Maryknoll, as well as my subsequent travels to Africa, Asia, Latin America, and the Middle East, were crucial to my development as a person and a thinker, for they broadened my experience beyond the Jewish world. Paradoxically, they also drew me to a deeper understanding and commitment to Jewish life as a self-critical Jewish religious thinker, and resulted in, among other works, my books *Toward a Jewish Theology of Liberation* and *Beyond Innocence and Redemption: Confronting the Holocaust and Israeli Power*. The experience of being with

Christian theologians and activists who were attempting to confront empire—empire that often carried the label "Christian"—forced me to confront the post-1967, post-Lebanon, and post-intifada Israeli state. Were we, a previously oppressed people, now to become the oppressors? As survivors of Christian domination, were we now to sponsor a Jewish state ruling over the Palestinian people? Could our love for and return to Jerusalem, so fervently prayed for over the millennia, become instead a celebrated militancy and the creation of an imperial Jerusalem?[8]

Surely this is what I witnessed in 1973 when I first traveled to Israel, and what I understood more deeply during a visit in 1984. In 1973 I saw these Palestinians about whom I had read and who had so angered my Hebrew school teacher in 1968. When I arrived in Israel I knew immediately that something was profoundly wrong. It was clear that in Israeli society Jews were more than equal; they were dominant over a minority who were considered second class, a minority who were, to understate the case, unwanted. By 1984, however, when I returned after a decade and a half of the occupation of East Jerusalem, the West Bank, and Gaza, the situation was even clearer. Israeli Jews, with the support of almost the entire Jewish world, had embarked on a policy of expropriation and displacement reminiscent of policies that had been pursued against us in the past. I witnessed a bravado and a militarism among Jews that were alien to my upbringing and my early Jewish training. And as I met Palestinians face-to-face for the first time—with their families, aspirations, and dreams—I wondered if this treatment of another people, the desire to end their presence in our midst, might spell as well the end of our own tradition of suffering and struggle. Could we permanently dispossess another people and call this our own liberation? Were we becoming mirror images of those who oppressed us so insistently and totally, with all the attendant justification we were now developing? And did the vehemence with which we held forth on the question of Israel and the Palestinians have anything to do with—in fact might it spring from—our unresolved history with the West and with Christianity? I wondered whether our defeated "enemy," the Palestinian, really was a stand-in for the defeat we longed to deliver to those who had oppressed us for over a thousand years.

Meeting the "enemy" in what I came to see as Israel/Palestine and working with the "enemy" at Maryknoll made such designations more difficult. Palestinians, indigenous to the land, were displaced by my people. Who then was the enemy of whom? And if the emergency years of the post-Holocaust period can for the moment be put aside, how can we describe the decades after 1967, which have seen the constant expansion of the state of Israel and the renewed exile and suffering of the Palestinian people? My experience of Christians around the world also indicated a renewal of thought and image. Many of the Christians I met were victims of the same dominant Christians who had victimized us. Did not a majority of Christians experience the empires blessed by Christianity as a violence that uprooted them physically and psychologically and forced them to assume the religion of their oppressors? If we can see that in the recent past we as Jews were almost annihilated in the heart of Christian Europe, could we also see that a majority of Christians were in fact conquered by the gospel? And just as important, the struggle continues in the present. In my classes over the years at Maryknoll and in my travels throughout the world with those conquered by the gospel—those who fight today as Christians for freedom from oppressive power—the stories of the Holocaust, so vivid in my history, were too often replayed. I could not help but bring these contemporary stories of torture and the disappeared, of resistance and massacre, to this ominous place, Auschwitz.

As I left for Auschwitz, these experiences mingled freely and in contradictory ways. The Jewish past was haunting; the contemporary Jewish community, at least its leadership, was relentless in pursuing dissenters, one of whom was me. At one level, teaching at a Catholic school of theology with a global outlook provided a way of expanding my horizons and a safe haven to pursue my thoughts and activities. But if the Jewish world was failing in its response to the Palestinians, Christianity, at least in the West, was similarly failing in its responsibility to its own history of oppression and empire. Was the failure of the Jewish community to come to terms with its misuse of power after the Holocaust mirrored by Western Christianity's unwillingness to confront its misuse of power in the event of 1492, which continues with so many consequences today? 1492 symbolizes the rise of Europe and the globalization of Christianity, when two thirds of the world, settled, cultured, and with their own religious systems, became poor and to a large extent Christian. Realizing that the churches supported and benefited from this expansion of Europe and European Christianity, and in some ways support and benefit from this legacy today, I wonder what real possibility there is for Christian renewal.

Perhaps it was coincidence that my journey to Auschwitz took place during the five hundredth anniversary of Columbus's voyages, which ultimately brought so much suffering to the Americas and elsewhere. Was it a coincidence that to embark on such an expansion of Europe, the Christianization of Spain spawned years of inquisition that began with the expulsion of Jews and Muslims? Exploring these issues in classes at Maryknoll helped crystallize my thoughts. Could the havoc wrought on those outside of Europe, by Europeans in the name of Christ in 1492 and after, be the same violence suffered by Jews within

Europe in 1492 and after, culminating in the devastation of our people at Auschwitz?

Preparing a lecture two days before leaving for Auschwitz, I could not shake this haunting thought, which is in fact a crystallization of my experience in the Jewish and Christian worlds: that there is a continuity of 1492 and Auschwitz; they are intimately linked together, and the consequences of this continuing symbiosis have been faced by neither community in their activities or religious thought. The continuity poses a series of questions, historical and contemporary, not the least of which is whether the movement of destruction and oppression will extend and expand into the future or whether there is a path beyond 1492 and Auschwitz. Are we as Christians and Jews destined to remain in the terrifying dynamic of 1492 and Auschwitz?

2

Auschwitz, Israel, and the End of Jewish Innocence

Our guide had warned us that though we as Jewish scholars and intellectuals had for years thought and written about Auschwitz, our arrival at that place would contain many surprises. Leaving for Auschwitz on the one-hour bus ride from our hotel in Krakow, I thought of our journey in different ways. We were for the most part silent, surveying the surrounding countryside and the villages, wondering how the occupants, then and now, felt about Jews and what responsibility, if any, they had in the mass murder of Jews. The scenery transported us back half a century when Jews like ourselves traveled to Auschwitz to die.

We had previously been informed that although Auschwitz is often portrayed in Jewish literature as a barren burial ground, it is in actuality almost completely intact. Building after building remains standing, so from the roadway Auschwitz appears almost a picturesque village. The Nazis had originally planned to conceal their crimes at Auschwitz, but the speed of the Soviet military advance in early 1945 made this impossible. Though partially successful in destroying the principal gas chambers and crematoria, the Nazis left most of the buildings intact: watch towers, barracks, electrified barbed-wire fences, guardhouses, the railway lines. The gate through which the prisoners entered, with its German sign "Arbeit Macht Frei" ("Work Makes One Free"), remains as it was then. Haunting as is this picture of Auschwitz, standing as it was in the time of mass murder, one is unprepared for the jarring juxtaposition of tourist attractions with the site of mass death. To accommodate these visitors Auschwitz has, among other things, several book shops, a cafeteria, a tearoom, a lost-luggage counter, a post office, and a hotel. I could not help but ruminate, as no doubt others did as well, on the difficulty of journeying to the dead in the context of a modern tourist site.[1]

There remained yet another sorting out to do as well. The intact Auschwitz was in the language of the camp "Auschwitz," a concentration camp essentially for non-Jewish Poles and other Eastern Europeans; Auschwitz-Birkenau, a death camp, was the final destination for more than a million Jews. Situated approximately two miles from Auschwitz, Auschwitz-Birkenau is as Jews imagine it: destroyed, barren—the fields littered with the ashes of incinerated Jewish bodies. Auschwitz contains the museum that narrates the story of dispossession and death and thus is the more frequented site. Because the tour of Auschwitz takes two or three hours to complete, most visitors do not make their way to Birkenau. Thus we immediately stumbled upon a dilemma: Birkenau, nearly devoid of tourists, evokes the reality that Auschwitz, busy and built, diverts. On the other hand, the overwhelmingly Jewish aspect of the Holocaust is relatively neglected by both the visitors and the museum staff itself. Should we suggest a focus on Auschwitz-Birkenau for the mostly non-Jewish visitors, so as to inform them of our understanding of the tragedy, or should we suggest leaving it as it is for the Jews and others who find their way past the crowds and the museum? Should the administration at Auschwitz transform Birkenau into a tour site or maintain it as a memorial?[2]

In a sense, these were administrative policy decisions with ramifications for the technical side of how to devise a present narrative history of Auschwitz and Birkenau. But already by the afternoon of our first day we sensed that the presentation of the camp was involved in much deeper questions of Jewish and Polish, Jewish and Christian memory. Standing in the guard tower of Birkenau overlooking the train tracks and the platform where Jews disembarked, and from there seeing also the rubble of the crematoria, reciting the Kaddish, the Jewish prayer for the dead, one knew the larger issues involved.

Joining in the prayer, *kippah* in place, was Richard Rubenstein, my teacher, who had years earlier proclaimed his inability, because of Auschwitz, to believe in the Jewish God of history. I wondered whether Rubenstein would join the others and, as he did, I found no contradiction. He had returned to the grounding of his religious life—indeed its shattering—as an intellectual and as a Jew. Nearing his seventieth birthday, it seemed to me at last that Rubenstein, although maintaining his perspective and his anger, was folding his own life into the larger framework of Jewish history.

Surely Rubenstein, with others of his generation, had analyzed the consequences of Auschwitz for the Jewish world and beyond. At the guard tower, we as a delegation surveyed a past event of enormous import. Still this event was more than historical, for through the interpretation, indeed the *naming* of mass death as Holocaust, we were also marking a Jewish present defined by the past. Who could be at Auschwitz without thinking of one of its former inmates, Elie Wiesel, or recalling the seminal work on the Holocaust of two of our delegates, David Roskies' *Against the Apocalypse: Responses to Catastrophe in Modern Jewish Culture* and Alvin Rosenfeld's *A Double Dying: Reflections on Holocaust Literature*? Could one be at Auschwitz as a Jew and not see it at least partially through the prism of Rubenstein's *After Auschwitz*?[3]

Thus the site of mass death was past *and* present, a place of endings *and* beginnings. In diverse ways Wiesel, Roskies, Rosenfeld, Rubenstein, and many others carried this death into an unpredictable present. Still the haunting question remained, as suggested by the title of our gathering, "The Future of Auschwitz." If there was a past and present at Auschwitz, was there also a future? And was the present, as articulated in *After Auschwitz* and by those other historians and theologians, already also a past with new issues diminishing its relevance for the future? It was a troubling thought as I walked along the railroad tracks inside Birkenau, but one I could not shake. The Jewish world, once overwhelmed by Auschwitz, had now embarked on a way of life that impacts the lessons we draw from this experience. And these lessons, unspoken by our delegation, remained to be articulated. But with what words and in what place? Could I speak of our power in Israel vis-à-vis Palestinians while standing at the pond of ashes where burned bodies by the thousands were dumped? Or as I touched the pile of silverware confiscated from Jews and scattered in the field near the pond, was it imperative to speak?

Clearly, if at least in the beginning unmentioned, Israel was in the air at Auschwitz. It is almost impossible to be at Auschwitz, the site of our destruction, without thinking of the place that many Jews believe to be a response to Auschwitz. The utter powerlessness of the victims of Auschwitz was before us, and the modern methodical and powerful way of disposing of Jews developed by the Nazis was evident everywhere. Israel was also physically there, for during the afternoon of our first day at Auschwitz we happened upon an official delegation from Israel with a cabinet minister delivering a speech. Soldiers from the Israeli armed forces stood at attention, each holding an Israeli flag. Television cameras were recording the event for Israeli television, and a group of about thirty Israeli visitors gathered around singing their national anthem. Spoken in Hebrew, the message was clear: Israel is our security against the occurrence of another holocaust.

On the second day of our time at Auschwitz, Israel was placed even more vividly before us. It happened in the morning as we waited in the hotel lobby before boarding our bus for Auschwitz. Standing with members of our group who were politically progressive, we were joined by someone who had just heard a report on the BBC that a plane carrying Yassir Arafat, chairperson of the Palestine Liberation Organization, was missing in a desert area inside Libya. It was presumed that his plane had crashed and that Arafat was dead. As I listened to this news, I was stunned. My first thought was simply, "I am at Auschwitz and Arafat is dead." My second thought was of the Palestinians I had come to know over the years and how important Arafat was as a symbol of the Palestinian struggle for nationhood. Obviously, Arafat is controversial inside and outside of the Palestinian community, but his place in Palestinian history is secure. As people talked about the news I withdrew into silence, thinking that perhaps we should all observe a moment of contemplation in his memory and out of respect for the Palestinian people, who had suffered so long and had now lost their leader. However, I quickly realized that such a suggestion was not only out of place with our delegation, but could not be received with any depth. Instead, the discussion revolved around the probable effect of Arafat's demise on Israeli public opinion. At that moment, immersed in electoral politics, Israel would soon choose either a continuation of the Yitzhak Shamir-led Likud government or turn to a Labor government under Yitzhak Rabin. Would Arafat's death and the ensuing uncertainty of Palestinian leadership reinforce Shamir's policy of occupation and settlement, or would it convince the Israeli public to compromise on the territories, thus lessening to some extent the harshness of the occupation and the policy of settlement, to Rabin's benefit?

As we boarded the bus minutes later, I was shocked, almost numbed, by the superficiality of the discussion. In remembering Auschwitz, had we forgotten what it was like to be on the underside of someone else's history? Could we not remember the importance of our own leaders to our people nor recognize that, despite the dislocation and bloodshed, or rather because of it, Jewish history and Palestinian history were now intertwined and the death of Arafat had a deeper meaning to us as Jews than its impact on a political election? In our ability to mourn our own, represented at that moment by our journey to Auschwitz, we had forgotten how to mourn with others at their loss, which was in a paradoxical way *our* loss as well.

But this is in a sense to get ahead of the story. As we drove to Auschwitz on that second day, I realized that to understand the reaction to the story of Arafat's presumed death we had to understand the way we remember the death of our own. And this remembrance had in the beginning little to do with the importance of Israel or the demonizing of Palestinians. If the analysis of the massacre of European Jews was understandably self-involved from the outset, this preoccupation with the Jewish community led to questions, sometimes radical questions, that were shared across community boundaries. In a strange way, some of the earlier reflections on the Holocaust, as illustrated in the work of Hannah Arendt, were deep and radical, and less isolating and demeaning to others than some of the more current writings on the event. Two crucial thoughts resonated within me: first, that our distance from the Holocaust, instead of initiating a process of healing, had in fact hardened our anger; and second, that the extreme isolation we experienced in Auschwitz as it occurred in history was carried forth almost fifty years later, at the same time that we were more politically integrated and secure than perhaps any time in the history of the Jewish people. If our objective circumstances had changed radically in nearly half a century, our subjective understandings remained as they were, or perhaps were even worse than at the time of the liberation of the death camps.[4]

God and the Death Camps

In some sense the radicalization of Jewish anger and isolation can be seen as a generational issue in reverse. The literature of survivors was for the most part autobiographical and descriptive in its portrayal of the depravity inflicted upon Jews; it was analytical about how Jews perished and struggled to survive within that depravity. A recurring theme in the early literature is the difficulty of describing the world of the camps to those outside them in time and place. Some refer to the camps as the concentration camp universe, as if it were another planet. A French survivor, David Rousset, labeled Auschwitz "The Other Kingdom." Though the particular event was emphasized and the particular people named, the struggle within the concentration camps and the death camps was often proposed as a universal question as well. One thinks of Bruno Bettelheim's early work *The Informed Heart: Autonomy in a Mass Age*, published in 1960, as well as Victor Frankl's *Man's Search for Meaning*, published in 1959. As survivors and psychologists, Bettelheim and Frankl thought that the camps raised issues germane to Jewish survivors and to all people interested in the human condition in extremis. Similarly, Hannah Arendt's *The Origins of Totalitarianism*, published in 1951, and *Eichmann in Jerusalem: A Report on the Banality of Evil*, published in 1963, engage the dialectic of particular and universal, in a sense opening up the contemporary history of the Jewish people to those interested in the fundamental questions of the human search for meaning, community, and justice.[5]

In the realm of Jewish theology, Abraham Joshua Heschel, who fled Europe in the 1930s, complemented this early work. In his books *Man Is Not Alone: A Philosophy of Religion,* published in 1951, and *God in Search of Man: A Philosophy of Judaism,* published in 1955, Heschel outlined the continuing human dilemmas exaggerated by the ferocity of the contemporary world. Heschel is fascinating in this regard; the experience of the Jews is a particular example of the experience of the human, while the Jewish reclamation of the human and of God is a particular journey, yet one that is shared also by non-Jews. In writing as a Jew, Heschel called for a new alliance to rescue the human, including those whose humanity was being assaulted in the present. His presence in the civil rights movement and his protest against the Vietnam War, his friendship and dialogue with the Protestant theologian Reinhold Niebuhr and the Catholic monk Thomas Merton were for Heschel an extension of the Jewish experience, undiminished and in fact enhanced.[6]

I met Heschel in 1972 when he was invited to lecture at my university. One could almost see the suffering and hope in his face as one formed in the pre-Holocaust world of Eastern Europe and the Holocaust event itself. When we learned of his death several weeks after his visit, I was not surprised. Heschel had looked tired and even older than his sixty-five years. When a student asked him to explain one of his basic theological themes, Heschel looked at the student and gently told him how difficult it was to write and that he should therefore take time to read the words Heschel himself had written. Yet when he spoke these words, they seemed almost resigned, as if he had written all that he could and that it was somehow inadequate. Perhaps it was simply that Heschel came from, and in a sense sought to continue, an Eastern European world that had in fact been destroyed. Could the fatigue evident in his face and body betray this inability to pass on to the next generation a world that no longer existed?

One of Heschel's students at Jewish Theological Seminary in New York was Richard Rubenstein, and I recall that on the day of Heschel's visit Rubenstein was nowhere in sight. Later I learned that Heschel and Rubenstein had parted on less than amiable terms. Surely their differences, at some level, were in the realm of personality, but the larger divergence is evident in their writings. As Heschel wrote essays extolling the memory of the world of Eastern European Jewry and the beauty of the Sabbath and sought to revive the image of the human and God, Rubenstein probed the destruction of that world and these images. The shift can be found in the preface to *After Auschwitz,* in which Rubenstein distances himself from previous theologians and, without naming Heschel, declares independence from theologians like him. Rubenstein writes:

> It would have been better had six million Jews not died, but they have. We cannot restore the religious world which preceded their demise nor can we ignore the fact that the catastrophe has had and will continue to have an extraordinary influence on Jewish life. Although Jewish history is replete with disaster, none has been so radical in its total import as the Holocaust. Our images of God, man and the moral order have been permanently impaired. No Jewish theology will possess even a remote degree of relevance to contemporary Jewish life if it ignores the question of God and the death camps. That is *the question* for Jewish theology in our times. Regrettably most attempts at formulating a Jewish theology since World War II seem to have been written as if the two decisive events of our time for Jews, the death camps and the birth of Israel, had not taken place.[7]

Rubenstein's *After Auschwitz* carries through these insights in radical and enigmatic ways, thus giving birth to a theology of the Holocaust, Holocaust theology, that moved and divided the Jewish community. The division between Heschel and others of his generation is delineated in the preface and the argument that follows: either the Jewish God of history does not exist and therefore should not be considered, or this same God abandoned Jews in their terrible moment of distress and thus should be, in conscience, abandoned. Though Rubenstein then and even sometimes today is grouped with the "death of God" theology movement of the 1960s, his point in *After Auschwitz* is both similar to and distinct from that generation. The question of God's existence is forever debatable; God's objective assistance can be analyzed and judged. After the Holocaust, in which six million innocent Jews were killed, could Jews pray to such a God?[8]

This mutual abandonment of the Jewish people by God and of God by the Jewish people in and after the crisis of the death camps caused Rubenstein to reflect on the history of the Jewish people. For Rubenstein, Jewish tradition, leadership, and theology left the people unprepared for and unable to protect themselves from the violence of the Nazis. Rabbinic Judaism, which emerged in the Jewish defeats of 70 and 135 C.E., was a theology and a politics of a defeated people. In Rubenstein's view, this system left Jews exposed to the violence of many oppressors, the latest of which were the Nazis. The rabbinic system spoke of God's presence even in tribulation and Jewish suffering as a way of demonstrating how far Jews had wandered from divine law.

The rabbis were also Jewish political leaders who because of Jewish theology and Jewish powerlessness often acceded to and bargained with the enemy. In the Holocaust they bargained until it was too late. Thus the entire framework of Jewish life is shattered, and for Rubenstein it is only illusion to carry on with that form in the present.[9]

Rubenstein goes still further in his questioning. If the bond between God and the Jews is broken, and if the bond between Jewish leadership and theology has betrayed the Jewish people to Auschwitz, all that is left is the possibility of human solidarity in the face of overwhelming evil. And yet the death camps were built and operated by human beings. The Enlightenment overthrow of God, which promised a harmonious humanity, paradoxically in Rubenstein's view made the death camps possible. Though developed more thoroughly in his book *The Cunning of History: Mass Death and the American Future*, published in 1975, even in *After Auschwitz* Rubenstein hardly romanticized the fact that after Auschwitz we live in a functionally godless world. Citing Hannah Arendt, Rubenstein writes that in a world devoid of God "the realm of the impossible ceases to exist in such a world; the limitations of reality become a parenthesis to be overthrown."[10]

If anything, Rubenstein's probe of the deepest questions confronting the Jewish people touched off a ferocious debate within the Jewish community. One can see the onset of this debate in its rawest form at the first International Scholars Conference on the German Church Struggle and the Holocaust held at Wayne State University in 1970. Here Elie Wiesel, whose autobiographical account of his experience in Auschwitz, *Night*, had just been translated into English, discarded his prepared remarks to respond directly to a presentation by Rubenstein earlier in the conference. With Rubenstein present, Wiesel challenged Rubenstein's inability to believe in God, or rather, confronted the way Rubenstein spoke of God's responsibility. To be sure, Wiesel affirmed the difficulty he had speaking of God, stating, "I rather speak of men who believed in God or men who denied God." Wiesel found it strange that the philosophy denying God came from other than the survivors themselves. "Those who came out with the so-called God is dead theology, not one of them had been in Auschwitz. Those who had never said it. I have my problems with God, believe me. I have my anger and I have my quarrels and I have my nightmares. But my dispute, my bewilderment, my astonishment is with men."[11]

Instead of representing the brokenness of the tradition, the Holocaust for Wiesel brought out its many strengths. To Rubenstein's insight that the death of millions of innocents for no reason other than that they were Jews deprived Jews even of martyrdom, Wiesel is equally strong in his response: "That is not true. Many Jews, especially the rabbis, could have saved their lives. . . . I think there were two, out of at least fifty thousand rabbis in Eastern Europe, two who chose to escape individually. All the others preferred voluntarily, knowingly, to go with their Jews. How did these rabbis maintain their Jewishness and their humanity? *That* is the wonder. After all, the system was so strong and the whole world was an accomplice!" Finally, Wiesel returns to the question of God, asserting that what the Germans wanted to do was to substitute themselves for the Jewish God. "All the terminology, all the vocabulary testifies to that. And in spite of all, here were these men who remained human and who remained Jewish and went on praying to God. And here I will tell you, Dick, that you don't understand *them* when you say that it is more difficult to live today in a world without God. No! If you want difficulties, choose to live *with* God."[12]

If there was a profound disagreement as to the relevance of the Jewish God and tradition, accentuated in the years ahead to a bitter division, one cause brought Wiesel and Rubenstein together—the state of Israel. Yet even here the bonding betrays significant divergence.

In his talk at the 1970 conference, as earlier in *After Auschwitz*, Rubenstein affirmed the necessity of the state of Israel. According to Rubenstein, in a functionally godless world where even human solidarity is broken, the return of a Jewish population to Israel is a significant event. At the outset, Jews in Israel represent an act of defiance toward a world that has abandoned them and rejection of a tradition of normative Judaism that sought protection in God and bargaining with the oppressive other. Developing a protective state is for Rubenstein an imperative of the Holocaust and a return to a more earthy—pagan— Jewish existence. After Auschwitz, the exile from the Jewish land of origins has come to an end in Israel. "The deepest and most profound of all striving in the individual and the group may indeed be the striving to return to one's place of origin," he stated. "Theologically, that striving may be conjoined with a return to the archaic gods of the place of origin." For Rubenstein, this means the return of the Jews to the "gods of the earth, not the high gods of the sky," pagan gods rooted in the earth rather than the rabbinic god of exile and wandering. Rediscovering the Jewish place on earth and the gods that go with it increases the ability of Jews to defend themselves and necessarily escalates the cost of taking Jewish lives. Still, on the issue that ultimately catapulted Holocaust theology into the normative Judaism of our time, Rubenstein again dissents. He finds that the 1967 Six-Day War represents a necessary military victory against a determined foe rather than a miraculous response to the possibility of a second Auschwitz. As he emphasized in his talk, "*The Six-Day War, tentative as its conclusion may have been, is no royal road back to the God of History.*"[13]

But it was in fact that war which overwhelmed Rubenstein's questions and shifted the emphasis in the discussion of God and land in favor of Wiesel. For Wiesel and others like Emil Fackenheim, the lightning victory was a kind of miracle suggesting the possibility of God's presence; and if this was too strong, it at least demonstrated commitment to the continuation of Jewish life. For Wiesel, Rubenstein was breaking a Jewish continuity at a time of great crisis, as the Jewish people themselves were affirming that continuity. Thus Wiesel saw the 1967 war as a miracle that bode well for the future of the Jewish people; it was not an answer to Auschwitz, but neither was it simply an act of survival or escalating the cost of taking Jewish lives, as Rubenstein wrote. Rather, it was a victory of hope over despair, perhaps even a victory of faith. Wiesel concluded his talk on this understanding of faith after the Holocaust: "But to be a Jew is to have all the reasons in the world to destroy and *not to destroy!* To be a Jew is to have all the reasons in the world to hate the Germans and *not to hate them!* To be a Jew is to have all the reasons in the world to mistrust the church and *not to hate it!*" This was true of the Israelis as well: "Look at Israel; Israelis do not hate the Arabs."[14]

Reflecting on the experience of the Holocaust and its meaning for contemporary Jewish life in 1970, Rubenstein and Wiesel encompass many of the themes that later become part of the acceptable post-Holocaust Jewish discussion. In fact, over the years they blended into a series of seemingly contradictory but in reality complementary aspects of a new Jewish theology. To be sure, the rough edges of Rubenstein—his admitted paganism, for example—were smoothed, and the innocence of Wiesel—the inability of Jews to hate, for example—was contradicted by experience. Even the boycott of Rubenstein by Wiesel and others initiated after the International Scholars Conference was at least partially revoked; in 1987 the Jewish Theological Seminary, Rubenstein's alma mater, granted him an honorary doctorate, citing among his other works *After Auschwitz*. Still the pain of this bruising battle was evident as I listened to his lectures after his return from this conference, and even two decades later as I talked with him at Auschwitz. It was a battle that left Rubenstein bitter toward the Jewish community and ultimately estranged his children from the Jewish fold.

At Auschwitz it was clear that essential aspects of the struggle had been settled—at a cost to be sure—and a new struggle had arisen whose stakes were higher, a struggle for the most part unanticipated by Rubenstein and Wiesel in 1970, the struggle over Israel. In 1970 Rubenstein's presence on the delegation would have caused tremendous problems; in 1992 he was accepted as an honored theologian. The fact of his break with normative Judaism when it was unpopular was later accepted because his critique of normative Judaism rather than his conclusions had ultimately been vindicated by the triumph of Holocaust theology. And Rubenstein had held the line on Israel, the new crisis point, and thus stood guard over a tradition he critiqued and paradoxically helped to recreate.

A Silence on Israel

In a strange way, by the end of our second day at Auschwitz, after the Israeli delegation we had witnessed and the reports of Arafat's death, it seemed to me, at least, that the issue in the background was Israel as much as Auschwitz. Though they had been tied together in 1970, they were joined in the present in a much different way. In 1970 the Jewish community was still celebrating the victory of 1967; intervening years had seen the Yom Kippur War, the Lebanon War, a decade of Likud expansionist policies and, of course, the Palestinian intifada. The miracle was over, and a nightmare was threatening to descend. Even this crisis point had undergone a tremendous transformation of definition: Rubenstein and Wiesel in 1970 postulated the possibility of an Arab victory over Israel in 1967; twenty-five years later, Israel stood as a powerful military occupier, expropriating land, disciplining and displacing Palestinians through the use of the army, which features, among other things, torture and death squads. Was there a sense at Auschwitz, at least subconsciously, that the Jewish liturgy of destruction, about which David Roskies has written so hauntingly and which Rubenstein and Wiesel have articulated so movingly, now includes the Palestinian people whom we have displaced?

On the third day of our visit, the issue of Israel came to the fore, as one of the delegation's tasks was to recommend to the museum officials, after surveying the grounds and the museum exhibits, what improvements might be made. The discussion was wide ranging. For example, the delegation felt that the museum displays and monuments did not show clearly that over 90 percent of those who were murdered at Auschwitz-Birkenau were Jews, and that too many symbols and events of a noncommemorative nature predominated, sometimes without authorization of the staff itself. It was also noted that the book shops had an inadequate selection of books and audiovisual material on Jewish civilization and the Holocaust; the restaurant lacked food prepared according to Jewish dietary law, thus making it difficult for orthodox Jewish visitors to eat at Auschwitz. However, the delegation noted with gratitude that an updated, corrected, and improved visitors guidebook had been issued and that signs in Hebrew were being introduced.[15]

Up to this point the discussion had for the most part been freewheel-ing. When it came to proposing the narrative we would contribute—that is, how, starting from the beginning, the story of Auschwitz should be told—the whole matter became more complex. Would we begin with the Europe of the 1930s and the rise of Nazism, or in the nineteenth-century *shtetls* of Eastern Europe, portraying the vitality of their life be-fore the catastrophe? Would we analyze the Germany of that period through the defeat of World War I, the depression, the combination of anti-Semitism and modern technology? Should we see the rise of the Nazis and the Holocaust as unique or within the context of global his-torical patterns? Another option would be to abandon the modern em-phasis and look almost exclusively at the travails of Jewish history, the beginning of our two-thousand-year exile from the Holy Land, and the persecutions that attended that exile culminating in the Holocaust.

These thoughts on history naturally brought us to the present. Many of the national exhibits as well as the museum staff itself encountered this problem: as difficult as the history and the need to place it in an un-derstandable and manageable narrative was the question of how to conclude the narrative itself. If the past was darkness, if Auschwitz was as Wiesel described it, night, and as Roskies defined it, a liturgy of de-struction, was there day after night, a liturgy beyond destruction? As a delegation we were commenting on the destruction, yet we were also objective witnesses to a Jewish life after Auschwitz. How could this life after Auschwitz be described without minimizing the deaths and with-out in any way suggesting that these deaths somehow led to life? It was at this juncture that the least was said and the suggestions were most hesitant; a silence pervaded the room. In a strange way we found it eas-ier to describe Jewish death than Jewish survival.

When the proposals were finally articulated, they were tentative and diverse. One delegate suggested that contemporary communities of Jews around the world be highlighted; another proposed that diverse surviving communities in Israel be featured. But when the chair asked whether Israel itself, as a state, should be shown as *the* response to Auschwitz, the central theme of Holocaust theology, the vote against the proposal was a quick and decisive one. Although this reaction was hardly anti-Israel, it was clear that the delegation felt a discussion of Is-rael was best avoided. The decision was to propose the termination of the narrative at Auschwitz; the surviving Jewish communities includ-ing Israel should be spoken of in a different venue. Auschwitz should not be used instrumentally even to promote the cause of Israel.

In the larger sense, however, it was clear that Israel could no longer be spoken of in a clear and unified voice, for such a discussion was rec-ognized as potentially divisive as well as embarrassing within the group and within the larger Jewish community. To emphasize Israel, to highlight a country that had entered its third decade of occupation, with its policies of expropriation and displacement, was to risk emphasizing what international bodies and organizations like the United Nations and Amnesty International had disclosed as illegal. In an even more fundamental way, it risked raising questions recently pursued by Israeli historians of a connection closer in time: Auschwitz and the founding of Israel, the displacement of Jews and the displacement of Palestinians by Jews. The inability to celebrate what had been celebrated before and the ensuing silence were important in gauging how far we in the Jewish community had traveled since the liberation of Auschwitz.[16]

Still I felt in the room among our delegation something more significant than a desire to keep others from critiquing Israel. Instead, I experienced an inability to discuss the subject of Israel outside of its more superficial aspects such as electoral politics. I could not help but feel that we had reached a dead end on the question that had radicalized our energies—and militarized our language and activities—over the last decades. Were we, after these seemingly endless decades of battles— intellectual, theological, and military—left where we had emerged from, Auschwitz?

In the midst of the silence I wondered whether in a paradoxical way Auschwitz had perhaps become for Jews a place of safe haven. For if we dwell in Auschwitz, if we freeze our history at Auschwitz, we silence the questions others have of us and in fact we have of ourselves. In this way Auschwitz becomes for us a place where we can hide our accountability in the present, even as we demand it insistently of others for their past actions. And so it became clear: we as a delegation were in danger of becoming guardians of a Holocaust orthodoxy that admitted only the questions we posed to others, denying as anti-Jewish questions posed to ourselves.[17]

Accusing Images

After I returned to my room that evening, these thoughts haunted me. When traveling I often take books and articles to read on the plane and during sometimes sleepless nights. Perusing my reading material, I found an essay given to me by a sponsor at a previous speaking engagement. It was titled "On Gaza Beach" and was written by a Jewish Israeli, Ari Shavit, who in the spring of 1991 was performing his annual reserve duty as a guard in the internment Camp Gaza Beach for Palestinian political prisoners. In the essay Shavit continually juxtaposes the historic suffering of Jews with the contemporary suffering of Palestinians, sometimes protesting the "impossible" comparison, other times embracing it. In a particularly moving passage Shavit writes:

> And yet the unjust analogy with those other camps of fifty years ago won't go away. It is not suggested by anti-Israel propaganda. It is in the language the soldiers use as a matter of course: when A. gets up to do guard duty in the interrogation section, he says, "I'm off, late for the Inquisition." When R. sees a line of prisoners approaching under the barrels of his friends' M-16s, he says with quiet intensity: "Look. The *Aktion* has begun." And N., who has strong right-wing views, grumbles to anyone who will listen that the place resembles a concentration camp. M., with a thin smile, explains that he has accumulated so many days in reserve duty during the *intifada* that soon they will promote him to a senior Gestapo official.
>
> And I, too, who have always abhorred this analogy, who have always argued bitterly with anyone who so much as hints at it, I can no longer stop myself. The associations are too strong. . . . Like a believer whose faith is cracking, I go over and over again in my heart the long list of arguments, the list of the differences. There are no crematoria here, I remind myself, and there was no conflict between people there. Germany, with its racist doctrine, was organized evil, its people were not in danger, and so on. But then I realized that the problem is not in the similarity—for no one can seriously think that there is a real similarity—but that there isn't enough lack of similarity. The problem is that the lack of similarity isn't strong enough to silence once and for all the evil echoes, the accusing images.[18]

The accusing images of which Shavit writes are found throughout post-Holocaust Jewish literature. During the Israeli invasion of Lebanon in 1982, Jacobo Timerman, who had been imprisoned in Argentina as a dissident Jewish journalist and upon his release went to Israel, wrote:

> Yes, we have killed our moral integrity. I feel that quite soon the Diaspora Jews will begin to experience the consequences of the process started by Menachem Begin, when they are denied the right to symbolize the pain of this century, the right to represent the universality of the victim. We are victims who have created our own victims in acts of cruelty. From now on, our tragedy will be inseparable from that of the Palestinians. Perhaps some of us will try to side-step the Israeli moral collapse by resorting to statistics and comparing Auschwitz to Beirut. It will be in vain. The victims of Auschwitz would never have bombed Beirut. Our moral collapse cannot be diluted by statistics.[19]

The same year that Timerman was covering the Lebanon War, a survivor of the Warsaw Ghetto and Buchenwald staged a hunger strike protesting Menachem Begin's policy of bombing Beirut. The protestor's son was an Israeli paratrooper. Outside Yad Vashem, the Holocaust memorial in Jerusalem, he read a statement: "When I was a child of ten and was liberated from the concentration camp, I thought that we shall never suffer again. I did not dream that we would cause suffering to others. Today we are doing just that. The Germans in Buchenwald starved us to death. Today in Jerusalem, I starve myself, and this hunger of mine is no less horrific. When I hear 'filthy Arabs' I remember 'filthy Jews.' I see Beirut and I remember Warsaw."[20]

These images are hardly confined to Israeli policy and warfare in 1982. In fact, they reach back to the founding of Israel in 1947–48, when the wounds of Auschwitz were fresh. On April 9, members of the Irgun Zvai Leumi and the Lehi, both Jewish right-wing terrorist organizations, attacked the Palestinian Arab village of Deir Yassin, located on the outskirts of Jerusalem. Over two hundred villagers were massacred; the rest were paraded through Jerusalem and then forced to cross into Jordan. In response to the government's attempt immediately to place new immigrants in the now-abandoned village, Martin Buber and three other Jewish scholars, Ernst Simon, Werner Senator, and Cecil Roth, wrote to the Israeli Prime Minister David Ben Gurion to halt the resettlement:

There are certain symbolic acts in the life of a nation that must be avoided, and there are certain educational values that must be preserved. In the case of this great and ancient nation, and this state, so small and so young, this is even more imperative. We hope that time and constructive acts of friendship will heal even this sore wound, which is far too fresh— just as fresh as our own memory of the tragedy of April 13th, when the medical convoy to Hadassah on Mount Scopus was massacred (24 hours after the massacre in Deir Yassin). The time will come when it will be possible to conceive of some act in Deir Yassin, an act which will symbolize our people's desire for justice and brotherhood with the Arab people. We are already now proposing such an act. But in the meantime, it would be better to let the lands of Deir Yassin lie fallow and the houses of Deir Yassin stand uninhabited, than to carry out an act whose negative symbolic impact is infinitely greater than the practical resolution it can offer. Resettling Deir Yassin within a year of the crime, and within the framework of ordinary settlement, would amount to an endorsement of, or at least an acquiescence with, the massacre. Let the village of Deir Yassin remain uninhabited for the time being, and let its desolation be a terrible and tragic symbol of war, and a warning to our people that no practical or military needs may ever justify such acts of murder and that the nation does not wish to profit from them.[21]

A few months later the possibility of resettling the village was again mentioned, this time in the course of a Knesset debate on the return of 100,000 Palestinian Arab refugees to Israel:

YAAKOV MERIDOR (HERUT): "Soviet Russia knew how to solve the problem of the Volga Germans during the war. There were 800,000 Germans in that region. . . . They transferred them to the east, beyond the Urals. If there should be a second round of fighting, where shall we transfer this fifth column? With the coastal region being only 10 miles wide, how shall we do it? Or perhaps we'll have to evacuate Tel Aviv so as to settle them there and keep an eye on them."

TEWFIK TOUBI (COMMUNIST): "You're preparing another Deir Yassin!"

MERIDOR: "Thanks to Deir Yassin we won the war, sir!"

A. BEN-ELIEZER (HERUT): "Don't be so sad."

A. CIZLING (MAPAM): "Don't boast about Deir Yassin."

E. RAZIEL-NAOR (HERUT): "There's nothing to be ashamed of . . . !"

ZALMAN ARAN (MAPAM): "As a member of the Knesset I must comment on one interjection that was heard here yesterday from the Herut benches. The interjection was, We are not ashamed of Deir Yassin."

A. BEN-ELIEZER: "How many Deir Yassins have you been responsible for?"

ARAN: "For your sakes, I should like to say that I don't believe you're not ashamed of Deir Yassin."

BEN-ELIEZER: "You don't have to bring up something that you yourselves performed."

ARAN: "I don't know that we performed any Deir Yassins."

BEN-ELIEZER: "If you don't know, you can ask the Minister of Defense!"

ARAN: ". . . If I thought that the State of Israel would be capable of Deir Yassins, I would not only not wish to be an Arab here—I wouldn't want to be a Jew here!"[22]

I wondered at Auschwitz and wonder now why these accusing images did not lead to a Jewish theology, or if not a theology, at least a more critical communal reflection after Auschwitz. As he expressed in his 1970 presentation, Wiesel saw the beauty of Jewish survival, a faith, if you like, in the inability to hate those who persecuted us in the past and our "enemies" today. For Wiesel, as for all Holocaust theologians, Jews were and are reluctant warriors, innocent victims forced to defend a beleaguered homeland. And while not vilifying Jewish Israeli soldiers, can we say even after these descriptions by those connected with the Jewish military that Jews are only innocent and never hate? Why did Wiesel and others feel that a Jewish army would somehow be different, perhaps inherently so, from the common cruelties of armies at war? Did Jewish theologians think that the Jewish ethical tradition, honed in suffering, could survive intact when wielding power? Perhaps it simply is a continuation of the Jewish understanding of exceptionality, now embodied in a nation-state; once chosen by God to be a light unto the nations, the modern continuation of this chosenness is found in the state of Israel. If America is described as the first new nation, Israel was somehow to be the first innocent one.

Still there was, at least initially, a choice, for the accusing images could be used correctively—if not returning one to innocence at least forcing a correction. Instead, those images were vanished from Jewish public discourse, as if they, and the reality they suggested, were illusory. It could be that they were censored in the emergency years of the post–World War II period, when hundreds of thousands of Jews sought refuge in Palestine, because Jews could hardly afford an ivory tower reflection on the ability of a suffering people to abuse newfound power. If this is so, then why after this true state of emergency was over, when the Jewish community in Israel became relatively secure, did the concealment of these images not wane, but in fact accelerate? I had noticed this before and experienced it again at Auschwitz—that the distance from Auschwitz has deepened our anger, and the orthodoxy that has developed around Auschwitz and Israel seeks control of images, especially external and internal accusatory images, that nonetheless continue to appear. Perhaps the need to avoid these images, indeed to repress them, is an attempt to hide the realization that they can never be finally and completely buried.

At Auschwitz we all knew that the redemption promised by Israel after the Holocaust was in fact an illusion. "Arab" intransigence was part of a larger problem. A Jewish state with power was fundamentally altering the loss we mourned at Auschwitz of a flawed and beautiful people seeking a place in the world among other peoples. Auschwitz had put us on the march, and Israel had militarized our soul as well as our theology. Behind Wiesel's innocence was Rubenstein's idea of Israel escalating the cost of taking Jewish lives; but were we as delegates from Europe and America in danger of losing our lives? If Israel was our redemption, why were we in fact living quite comfortably in the dias-pora that Israel was supposed to end? These accusing images reveal to us that the challenge of the Jewish community is not only living up to the lessons of the Holocaust, but also deriving lessons from the Pales-tinians, against whom we have used our power. How could we face this challenge without the accusing images being owned and discussed by us even, and especially, at Auschwitz?

So here the issue remains as to how Israel functions for we Jews who live outside this "redemption." There was one Israeli on our delegation, a researcher at Yad Vashem, who symbolized the ambivalence the delega-tion felt about Israel. We became friendly, and on the first day I visited his hotel room, sharing hot chocolate and biscuits he brought from Israel. I remember him rummaging through his huge suitcase to find a small pot to boil water; he brought this as well because of his many travels throughout Eastern Europe and his schedule, which often found tea shops closed. He was a delightful person with a deep sensitivity. We talked of his German parents, who had escaped to Israel, and his work—almost an obsession—in finding the last survivors of the Holocaust and recording their stories for posterity. Later during the conference he asked to address our delegation in Hebrew, his native language. Only two of us admitted to our lack of facility in the language, so he began. After two minutes or so he was asked to continue in English, his third language. Later we met, and when he inquired why I thought he was asked to shift from Hebrew, my response had two parts, the first of which had to do with his Hebrew, which was quite different and more extensive than most of his listeners could follow. The second observation was linked to the first: our journey to Auschwitz was not about the concrete reality of Israel, which he embodied, for the accusatory images were too strong. Rather, our journey was about our own lives and communities in Eng-land and America. We wanted his speech in our language; in a strange twist, the Holocaust was to justify our lives in the diaspora. In Holocaust theology, Israel originally functioned as a dreamlike symbol and now could no longer be discussed. This sensitive Israeli threatened to expose the dream as a nightmare reality too explosive to be contained.[23]

In short, we wanted to see ourselves in the image of suffering in the Holocaust and the dream of empowerment in Israel, rather than within the messy realities of state power, because our status and identity in America was bound up in these two events. That is, the image of us as innocent victims calls forth a special status: we are freed from normal judgment and accountability. However, to retain the sense of being in-nocent victims, our empowerment must be innocent as well, thus again protecting our special status. If our empowerment contains the usual elements of empowerment, then our claim to be victims is challenged.

As John Murray Cuddihy, a Catholic sociologist of religion, writes, "There is an almost conscious search on the part of Jewish writers to find a rhetoric, and metaphors, and analogies that will hold on to both images at once: the Jew as agonized, good and victim together with the Jew as victorious soldier." He continues:

> The self-image of the Jew as morally superior to the goyim is embedded in the situation of Jewish emancipation. Being marginal and relatively powerless, in other words, being *luftmensch*, enabled Jews, especially Jewish intellectuals, to become more moralistic, very critical of the Diaspora. Ideologies like Marxism, Freudianism, Hebraism, and Reform ended with the founding of Israel. In becoming Israelis, Jews dirtied their hands. But, despite *les mains sales*, the old-time theodicy of victimage continued, especially in the Diaspora. There is a strain, a conflict, between two rhetorics—between the Diaspora Reform rhetoric of the Jew as ethical, moralistic, and pacifistic and the Israeli rhetoric of *Sabra* victory and pride, between, if you will, *New York Times* editorial talk and the talk of Menachem Begin and General Ariel Sharon.[24]

Thus Cuddihy finds that Jewish theodicy is unaware of its morally problematic claimed status as victim. "Jews blame the victimizer, the anti-Semite. They see the anti-Semite as blaming the victim, the Jew. This they take to be very problematic and irrational. Yet when Jews' own historical actions in the Middle East, for example, create a stateless people who, in turn, blame the Jews and the Israelis, what does Jewish theodicy do? It blames the victims, the Palestinians, and sees nothing irrational in this. This presumption of blamelessness is irritating because it violates reciprocity." Cuddihy sums up his remarks by reference to Wiesel's essays after the 1967 war, which he no doubt would apply to his presentation at the International Scholars Conference as well. "This public *kvelling* and sanctimonious moralizing are rolled into the familiar Wieselian bolus. It is irritating."[25]

For a non-Jew this behavior is no doubt irritating. But for a Jew, conscious of past and present, the inability to move beyond this moralizing is tragic. It means in the first place the continued oppression of the Palestinian people at the hands of Jews; in the second, the addition of occupier to the many roles Jews have assumed in our history. Could we in the oppression of the Palestinian people be bringing to an end the history of suffering and ethics, which is our burden and our gift? The inability to speak of this course we have embarked upon means that there is no way that we can become conscious of the choices we are making and thus perhaps at the last moment choose another way. In this light, the silence of our delegation on the question of Israel was less a choice to separate the two events of Holocaust and Israel than it was to allow our present history to proceed unquestioned. It meant choosing the present course, as if the accusing images were created by anti-Semites rather than illustrating an internal recognition of who we have become. One wonders if our silence can maintain our status as victim when we and the world around us know that in fact we are creating our own victims. Can this silence protect our identity as an ethical and socially concerned people when our actions destroy this veneer?

At Auschwitz I wondered how long we could carry on this facade, sitting in judgment of the Nazis and the Poles and the Christians and the Palestinians and anyone else who had persecuted us then or challenges us today. Surely, though, to lie to others we must lie to ourselves. The lie began when we repressed the initial intuitive understandings of what we were doing to another people. That is, in 1947–48, in 1982, in 1988, Jews realized by reference to our own history of suffering that what had been done to us we were now doing to another people. These prepolitical and pretheological understandings were and are present precisely because we have a history of suffering and ethics; they serve as a warning that we are on a road that can only betray that history. Once that warning is suppressed and then repressed through political and theological discourse, other possibilities become obscure or unreachable. A cycle is created: in denying to ourselves what we are doing, we seek to deny it to others as well. Over time the cycle itself becomes a reality, until our activity and the intuitive understandings of that activity are on the one hand explainable in the language of cliché and on the other hand are so buried that an objective discussion becomes possible. Finally, because the cycle itself is so rote and under attack, the only response is silence, the silence I experienced at Auschwitz.

3

Auschwitz and Palestine in the Jewish Imagination

As our visit came to a close and I left Auschwitz for meetings in Rome, the silence on Israel and its consequences haunted me. If our empowerment in Israel, rather than liberating us, binds us in occupation and the diminution of Palestinian life, how do we move forward into the future? And if Auschwitz is a memorial to our dead, never to be forgotten or trivialized, how do we keep Auschwitz from becoming simply a functional symbol to keep us untouchable, which in another way is to forget and trivialize the dead? How do we keep Auschwitz and Israel from becoming a kind of show to be trotted out when necessary to buoy our own position and banished when the story told is not the one we want to hear? At least to the Israeli author Tom Segev, this is what pilgrimages to Auschwitz are becoming—an emotional play divorced from history. After joining a recent youth tour of Auschwitz, Segev writes, "[That journey] exuded isolationism, to the point of xenophobia, rather than openness and a love of humanity." For the Israeli youth it has become a pilgrimage to a perpetual exile rather than a place of mature examination and analysis.[1]

A similar point is made by Joan Ringelheim, research director for the permanent exhibition of the United States Holocaust Memorial Museum in Washington, D.C. As a Jewish feminist, Ringelheim has spent the last decade trying to analyze the plight of women during the Holocaust but has found it difficult to discuss the Holocaust as a historical and analyzable subject. Seen as unique and exclusive, the Holocaust is too often spoken about as a metaphysical evil, thus removing it from the possibility of human explanation or understanding. In so doing, the Holocaust comes to be seen, at least in Ringelheim's view, as "ontologically separate from human history"; at the same time, it is used to make other events or other people's experience prior to, during, or after the Holocaust seem relatively trivial. Ringelheim writes that under these conditions, "it can be difficult to discuss the many contours and crevices of Holocaust experiences, both Jewish and Gentile; and even more extreme, it becomes difficult to say anything at all because it is thought that speech (or any other form of representation) inadequately expresses, or even subverts, the experiences." Rather than concentrating on the exclusive and unique, Ringelheim seeks an expansive understanding of suffering, for the Holocaust was not only "an exercise of unrestrained power over and terror against Jews." Other victims such as communists, socialists, homosexuals, and gypsies either are unnamed victims or are denigrated to a lesser status in much of the literature and the public perception. To Ringelheim "there has been an implausible silence about them."[2]

For Ringelheim, enlarging the scope of analysis concretizes the event of Holocaust in history, at the same time posing the possible connections of racism (including racism in the form of anti-Semitism), sexism, and genocide. Was it coincidence that our delegation was overwhelmingly male and that the other victims of Nazism went largely unmentioned or were diminished in importance? One cannot help but feel that Ringelheim's exploration of the past, though lacking in specifics, is also linked to the opening of a Jewish future. By understanding the uniqueness and commonality of Jewish suffering, the Jewish community may begin to examine critically its contemporary life and power in the United States and Israel.

Over the years I have reflected on these questions, but at Auschwitz a new urgency emerged. Rather than provoking thoughts of perpetual exile or exclusive suffering, Auschwitz encouraged a crystallization and a closure to me. At Auschwitz, certain aspects of Jewish life became so highlighted that there was no turning away or delaying decision by placing them in a dialectical pattern.

Several options presented themselves to me with new force, beginning with the question of Zionism. For example, in 1982 at the height of the war in Lebanon, Henry Schwarzschild, who with his family fled Berlin in the 1930s, resigned from the editorial advisory board of *Sh'ma*, a Jewish journal. In his letter of resignation Schwarzschild wrote: "I have experienced the war on Lebanon of the past few weeks as a turning point in Jewish history and consciousness exceeded in importance perhaps only by the end of the Second Commonwealth and the

Holocaust. I have resisted the inference for over thirty years, but the war on Lebanon has now made clear to me that the resumption of political power by the Jewish people after two thousand years of diaspora has been a tragedy of historical dimensions. The state of Israel has demanded recognition as the modern political incarnation of the Jewish people. To grant that is to betray the Jewish tradition."[3]

Schwarzschild concludes that to him the price of a Jewish state is Jewishly unacceptable and that the existence of this (or any similar) Jewish ethnic-religious nation-state is a human and moral disaster and violates the value for which Judaism and Jews might exist in history. "The lethal military triumphalism and corrosive racism that inheres in the State and in its supporters (both there and here) are profoundly abhorrent to me. So is the message that now goes forth to the nations of the world that the Jewish people claim the right to impose a holocaust on others in order to preserve its State." Thus Schwarzschild disassociates himself from an Israel that has betrayed Jewish history.[4]

There is also the possibility, different in time and location, represented by Gadi Gofbarg, a Jewish Israeli artist. Born in São Paulo, Brazil, and having received a Zionist education in his youth, Gofbarg immigrated to Israel in 1970. By the 1990s, however, Gofbarg was, in his terms, "divorcing Zionism," a most difficult affair for one steeped in its ideology as a child and now in his adulthood living in Israel. As Gofbarg relates, it was his experience in the Israeli army that prompted the break with Zionism.

Soon after arriving in Israel, I entered the army. After serving in the army for three years, I was drafted into the 1973 war as a reservist for several months. During the war we found ourselves occupying a Syrian village in the Golan Heights which had been emptied of its inhabitants. The villagers' beds were still warm. The cats and dogs which they left behind were starving and afraid of us. The army made itself at home, but I found I couldn't sleep in someone else's house. I also remember spending a night during the war in a bombed out school, warming myself by a fire made with pupils' desks, watching the flames slowly consume that wood with children's names etched in it.

My experience during the war introduced the missing element to the official Zionist version of events. For so many years I had heard stories in which the "Arabs" were mentioned only as crazy assassins who were going to push the Jews into the sea. I was shocked into a different awareness by all that evidence of humanity. The "enemy" became real people to me: they slept and ate and their kids went to school. I entered their homes, smelled their foods, and burned their children's desks.[5]

For Gofbarg, this in fact is the story of Zionism: "Zionism precipitated the creation of the Jewish state contingent on the destruction of Palestinian society, or as a poet has written, 'everything that has a front has a back . . . .' And if in the front the desert was blooming, in the back Palestinian olive trees were being uprooted, and if in the front Israeli culture was flourishing, in the back Palestinian culture was withering, and if in the front Israelis had dignity, in the back Palestinians were humiliated. The Israelis have made their pleasure contingent on Palestinian suffering."[6]

As insightful as Schwarzschild and Gofbarg are, I wonder after my travel to Auschwitz whether disassociation and divorce is enough, or if in fact it is even possible. If Rubenstein and Wiesel are correct, which I think they are, that Israel is a central component of Jewish life, how can one be removed from it? Even if one desires this and seeks it out, this in itself, even with many others joining in, would not halt the historical fact of Israel's existence and continuation.

A third option that suggests itself is that of progressive Jews who argue for the essential rightness and goodness of Israel, but lament the "aberrations" of, say, the war in Lebanon or decades of occupation. If the occupation ends, then the aberration ends. With minor variations these are the views of Michael Lerner, editor of the Jewish journal *Tikkun*, and Amos Oz, Israeli novelist and political essayist whose writings include *The Slopes of Lebanon*. One might call Lerner and Oz "doves" in the Jewish spectrum on Israel; they represent the consensus of Jewish progressives on this question.

Although the likes of Schwarzschild and Gofbarg were unrepresented in our delegation, several members were in agreement with much of what Lerner and Oz have to say. And certainly both have strong arguments with Israeli policies. For example, at the beginning of the Palestinian uprising in March 1988, Lerner wrote forcefully of the policy of might and beating promulgated by Yitzhak Rabin, then Minister of Defense: "That is why we say in unequivocal terms to the Israeli government: Stop the beatings, stop the breaking of bones, stop the late night raids on people's homes, stop the use of food as a weapon of war, stop pretending that you can respond to an entire people's agony with guns and blows and power. Publicly acknowledge that the Palestinians have the same right to national self-determination that we Jews have, and negotiate a solution with representatives of the Palestinians!" By January 1993, Lerner, after reports of the killing of an Israeli policeman in Gaza, counseled a unilateral Israeli withdrawal from the territory. His disclaimer of complicity, delivered in a condescending tone, is instructive: "Unilateral withdrawal can be sold to the Israeli population as an act of strength and even retribution. If the Palestinians would prefer to live in a Lebanon-type situation, that's their problem. Better to kill each other than to kill us. We've had enough!" In fact, Lerner further expresses what many Jewish progressives may also see as the most desirable solution to the "Palestinian problem" when he acknowledges the fantasy "of how nice it would be for Israel if all the Palestinians were living in Los Angeles or Queens."[7]

If Lerner and other progressive Jews strongly associate with Israel while confronting some of its policies, they also want to disassociate from the Palestinian people. Although in their view the state of Israel should not oppress the Palestinians, Jews have the responsibility to end the occupation and nothing more. Amos Oz articulates this understanding when he describes the relationship of Jews and Palestinians as an unfortunate marriage in need of a "fair and decent" divorce. Oz continues: "There are those on the left who are secretly enchanted by the Palestinian presence and are somehow attracted to their claims. I, for one, have never been impressed or attracted by Palestinian culture. I profoundly regret to say that the Palestinian National Movement is one of the ugliest and stupidest national movements in modern history."[8]

In a somewhat different perspective, A. B. Yehoshua, the Jewish Israeli novelist and political commentator, writes that the "concept of historic right has no objective moral validity when applied to the return of the Jewish people to its land." Rather, as a committed Zionist, Yehoshua argues that the Jewish people have a "full moral right to seize part of Eretz Israel, or any other land, even by force," on the basis of a right he calls the survival right of the endangered. His underlying proposition is as follows: "A nation without a homeland has the right to take, even by force, part of the homeland of another nation, and to establish its sovereignty there." Thus Yehoshua, unlike most Jewish progressives, admits of what might be termed a necessary theft, a "moral invasion," as it were. But to hold the Palestinians responsible for resisting that theft or to expect them to accept it is in Yehoshua's eyes ridiculous, as is the extension of that theft to the rest of historic Palestine in the possible annexation of the occupied territories. For Yehoshua, the basis for the Jewish right is the seizure of a part; and thus if Jews intend to extricate themselves from the "situation of a people without a homeland by turning another people into a nation without a homeland, our right to survival will turn to dust in our hands."[9]

Whatever one thinks of Yehoshua's foundational argument that the survival of the Jewish people is linked to a territorial sovereignty, a position that should be probed in a deep way by Jewish thinkers, his position moves well beyond the typical expression of Jewish innocence and Palestinian demonism. Though his book bears the English title *Between*

Right and Right, his argument speaks of Jewish necessity, the dispersal of Palestinians, and the right of Palestinians to resist. Thus the title might be better rendered as *Between Jewish Necessity and Palestinian Rights to a Homeland*. Accordingly, it could be that the formation of Israel was necessary in its historical moment and at the same time wrong vis-à-vis the Palestinian people. The original sin, then, was European anti-Semitism, not Palestinian resistance to a Jewish state. But even here, if one accepts Yehoshua's analysis of historical necessity in seizing only a part of the land, the framework he maintains is strictly separatist. That is, the necessity of survival, the formation of a Jewish state, is extended beyond the historical moment into a relentless future: to survive physically and culturally Jews must be separate in their own land for the remainder of world history. The moral invasion is to flee the fire and to build a new home among others who have fled the same fire. Those who fled the Jewish fire must rebuild their own homes somewhere else.[10]

Here the "two state" position, although seemingly progressive, argued from a survivalist or innocent perspective, needs to be questioned within the framework of solidarity. The entire burden of proof is placed on the Palestinians. For example, the two-state position as argued by most Jews, including Lerner, or Yehoshua, and others like Yossi Sarid, a member of the Israeli Knesset, places primary responsibility on the Palestinians to, among other things, demonstrate their ability to live peacefully with Israel, to renounce their fundamental claims of sovereignty over all of Palestine, to guarantee a demilitarized state with Israeli security positions within Palestine and the right of Israeli invasion if militarization occurs. At the same time, it also limits forever the size of Palestine to less than one-fifth its original land mass in the least significant part of Palestine. Among other things it assumes, at a foundational level, that Israelis should be afraid of Palestinians, but Palestinians have nothing to fear from Israelis, a position that many Palestinians in their diaspora no doubt find surprising, if not untenable.

For all its force, the progressive Jewish position as represented by Lerner, Oz, and Yehoshua is also troubling. If it is impossible to disassociate Zionism and the state of Israel, is it possible to disassociate from a people whom we have displaced? Zionism and Israel are an authentic part of Jewish history; are not the Palestinians, then, also now a part of our history? Has not our Jewish liturgy of destruction become an inclusive liturgy of destruction, which now enfolds the Palestinian people suffering under our rule? Thus it seems that simply to separate each side from the other misses the fundamental point: the course of past history cannot be altered, and it is this history that must be dealt with as it is, rather than pretending to a history we prefer. In fact, the fundamental lesson seems to be in association and togetherness, a history of Jew and Palestinian bound together, which disallows retreat to any sense of Jewish innocence and redemption. Disassociation and divorce allow the fundamental lesson to go unheeded: that with power we as Jews do much of what has been done against us. Would disassociation and divorce promote on the progressive side what Cuddihy earlier accused Wiesel of, the irritating propensity of trying to have it both ways, innocence and power?

Lurking in the background of these thinkers is the Holocaust, though their present preoccupation seems on the surface to lie with Israeli policies. If the association of Holocaust and Israel is to be complete, then one cannot address Israel in a different way without addressing the Holocaust in a different way as well. It is clear that the Holocaust theologians are correct: the Holocaust and Israel are indeed linked. However, they are linked essentially and at their deepest parts not in a linear way, one leading to or following from the other. Nor are they linked as a justification for behavior and a founding principle of empowerment. Rather, they join in the lessons of the effects of powerlessness and the consequences of power, and in the connections of the breakdown of community and movement toward violence and domination. They are further linked with the deep questions of purpose and history, of beauty, tragedy, and God. In the end, Holocaust and Israel represent the paths chosen and unchosen within history. They are another way of asking how we as individual Jews and as a community seek to live in the world.

Ending Auschwitz

As I walked around Rome the day after leaving Auschwitz, these thoughts resonated within me. I visited the Colosseum, where sport was made of human lives, and then St. Peter's in Chains, where Michelangelo's statue of Moses is housed and where Freud, when in Rome, used to sit for hours and meditate. The Counter-Reformation churches are also beautiful if one overlooks their attendant history; in fact, I reflected continually while in Rome on the beauty and tragedy of history. In Rome the tragic, at least for the moment, had relinquished precedence to the beautiful; people were everywhere on the streets, enjoying the sun and each other. Coming from Auschwitz, should I be permitted to enjoy this beauty? Could I enjoy it as if Auschwitz had not occurred? I recalled the writer Ben Hecht's commentary on Jewish laughter after the massacre in Europe. Writing in the late fifties, Hecht recalled Hitler's desire to make sure that when he was through with the

Jews, no Jew would ever laugh again. At one level Hecht found Hitler to have failed and on another to have succeeded. After Hitler, Jews could laugh again, but their laughter is tempered by the tragedy over which Hitler presided. Thus beneath the laughter lies a sorrow too strong to forget. When I read this commentary many years ago, I understood Hecht immediately and even more so after my visit to Auschwitz.

Perhaps laughter seems a small matter, but if one sees laughter within healing, then it is more to the point. Walking around Rome I visited places of triumph and tragedy as a tourist; it was for the most part another people's history. But what I could not shake was our own history and the need for some kind of healing. I wondered if our delegation brought us a step closer to that healing or perhaps moved us farther away from it. I also wondered in a paradoxical way whether we as a people wanted to be healed of our trauma. Perhaps such a healing would pose too many questions to our status and identity. After all, so much of our public and private life is consumed by this tragedy; if we are healed of it, what will become of our status and identity? Do we fear that healing might have us drop our guard and suddenly thrust us back into a world of holocaust? This is a central theme of Holocaust theology, that holocaust is not only past, but part of our future as well. Of course, healing would minimize our special status as victims and make us accountable to the world for our present actions. Perhaps we fear that after the Holocaust and modern life there is nothing compelling left of Jewish life; thus anger, isolation, and fear serve a purpose of continuing what might otherwise be dismissed as irrelevant. Could the desire to remain unhealed be fueled by the age-old question of assimilation—that once healed, Jews will simply assimilate into the general population? Perhaps Auschwitz was as Hitler intended it, though in a very different way—the terminus of Jewish history. Despite our previous celebration of Israel and now our silence concerning its actions and policies, Auschwitz may indeed triumph in the end.

This was my intuitive sense as I walked the streets of Rome—that Auschwitz was in fact killing us as a people long after the crematoria were destroyed. A phrase continually recurred in my mind, which initially I tried to shake, for I could not yet make sense of it. Formed to some extent by *After Auschwitz* and my participation in the delegation on the future of Auschwitz, the phrase that suggested itself was "ending Auschwitz."

This phrase was, at least initially, difficult to decipher. Surely it means "never again" an Auschwitz for the Jewish people, a common Jewish understanding, and "never again" anything that approximates this for other peoples as well, the latter being a less emphasized understanding proposed in early Holocaust theology. "Ending Auschwitz" carries both of these understandings as a given, with the present as central as the past. Yet something remains to be articulated; by "ending Auschwitz," I mean that this episode in our history has created such anger, isolation, and a pretense of nonaccountability that it erodes the basic sensibilities and fundamental ethics of our existence. *That is, Auschwitz has become a burden to the Jewish future, a burden that we as a people now further.* If the burden was thrust upon us, unexpected and unwanted, in a sense we now assume and expand it in a way unforeseen by the victims of the Holocaust. The point is less the historical fact of our suffering; rather, it is how we use this suffering in the present. To me the choice is clear and in the main already decided—whether we use our past suffering as a way of understanding and entering into the suffering of others or instead use it as a blunt instrument against others, protecting our suffering as unique and incomparable to the sufferings of others.

"Ending Auschwitz" thus has its dangers because it proposes, first and foremost, an accountability before ourselves and the world. Continuing Auschwitz provides an isolating buffer to fend off many questions related to our empowerment. These are questions with which I believe most Jews struggle, though often they are suppressed and repressed, both internally and communally. To continue Auschwitz as a central overriding memory is in a sense to postpone—permanently if possible—the explosive realities within our community as they relate to power and injustice, and to postpone—again permanently—decisions concerning our future as a people. We are aware, subconsciously at least, that for the majority of Jews the Holocaust and Israel are not the central realities of our lives as we live them today. Rather, they are ideological and theological sensibilities with tremendous emotional content that are already fading and are destined to recede even more in the future. What, then, is the future of Jewish life? "Ending Auschwitz" poses this question in a more immediate sense than perhaps the Jewish community can handle. But surely the continuation of Auschwitz as an anchor of memory limits our ability to raise the questions we need to ask about the history we are participating in and creating.

If we end Auschwitz, who, then, are we? Pre-Auschwitz Jewish life is often viewed as a life of the weak and defenseless; post-Auschwitz Jewish life is seen within power and assertion, chutzpa, as the American Jewish lawyer Alan Dershowitz sees it, or within a renewed rabbinic framework in the shadow of the Holocaust and Israel. Yet the most important aspect, the healing of our personal and communal lives—the healing of our history—remains for the most part unaddressed. The

Holocaust and Israel may be viewed as anchors of Jewish identity, or we may celebrate the renewal of Torah study and synagogue observances, limited as it is, as significant to our future. Unfortunately, neither possibility addresses the deepest aspect of our lives as Jews. If the great majority of Jews alive today live within a Holocaust/Israel framework but have experienced neither reality, so too Torah study and Jewish renewal are experienced by a few and mostly to promote self-identity rather than out of religious conviction. In view of our history, these understandings cannot be abandoned, but neither can they provide us with a future. Whether we continue Auschwitz or end it, Jewish life still lacks depth in the present.

At the same time there is an anger and isolation that should concern us, and the accusatory finger, so easily and self-righteously pointed outward, should appall us. Therefore, to end Auschwitz is less to abandon our history than to claim it as it was *and* is in its fullness and to once again enter into a world that has often been hostile without the defense of our victimization, without the badge of special privilege, and with the realization of our newfound power. For in the displacement of Palestinians, then and now, no matter the justification or the variations on limited self-rule, whether in the guise of "autonomy" or the illusion of justice in a forced confederation, we have taken our place alongside others in the world of empire and in a manner too often like all other victors.

Thus, to end Auschwitz is to admit that we are no longer innocent and that Israel is not our redemption. As the meaning of this phrase unfolded for me in Rome, it was important to see this statement less as a condemnation than an opening, as a confession in pursuit of renewed possibility in the world. It became clear to me that if our healing is predicated on a critical understanding of our past and present, it also necessitates concrete action to implement and further that understanding in the world. With regard to Palestinians, we can say that by recognizing the national and political rights of the Palestinian people in thought and deed—that is, by recognizing the trauma Israel has caused and the right of Palestinians to be healed of their trauma—we might also be taking a step in the healing of our own trauma of past suffering. Among other things, I think that such a recognition could also alleviate the difficulties that lie in the years ahead if we, a previously displaced people, act to displace permanently another people. "Ending Auschwitz" would also allow us, or perhaps even compel us, to think the unthinkable—that our future is bound up in an essential solidarity with those whom we have displaced, a solidarity with the Palestinian people.

Palestine before Israel

A few months after returning from Europe, I was invited to speak at a conference led by the Palestinian intellectual Edward Said on the topic "Palestine in the Jewish Imagination." Though I immediately accepted the invitation, I was puzzled by the topic. Was there a Palestine in the Jewish imagination, and, if so, where was this Palestine located historically and geographically? With Rubenstein and Wiesel, as with much of our delegation, Palestine is never mentioned except as a prelude to the state of Israel. Progressives such as Lerner and Oz use it sparingly, referring to the West Bank and Gaza. Few Jews if any see Jerusalem as part of Palestine, and no Jewish spokesperson or writer uses the term to refer to the territories now encompassing the state of Israel. The more I thought about it, the more I realized that Palestine was essentially banished from the Jewish vocabulary as a present reality. Arabs exist, Palestinians sometimes exist, but Palestine does not.

It occurred to me that the continuation of Auschwitz as a phenomenon in the present is linked to the end of Palestine in the Jewish vocabulary. The inability to imagine the possibility of ending Auschwitz is connected to our inability to imagine Palestine as a contemporary reality. Linear history shows a sequential reality: Auschwitz leads to Israel, Palestine gives way to Israel. But it seems that here again an essential point is lost. Just as the Holocaust and Israel intermingle in the present rather than replace each other, so, too, Palestine and Israel exist together, though in a somewhat different way. Physically the Holocaust is over; its existence continues in the contemporary Jewish imagination. Physically the Palestinians have lost their independence, yet they exist within and outside of the state of Israel. There is a Palestine in the imagination of Palestinians, and at least the physical remnant of an actual Palestine even within the borders of Israel. But the continuation of Auschwitz not only promotes the state of Israel in the Jewish imagination but banishes Palestine from it, and in so doing effectively banishes Palestinians as well. Without Palestine in the Jewish imagination, Palestinians cease to exist in their essential integrity and take on a sinister reality that can only threaten Jews; they become the "locals" who exist by Jewish sufferance rather than intrinsic right.

The absence of Palestine in the Jewish imagination thus becomes a symbol of Jewish power and the Jewish right to displace Palestine and Palestinians. If Auschwitz has become a burden to the Jewish future, which we as a people now further, the banishment of Palestine in our imagination has become the special authorization to displace another people. Thus the contrary possibility suggests itself: the renewal of Palestine in the Jewish imagination might force a decision against an overpowering Israel and point to a way beyond the perils of expansionism and subjugation or even the humiliating offers of limited autonomy. A corollary emerges: the only way for the renewal of Palestine in the Jewish imagination to take hold is through ending Auschwitz; or, put another way, ending Auschwitz and the renewal of Palestine are bound together. These two understandings might take us as a people beyond victimization and the role of oppressor, beyond being occupied and being the occupier. They might also lead Jews toward the possibility of a healing, where the trauma of Holocaust and the trauma of Israel are reconfigured beyond isolation and anger into a present that emphasizes hospitality and community. In this way the sequential understanding is abandoned without abandoning the realities of history. The renewal of Palestine in the Jewish imagination refuses the end of Palestine and the end of Israel, and looks to a new configuration of Palestine/Israel.

Still the question remains: If there is little or no Palestine in the Jewish imagination in the present, where can it be found in the past? Obviously, the Palestine that does exist in the Jewish imagination—that of Lerner and Oz—is inadequate. A truncated Palestine only continues its banishment and leads to a renewal of Jewish triumphalism expressed in military power and in a hoped-for return to innocence and redemption. It can only lead to a continuation of Auschwitz. But there was a Palestine before Israel that included Jews and that might address part of the crisis of the contemporary Jewish world. There once was a Jewish understanding of Palestine that recognized our needs and the rights of the Palestinians. Here the inquiry requires less a desire for a utopian return to pre-Israel/Palestine than for something in the mix of Palestinian and Jewish history that existed, and by existing today, even in a different form, might now help Jews envision a path beyond the present impasse.

Of course, one possibility for renewing Palestine in the Jewish imagination is to investigate the importance of Zion and Jerusalem in Jewish history. Pursuing this line, we can discuss, for example, the role of Zion in biblical and rabbinic literature. However important it is to discuss Jewish longing in a period of exile or even the mobilization of Jews from different parts of the world to go to Jerusalem under the sway of the sixteenth-century mystical messiah Sabbati Zevi, it tends at least in the present to promote Israel rather than Palestine in the Jewish imagination. Jewish longing leads to present-day Israel.[11]

Rather than exilic longing or mysticism, the Jewish reality in Palestine as it was lived before Israel is crucial, and thus the study by Tudor Parfitt, *The Jews in Palestine, 1800–1882*, is closer to the point. Surveying the demography of Jews in nineteenth-century Palestine, the Jewish settlements in Jerusalem, Hebron, Safed, and Tiberias, as well as relations among Jews, Christians, and Muslims within Palestine, Parfitt helps concretize a history that is almost lost to the Jewish people. To begin with, reading Parfitt one realizes that the loss of Palestine in the Jewish imagination involves not only the loss of Palestinian Arabs, but also Palestinian Jews. Parfitt's work also helps to situate a small but growing Jewish population in Palestine in the Ottoman Empire's mix of different and at times hostile religious neighbors. Here the Jews of Palestine are not simply wanderers who come to the Holy Land to study and die, but rather they are seen within the complexity of human motivation, including the struggle for economic and civic betterment.[12]

Yet nineteenth-century Jewish life in Palestine, instructive and important, is too much in the past in time and circumstance to be emphasized today. Rather, it is the last Jewish contact with Palestine that is relevant today, the struggle of the 1930s and 1940s when the Nazis were rising to power and when Auschwitz was created. Here in the time of the emergency, recognizing a need for an empowered Jewish presence in Palestine while seeking to make that presence one of coexistence, can be found at least the seeds of Jewish hope before the formation of a Jewish state.

The Jewish discussion of Palestine, and thus Palestine in the Jewish imagination, was somewhat different when counterbalancing powers were visible and involved. To be sure, the contours of the Jewish presence in Palestine were articulated differently before the triumph of state power in Israel, partially because victory seemed less sure and thus the cost of victory and defeat seemed more tangible. For example, some of the early bi-nationalist Zionists on the ground in a Palestine controlled by the British and peopled in the majority by Palestinian Arabs had a sense of perspective and a depth of questioning lost in the conquest of Palestine. Perhaps, then, this view of bi-nationalist Zionists, in the decades before the establishment of the state of Israel, with their admittedly European colonialist mentality toward the Palestinian population and their imposition of a growing Jewish population in Palestine, can speak to the reemergence of a Palestine in the Jewish imagination that moves beyond a dominant Israeli landscape and narrative. Does recalling the Jewish need to negotiate desire and power with friend and foe in pre-Israel Palestine lead to a contemporary Jewish understanding that a counterpower is absolutely necessary to mitigate Israeli expansionism, which in its ultimate expression could subsume almost everything in its path, including its own citizens and tradition? Perhaps the need to negotiate may one day lead to a desire to negotiate and to a crystallization of exactly what Jews really wanted and want today in a land once called Palestine. With all its difficulties and possibilities, one thing is certain: it is crucial to explore the complexities of a movement that for the last time in contemporary Jewish history functioned within the context of a diverse and unitary Palestine.[13]

An example of one such Jewish bi-nationalist is the American-born Judah Magnes (1877–1948), a Reform rabbi who settled in Jerusalem in 1922 and became the first president of Hebrew University. Magnes's dream, one he shared with other bi-nationalists such as Martin Buber and Hannah Arendt, was to create a Jewish cultural, educational, and spiritual center in Palestine to help provide a focus for the worldwide Jewish community in the modern period. Yet he quickly became aware of forces in the Jewish world that sought to divert that center with a policy of domination and statehood. In a letter to Chaim Weizmann, the influential Zionist leader, dated September 7, 1929, Magnes wrote of the options before the Jewish people in Palestine:

> I think that the time has come when the Jewish policy as to Palestine must be very clear, and that now only one of two policies is possible. Either the logical policy outlined by Jabotinsky in a letter in the *Times* which came today, basing our Jewish life in Palestine on militarism and imperialism; or a pacific policy that treats as entirely secondary such things as a "Jewish State" or a Jewish majority, or even "The Jewish National Home," and as primary the development of a Jewish spiritual, educational, moral and religious center in Palestine. The first policy has to deal primarily with politics, governments, declarations, propaganda and bayonets, and only secondarily with the Jews, and last of all with the Arabs; whereas the pacific policy has to deal first of all with the Jews, and then with the Arabs, and only incidentally with governments and all the rest. The imperialist, military and political policy is based upon mass immigration of Jews and the creation (forcible if necessary) of a Jewish majority, no matter how much this oppresses the Arabs meanwhile, or deprives them of their rights. In this kind of policy the end always justifies the means. The policy, on the other hand, of developing a Jewish spiritual center does not depend upon mass immigration, a Jewish majority, a Jewish State, or upon depriving the Arabs (or the Jews) of their political rights for a generation or a day; but on the contrary, is desirous of having Palestine become a country of two nations and three religions, all of them having equal rights and none of them having special privileges; a country where nationalism is but the basis of internationalism, where the population is pacifistic and disarmed—in short, the Holy Land.[14]

Magnes saw the difficulties of achieving his own desire that a Jewish spiritual and moral center develop in Palestine. Like other bi-national

Zionists—Martin Buber again comes to mind—Magnes had a colonial attitude toward Palestinian Arabs, whom he saw as "unhappily still half-savage," with their leaders "almost all small men." Paradoxically, Magnes combined this perspective with a respect for the same people he derided, as we will see in his plan for a compromise settlement on Palestine. Regardless, the question remained for Jews:

> The question is, do we want to conquer Palestine now as Joshua did in his day—with fire and sword? Or do we want to take cognizance of Jewish religious developments since Joshua—our Prophets, Psalmists and Rabbis, and repeat the words: "Not by might, and not by violence, but by my spirit saith the Lord." The question is, can any country be entered, colonized, and built up pacifistically, and can we Jews do that in the Holy Land? If we can not (and I do not say that we can rise to these heights), I for my part have lost half my interest in the enterprise. If we can not even attempt this, I should much rather see this eternal people without such a "National Home," with the wanderer's staff in hand and forming new ghettos among the peoples of the world.[15]

The following week Magnes wrote to Felix Warburg, an American Jewish banker, philanthropist, and community leader about recent disturbances in Jerusalem. Again Magnes combines condescension toward Palestinian Arabs and a critique of Jewish power:

> I must say that I have been amazed that not one official Jewish voice has been lifted in sympathy with such slain and injured Moslems or Christians who may have been innocent; that no money was earmarked for their injured. Of course, the Arabs were the aggressors and the most bloodthirsty. Do I also have to be shouting that? But do you not know that we, too, have had our preachers of hate and disseminators of lies, our armed youth, our provocative processions, our unforgivable stupidity in our handling of the Western Wall incidents since last *Yom Kippur*, making out of what should have been a police incident an international political issue? Politics, statesmanship, hobnobbing with the masters of empire, using high-sounding phrases instead of disciplining and purifying our community and trying to understand and make terms with our neighbors.[16]

Magnes then outlines his own framework for a settlement of the dispute between Jew and Arab. He begins with the understanding that Palestine does not belong to Jew or Arab, or even the three monotheistic religions on an exclusive basis. For Magnes, if Palestine is truly to be the Holy Land, it will have to belong to all of them.

We must once and for all give up the idea of a "Jewish Palestine" in the sense that a Jewish Palestine is to exclude and do away with an Arab Palestine. This is the historic fact, and Palestine is nothing if it is not history. If a Jewish national home in Palestine is compatible with an Arab national home there, well and good, but if it is not, the name makes very little difference. The fact is that nothing there is possible unless Jews and Arabs work together in peace for the benefit of their common Holy Land. It must be our endeavor first to convince ourselves and then to convince others that Jews and Arabs, Moslems, Christians, and Jews have each as much right there, no more and no less, than the other: equal rights and equal privileges and equal duties. That is practically quite sufficient for all purposes of the Jewish religion, and it is the sole ethical basis of our claims there. Judaism did not begin with Zionism, and if Zionism is ethically not in accord with Judaism, so much the worse for Zionism.[17]

Years later, in the January 1943 issue of *Foreign Affairs*, Magnes published an essay, "Toward Peace in Palestine," which details how this vision of a diverse and unitary Palestine might be preserved. It is important to note that Magnes was by now quite aware of the Nazi atrocities being committed in Europe. Thus Magnes argued for increased Jewish immigration to Palestine within the context of the emergency situation facing European Jews. Still, for Magnes the context of European Jewry had to be understood within the context of a land that, far from empty, was home to Palestinian Arabs.[18]

Magnes begins his article by linking the solution of the Jewish problem to the labor of Jews and non-Jews for a free and just society. To those Jews who seek to separate politics and religion or impose messianic religious ideas on the political reality in Palestine, Magnes is firm: "The fact remains that Palestine is small and not empty. Another people have been in possession for centuries, and the concept of Palestine as a Jewish state is regarded by many Arabs as equivalent to a declaration of war against them. To those who contend that Palestine is the Promised Land of the Jews, I would say that it is necessary to distinguish between messianic expectations and hard reality."[19]

To Magnes, the conception of Palestine as a Jewish or Arab state leaves little room for compromise and further oppresses the ordinary Jew and Arab who have "no hatred for one another and who will rejoice over the prospect of a reasonable settlement which might enable them to live together and to develop their common country in peace." Magnes explicitly rejects the Jewish and Arab proposals of population transfer and calls instead for a Union of Palestine, worked out at the first level by Jews and Arabs and guaranteed by the emerging American power which is "greatly trusted, having no territorial or imperialist ambitions here." Magnes outlines this Union of Palestine under three aspects: (1) union between Jews and Arabs within a bi-national Palestine; (2) union of Palestine, Transjordan, Syria, and Lebanon in an economic and political confederation. These lands form a geographic unit and constituted a political and economic union at several times between ancient Semitic days and the First World War. (3) Union of this federation with an Anglo-American Union that is assumed to be part of that greater union of the free nations now laboring to be born out of the ruins of the decaying world.[20]

Some of the details of this bi-national Palestine envisioned by Magnes are important to the question of the renewal of Palestine in the Jewish imagination. To begin with, a bi-national Palestine "must provide constitutionally for equal rights and duties for both the Jewish and the Arab nations, regardless of which is the majority and which the minority." Political equality should grow from a bi-national administration, so that "officials may be trained as soon as possible for the great tasks which confront them." According to Magnes, the British have failed to train Jews and Palestinian Arabs for the tasks they will soon inherit: "The time has come to put Palestinians, both Jews and Arabs, in charge of non-controversial government departments and to make them members of the Executive Council of Government." As for immigration of Jews to Palestine, a pressing matter as the European catastrophe mounted, Magnes agreed that whatever the yearly immigration allotment, the Jewish population should never be permitted to become more than one-half of the population of Palestine.[21]

Magnes envisioned Jerusalem, as part of the Jewish-Arab compromise, as the federal headquarters or capital of Palestine. Magnes saw Jerusalem, the Holy City of three religions, as once again assuming its destiny as a center of spiritual and intellectual exchange. If the three faiths had failed to create societies of righteousness and mercy, the "new Jerusalem, then, would symbolize a new relationship between Judaism, Christianity and Islam in their cradle of origin; and in the New Jerusalem they would work out together part of their common problems with the old-new East which contains among its other elements the vast, vibrating, spiritual powers of Russia, India and China."[22]

Though a rabbi and a thinker, Magnes was also an activist, and he spent his last years lobbying to rescue Palestine from partition and Israeli statehood. Indeed, on May 5 and 6, 1948, just months before his death in October and at a critical moment in the 1948 war, Magnes spoke at length with Secretary of State George Marshall and President Harry Truman, suggesting that the United States government withhold recognition from a declaration of Israeli statehood and establish an American trusteeship to provide an umbrella for an eventual bi-national political settlement. This trusteeship would permit a variety of political options with the central purpose of holding Palestine together as an "integral land." In Magnes's view, under trusteeship there could be a Jewish province, canton, or state, or an Arab province, canton, or state, but they would be held together in a federal union. The importance of the trusteeship was obvious to Magnes and was received with interest by both Marshall and Truman because it would allow Jews and Palestinian Arabs to work out, in Truman's words, their "own salvation." Unafraid to suggest means by which this goal could be reached, Magnes proposed to Marshall that the United States impose financial sanctions against both the Jews and Arabs in Palestine, and support the dispatch of a special United Nations representative to organize the Jewish and Arab municipal police to secure Jerusalem.[23]

Magnes—and by extension the bi-national Zionist tradition—is important to recall both for his weaknesses and strengths. When thought of in mainstream and progressive Jewish circles, the weakness of Magnes and the bi-national Zionists is usually seen to be an idealism about the willingness of Palestinian Arabs to share the land with Jews. That is, the weakness, idealism, is used to buttress the views of the necessity of a powerful Israeli state and its innocence. In this scenario, the original sin is the Palestinian Arabs' rejection of partition, which leads to the reluctant militarization of Jewish life in Israel. From the perspective analyzed here, Magnes's weakness is seen in more fundamental areas. At the outset he unilaterally accepts the concept of a Jewish homeland as inherently important for Jews *and* Palestinian Arabs, if the latter will only come to their senses. The Palestinian Arabs are seen through a Western lens, found wanting, and encouraged to grow into this more "mature" sensibility. Thus, with Jewish assistance, Palestine, perhaps even the whole of the Middle East, can become "productive" again. The infusion of scientific, technological, agricultural, and financial means is important to this development, and Jews can be the conduit for these advances. Clearly, Magnes is naive about the neutrality of American power, and even in opposing a military policy he underestimates the dynamic of Jewish power once established in the Israeli state. It also must be pointed out that Magnes's arguments were not always stated in complete honesty, a flaw that plagues the authenticity of Jewish progressive thought today: for Magnes, Western Jewish abilities would assure more than an equal place in a bi-national Palestine; they would eventually win over the Arabs to allow a dominant Jewish role.[24]

Despite these weaknesses, Magnes's strengths are also important. Because he was attempting to justify an insurgent power to a Palestinian and Arab world, Magnes recognized the need to justify and limit this insurgency so as to ensure the acceptance by the indigenous population and its leaders. And though his vision of a bi-national Palestine was perhaps inevitably skewed toward the West, Magnes realized that Palestine was located in the Middle East and that the future of Jews in Palestine was there, rather than in the Western-oriented nation Israel has become. His plan, unheard of today in Jewish circles, was one of federation with other Arab countries; he saw the future of the Jewish national home in the larger Arab context.

Magnes truly feared the military conquest for Jews and Arabs, fought it in words and ideas, and even lobbied a third power to prevent it. Thus, if we can say that Magnes showed a typical Western presumption vis-à-vis peoples of the East, he did in fact draw a line. And finally, Magnes envisioned a future Palestine with Jews and Arabs living and working together as two peoples with a constitution guaranteeing their civil rights and equality under law. Though this seems a rational plan within the context of Magnes's vision, it is today revolutionary when compared to the vision put forth by progressive Jews who seek only to distance themselves from a truncated and dependent Palestinian state.

Palestine and the Jewish Future

With the establishment of Israel in 1948, Palestine in the mainstream Jewish imagination was reduced to a problem of refugees to be settled in the larger Arab world. With the fall of Jerusalem, the West Bank, and Gaza in June 1967, Palestine assumed a different problematic in the Jewish imagination, that of administering occupied territories and monitoring disturbing demographic potentialities. Indeed, the victories of 1948 and 1967 occasioned celebrations among Jews around the world as a will to survival and the possibility of Jewish empowerment. However, unlike Judah Magnes, Jews gave little thought to the consequences of these victories, either for Palestine and Palestinian history, Palestinian Arabs and Palestinian Arab history, or for themselves and their history. The unification of Jerusalem under Jewish control in 1967 points this out vividly. One need only reflect on the differences between Magnes's vision of a shared Jerusalem in a unified Palestine, held together if necessary by outside military power, and the celebratory, almost mystical vision of a Jewish-conquered Jerusalem by Elie Wiesel almost two decades later. What Wiesel and other Holocaust theologians failed to account for was the cost of Jewish empowerment, again for Palestine, Palestinian Arabs, and also for Jews. In essence, the 1967 war sealed what had begun in 1948—the end of Palestine and the rise of a powerful Israel. The praises sung in Jerusalem hardly diminished the reality that continues to extend itself today; that is, the transformation of an insurgent force, fed by the state of emergency in Europe, to a dominant state power, built on the ruins of Palestinian life and land.

Here the question is hardly one of moving back before the existence of the state of Israel to a Palestine of the past. Rather, it is looking ahead to a Palestine/Israel of the future that involves a reintegration of that which has been split apart in the context of contemporary history. As with Magnes, the question of Jerusalem remains central. On the one hand, the joint governance of a Jerusalem that is capital to Israel and Palestine could lead eventually to a confederation of Israel/ Palestine. On the other hand, the refusal of Israel to admit Palestinian Jerusalemites—except in special circumstances—to participate in the "peace process" and the refusal to recognize diaspora Palestinians— both of which signal a recognition of Palestinian peoplehood and thus a past and possibly future Palestine—consign the Jewish and Palestinian future to an extension of and survival within the context of Israeli superiority. Political leaders in Israel, as well as mainstream and progressive Jewish religious thinkers, recognize quite rightly the significance of such recognition as it proposes an alternative narrative, one that challenges Jewish theological and political thought which glosses over the abuses of Israeli power.

Like other settler states, Israel seeks to substitute its narrative— Israel—for the indigenous narrative—Palestine—and more; Israel's hope is to destroy the Palestinian Arab narratives of Palestine so that they cease to exist. At the same time, Israel seeks to banish the Jewish subversive narrative, the inclusive liturgy of destruction, and Magnes's understanding of Palestine, for example. Military power is absolutely essential in this task as are its handmaidens—mainstream and progressive Jewish theologians and thinkers who celebrate the victory (not, of course, as a military conquest, but as a moral crusade over the forces of evil) and draw the limits of dissenting discourse. A new Jewish synthesis comes into being—thought and theology in service to the state. But what happens when this power is unmasked and the enterprise is seen for what it is? Yes, the powerful and its court always feel that the future is theirs, that dissenting narratives have been consigned to death or at least tamed and managed. However, the unmasking of power that dominates unleashes the most dangerous possibility of all, the renewal and expansion of dissenting narratives. If the dissenting narratives unmask the controlling state narrative, they may coalesce to challenge the configuration of political power.

Rather than relapsing into a pre-Israel world long since vanished, the end of Israeli domination has the possibility of issuing into a new Israel-Palestine diversity that combines elements of past and present

struggling toward a transformed future. Thus in this case, ending
Auschwitz is not the dismantling of Israel and the reinstitution of pre-
Israel Palestine as if history had stood still, but the movement beyond
pre-Israel Palestine and present-day Israel to a Palestine/Israel combining elements of both while also transcending both. Mainstream and
progressive thinkers who seek to continue Auschwitz see any discussion of a future beyond a dominant Israel as a war to destroy the Jewish
people. Despite the rhetoric, they seek to close off a future beyond the
status quo. But the new Palestine discussed here is less a war than a reconciliation with justice, less a battle than a healing, less a splitting than
a rejoining in justice of a history that has been, is now, and will be
shared by Jew and Palestinian Arab.

So finally the question is, What is it that might bring a Palestine of
the future into the contemporary Jewish imagination, a Palestine where
Jew and Palestinian Arab realize a mutually empowered destiny? Put
another way, what kind of Jewish thought, theological or otherwise,
can rescue the witness of the inclusive liturgy of destruction and the vision of Magnes, with all their limitations, into a contemporary, less limited vision of a renewed Palestine? In short, what elements need to be
added to incorporate aspects of the Jewish narrative and yet limit Jewish control of that narrative so as to give room for an equal and equally
compelling Palestinian Arab narrative?

Here we again enter difficult terrain. The replacement of a Jewish-
controlled narrative with one of equality with the Palestinian narrative
can be a charade when the power of the two communities is completely
unbalanced. It can serve to justify Israeli power if it speaks only of lim-
iting its advance in the present, the tendency of most progressive Jewish thinkers. Therefore, the equality of the Palestinian narrative spoken
of here should not be seen as moving toward a two-rights position that
solidifies Jewish conquest and allows for a Palestinian autonomy or a
state on 10–12 percent of pre-Israel Palestine. Rather, the raising of the
Palestinian narrative in the Jewish imagination is one that advises us of
the Palestinians' prior rights *that Jews transgressed* and the displacement
of Palestinians *that Jews caused*. The initial and prior Palestinian narrative therefore takes precedence over the European-Jewish narrative,
which, when transported into the Middle East, moves from suffering to
domination. Consequently, Jews may claim a state of emergency in Europe as the initial reason for actions in Palestine—thus the need for immigration. We may even claim, as Magnes did, a desire to return to
Palestine to found a Jewish national home as a legitimate Jewish hope,
but we cannot claim as a matter of right the political and cultural dispo-
sition of the Palestinian people and their narrative. From the perspective of Palestinians, the Jewish emergency, the desire for a "national

home," are both disasters and part of the Palestinian catastrophe. In sum, Jewish actions in Palestine were and are wrong vis-à-vis the Palestinian Arab people. This understanding is critical to the renewal of Palestine in the Jewish imagination.

For if Jews with our own situation and desires come to believe that what we did in Palestine and what we do to Palestinians is wrong, and that the continuation of these policies continues the wrong and even negates the positive aspects of a Jewish cultural, educational, and spiritual center that some Jews felt would accrue from the policy of settlement, then the Palestinian and Jewish narratives come together in a different way. Acknowledging the wrong is not simply stopping where the boundaries are drawn today but, with this new understanding, changing the boundaries—changing the internal and external landscape of Jews in relation to Palestine. It means to redress the wrong; it means reparations for the wrong done to Palestine and to Palestinians; and it means a fundamental solidarity with Palestinians as they seek to return and rebuild their own culture and homeland. This solidarity with the Palestinian people includes and moves beyond the question of Jews repeating what has been done to us and beyond a vision of renewed Jewish life in Palestine; it is to see Jewish life in Palestine as one important aspect of a pluralistic Palestine. It means the recognition that the Palestinian narrative and peoplehood is authentic, self-generating, and self-contained with or without a Jewish presence. It means that there was Palestine, not only a pre-Israel Palestine with an increasing Jewish minority, but a Palestine before Zionism, even bi-national Zionism, and there was still meaning, hope, despair—in short, everything that marks a human and communal existence.

Yet within this argument for a future Palestine in the Jewish imagination, one cannot end without stating the obvious difficulties of achieving this goal. Recent works on Jerusalem—for example, Amos Elon's *Jerusalem: City of Mirrors* and Avishai Margalit's essay "The Myth of Jerusalem"—as well as the more forceful discussion favoring a Palestinian state on the West Bank and Gaza, such as Yehoshafat Harkabi's *Israel's Fateful Hour* and Mark Heller and Sari Nusseibeh's *No Trumpets, No Drums: A Two-State Settlement of the Israeli-Palestinian Conflict*, demonstrate the continuing limitations of the Jewish imagination regarding Palestine rather than portending an expanding one. For example, Margalit's essay argues for joint sovereignty over Jerusalem separated, at least for now, from the "problem of the rest of the territories." Mark Heller reluctantly agrees to a two-state solution, but his tone is certainly condescending and almost fascist in its stridency. The question of a unified Palestine, when mentioned, is derided. Heller especially compares unfavorably and in fact fulfills the penetrating prediction that Hannah Arendt offered over forty years ago in her 1948 essay "To Save the Jewish Homeland: There Is Still Time," when she predicted that if a Jewish state was established by force, "the Palestinian Jews would degenerate into one of those small warrior tribes about whose possibilities and importance history has amply informed us since the days of Sparta," and in which she held out, at the last moment, the possibility of a unified Palestine. Margalit and Heller compare unfavorably as well with the contemporary Palestinian educator Muhammed Hallaj, whose recent essay "The Palestinian Dream: The Democratic Secular State" outlines the benefits to both Jew and Arab in a renewed Palestine.[25]

Next Year in Jerusalem

In the final analysis, most Jewish writing conspires against such a vision, and even in granting a small, demilitarized, dependent Palestinian state (often with these aspects secured by Israeli military power within the Palestinian territorial borders), the arguments are endlessly detailed and intricate. Could we say that these intricacies, this necessity to bargain Jewish claims with some recently acknowledged Palestinian claims, this leveling of terrain that is called dialogue, may be too little and too late for the Palestinian people?

It is in this context that the September 1993 mutual recognition and agreement on partial Israeli withdrawal from Gaza and Jericho, concluded between Israel and the Palestine Liberation Organization, should be seen. The dramatic handshake between Chairman Arafat and Prime Minister Rabin, seen around the world, enticed all but the most cynical of observers. Many wondered at that moment if a peaceful and just conclusion of this tragic conflict was truly at hand. Who could not assent to the words of Rabin when he said, "We wish to open a new chapter in the sad book of our lives together, a chapter of mutual recognition, of good neighborliness, of mutual respect, of understanding. We hope to embark on a new era in the history of the Middle East."

Yet as Rabin spoke, an ancient road was being widened and resurfaced, a road that would carry Palestinians, and perhaps Arafat himself, from Jericho to Gaza, but that would bypass Jerusalem. As Robert Fisk commented in *The Independent*, "The PLO leader would be granted just one very distant view of Jerusalem, five miles away, the Dome of the Rock and the walls just visible through a crack in the hills, close enough to taunt him with its presence, far enough to ensure despair."[26]

For me, at least, watching the ceremony on television in a hotel room in Lexington, Virginia, these five miles were as concrete and symbolic as the historic handshake. Had we as Jews come this far in our history

of suffering and struggle only to deny those whom we have finally recognized their healing and their destiny? Could we be so close to ending
Auschwitz and yet choose instead to continue Auschwitz by denying a
full, mutual, and interdependent empowerment to the Palestinian people? In the hours before the signing of the agreement the Israeli writer
Maxim Ghilan wrote in confessional tones to his Jewish and Palestinian
friends:

> What is now unfolding is far from just and will not, cannot, lead to a last-
> ing peace in the immediate. I therefore apologize to my Palestinian
> friends and contacts for what I have done during these last thirty-three
> years. If I helped delude them into thinking we could bring about, to-
> gether, a just solution—that is, a Palestinian state next to Israel—I did
> wrong. Now there can be partial peace for a while. But not justice. I feel
> swindled by destiny, by the present set of circumstances.[27]

Two days after the ceremony, the Jewish New Year began. The rabbis preparing their sermons had an unexpected task: to tell Jews why
people who had been demonized by the Jewish establishment should
now be seen as possible partners in peace. The Jewish community had
learned to demonize the other and now in a startling development
had to be reeducated. Is this not the fate of all orthodoxy, with its triumphal sensibility and certainty of truth, that one day it must be hum-
bled by the diversity of life and especially by the face of the other that
confronts the victor with blood and tears and even, amazingly, with an
outstretched hand?

This outstretched hand offered by Arafat was, at least to my eyes,
trembling with anticipation and a dignity that held forth the possibility
of a healing. Surely the time is now for a healing of Jew and Palestinian,
a healing of the damage rendered by expropriation, displacement, exile,
and death. A shared life in a shared land represents the beginning of
this healing. If the Jewish return to Jerusalem is a destiny fulfilled in
our time, it can only be celebrated when the Palestinians return to
Jerusalem as well. Perhaps at that time, a new, far-reaching agreement
will be signed that will bury a tragic past and annunciate a future of
equality and cooperation. Then the real celebration will begin. It is at
this moment that a new Jewish theology might emerge that takes us beyond the dead end that our delegation reached at Auschwitz and may
infuse with new meaning the ancient Jewish prayer, "Next Year in
Jerusalem."

4

Jews and Christians
after Auschwitz

If coming to terms with the Palestinian presence as essential to the future of Jewish life was difficult to address at Auschwitz, still another question confronted us even before we arrived, that of Christianity. None of us, including my Israeli friend, grew up among Palestinians. With the lone exception of the Israeli, we had, however, been born and raised among Christians and in a Christian culture. Though as adults we choose to live among Christians rather than in Israel, and each of us in our way has found a successful place within the Christian West, our feelings about Christians are on the whole ambivalent. The circumstances of food purchases and preparation for our group offer one example. Though most of us purchase and eat food within the dominant cultural setting of our respective lives, at Auschwitz only kosher food was provided to our delegation. Unavailable locally, our kosher meals were flown in from Switzerland at an exorbitant cost. The cost was high, the quality low, but the group organizer felt it necessary to distinguish us in this way as a Jewish delegation, whereas few of us ever sought this distinction at home.

More important than the logistics of our food were the discussions we had on the third day, before our conference concluded in silence on the question of Israel. Actually, the discussions might better be characterized as a series of outbursts that punctuated the more expected professional demeanor. I remember two such incidents. The first revolved around the question of Auschwitz-Birkenau and what might serve as proper memorial markers, for we had concluded these were sorely lacking. Should the memorials be a series of plaques noting the location of certain areas of the camps? The question of memorializing through worship also emerged, and it was here that the atmosphere grew heated. What kind of prayers should be recited at Auschwitz? Should a place of prayer be housed in one of the few standing buildings at Auschwitz-Birkenau, and if so, how should it be furnished? Should it be only for Jews or for anyone of goodwill who wanted to pray? Of course, there was the question of whether any prayers, other than for the dead, should be uttered in Auschwitz. But when one delegate suggested that—to satisfy the diverse interests of people, including Christians, and yet offend no one—a place of "reflection" could be the answer, an angry response followed. "Jews *daven*—Jews do not reflect!" was yelled out, as if silent vigils, presumably Christian, would offend the dead.

Following this was the example of a group of French Jewish survivors of Auschwitz who, during our first day there, arrived by train to commemorate their travails. The same delegate told us that at designated places they paused and "reflected," telling stories, reading poetry, or simply weeping for the loved ones they had lost. To him, Christians, not Jews, made pilgrimages, and this particular pilgrimage, with its method of stopping at places of significance, reminded him of Christians doing the Stations of the Cross. You could see the hurt in his eyes: had Jews survived Auschwitz only to adopt Christian language and ritual? That Jews who had survived Auschwitz decided on their own the reason and method to commemorate their journey was of less importance to him than its effect on his interpretation of Jewish history; in short, they were betraying the dead.

To many in our delegation, there was enough Christian history and presence at Auschwitz already without its supposed usurpation of Jewish life. Western Christianity laid the foundation of Auschwitz, with its anti-Jewish theology and polemic. The history of the Nazi period diverted too little from that general history, beginning in 1937 with the Concordat between the Vatican and Hitler. The Concordat guaranteed freedom of the Catholic religion in Germany and the right of the church to regulate its own affairs, so long as they were purely religious. In return for this agreement, the German Catholic Church abandoned its political organization, thus seriously weakening its political activity in Nazi Germany. During this era, in many ways this characterized most Christian churches, who bargained for their freedom and security at the expense of the Jews. The postwar experience of the Catholic presence at Auschwitz also left much to be desired: in 1979, on his first visit to Auschwitz as pope, John Paul II, while making particular reference to the suffering of

Jews and Poles, singled out for mention the converted Carmelite sister, Edith Stein, and Father Maxmilian Kolbe, a Polish Franciscan priest, who volunteered to go to his death so that a condemned prisoner would be spared. On his second trip to Auschwitz in 1982, John Paul II canonized Kolbe, despite the discovery of anti-Jewish tracts Kolbe had written.[1]

Though the elevation of Stein, who is commemorated with a plaque at Auschwitz-Birkenau, and the canonization of Kolbe, whose cell at Auschwitz is preserved with fresh flowers and liturgical candles in abundance, posed problems for the larger Jewish community, the background question as we arrived at Auschwitz was the ongoing crisis involving the Carmelite convent. The convent began on August 1, 1984, when a small group of sisters from the order of Our Lady of Mount Carmel, with the approval of Polish and Catholic Church authorities, moved into the *Theatergebände*, or Old Theatre Building, at the site of Auschwitz. By May 1985, however, when a Dutch Dominican priest launched an international appeal to Catholics asking them "to give a convent at Auschwitz as a gift to the Pope," Jewish groups in Belgium and France began to protest this Christian presence within sight of the massacre of over a million Jews. Almost a year later, in April 1986, a letter signed by prominent rabbis in Britain, France, Austria, Switzerland, and Romania, who together formed the Presidium of European Rabbis, urged the Pope to abandon the Auschwitz convent project, for it was offensive to the Jewish people. In response to the Presidium, over the years agreements were signed to relocate the convent, though the deadlines were never met. In fact, in November 1987 a new outcry occurred when a large cross appeared atop the Auschwitz convent building. When in July 1989 Rabbi Avraham Weiss and a group of Jewish demonstrators, protesting the convent's location, climbed over the convent fence and were ejected by Polish workers, the delicate negotiations escalated into an international confrontation.

If Weiss's provocations were not enough, Cardinal Josef Glemp's sermon on the celebration to mark the feast of the Most Holy Mary, Madonna of Czestochowa, at Josna Gora in August 1989 went further. In an apparent attempt to lessen tensions, Glemp instead reminded the Jewish community and the world of the persistence of anti-Jewishness. In the fourth section of his sermon, titled "Dialogue with the Jews," Glemp spoke the following words: "Given that so many issues have been distorted, dialogue is necessary, a dialogue which systematically clarifies difficult matters, not putting forward demands. We have committed our faults against the Jews, but one would like to say: 'Dear Jews, don't talk with us from the position of a nation above all others and don't lay down conditions which are impossible to fulfill.'" And later in his sermon: "Do you not, respected Jews, see that in your actions against [the sisters] you injure the feeling of all Poles, and our sovereignty obtained with such difficulty? Your power is the mass media, which are, in many countries, at your disposal. Do not let them act to kindle antipolonism." As controversial, though less quoted, is another section of the sermon:

> Despite all, life does not conform to established patterns and does not define relations between nations in friend-enemy terms. For us this is particularly true of the Jewish nation, which was never a neighbour but a member of our household and whose otherness both enriched us and caused problems. For many Jews, Poland was their Fatherland not only because of citizenship but also because of the authentic love they felt for it. We read in Jankiel (the Jewish character in the poem):
>
> > . . . Speaking, he continued to sob,
> > The kind-hearted Jew loved the Fatherland like a Pole.
>
> Along with the Jewish innkeeper who got the peasants drunk and those Jews who propagated communism, there were also people among the Israelites who gave their talents and their lives to Poland. We were not indifferent to one another, which is why phenomena like antipolonism and antisemitism came into being. In order to understand the complexity and the interpenetration of the Polish-Jewish problem, let us ask ourselves the following questions. Were there in Poland aversion to and quarrels with the Jews? There were. Were there in Poland Jewish businessmen who were disrespectful and scornful towards Poles? There were. Were there, during the occupation, Jews who collaborated and did not live up to the example set by the heroes of the ghetto? There were. Were there times in Poland when the suffering and victimization of the Jews were concealed? There were. Were there Poles who sacrificed their lives to save Jews? There were. The remembrance of the fiftieth anniversary of the outbreak of the Second World War puts us on the same side of the barricade, on the side of destruction and death. Jews, Gypsies, Poles—these peoples were condemned to annihilation in the Nazi strategy, but according to different plans and on different scales.[2]

Glemp's sermon thus combined a series of images, from the Jewish conspiracy to cut at the roots of Polish Catholic culture and control of the mass media, to a dialectical understanding of the historic interaction of the Jewish and Catholic Polish people. Both peoples had suffered; neither was innocent. In the Western media and in Jewish and Christian circles in Europe and America, the former thoughts were emphasized, and Cardinal Glemp's words and sometimes Glemp himself became an object of ridicule. When as a response to Glemp in September 1989, then Prime Minister Shamir, himself of Polish descent, suggested that Poles take in anti-Semitism with their mother's milk, the controversy escalated further.[3]

Though with new agreements in place by the time of our visit, as we drove into Auschwitz on the first day the convent controversy was on our minds. For both the Poles and the Jewish community, the convent and its cross symbolized much: the history of Christianity vis-à-vis the Jews; Jewish feelings toward the Polish people and vice-versa; a drama of two peoples suffering. If Auschwitz was a concrete embodiment of the attempt to annihilate the Jews, it was also the place of humiliation of the Polish people. Jonathan Webber comments that three million non-Jewish Poles died during the Second World War, seventy-five thousand of whom were murdered at Auschwitz. "As part of the wider Nazi treatment of the Polish population as a source of slave labour, Auschwitz was a specific element in the attempt at the systematic destruction of Polish culture and Polish national identity, in order eventually to provide Germany with more room to expand." For this reason Auschwitz represents symbolically to the Polish people the wider Polish fate if the Nazis had triumphed.[4]

Throughout the controversy, filled with such evocative symbols, certain details remained unattended. The convent and the cross, for example, now placed in the garden of the convent, overlooked Auschwitz, where mostly Polish Catholics were imprisoned and thousands killed. Virtually unmentioned in the controversy was a more incredible site pointed out to us at Auschwitz-Birkenau. In 1983 a former Nazi building, just outside Birkenau's barbed wire perimeter and clearly identified on Auschwitz-Birkenau maps as the "new commandant's office," was turned into a Catholic church as an extension of the parish of Oswiecim, the town where Auschwitz is located. Overlooking the road that took hundreds of thousands of Jews to the gas chambers, that church, which is much more visible at Auschwitz-Birkenau than the convent is at Auschwitz, venerates the Jewish convert Edith Stein. Clearly, this is much more provocative than the convent at Auschwitz.[5]

The symbolism of a Catholic presence at a site that in memory is claimed by the Jewish world was destined to create controversy. This was Richard Rubenstein's perspective when he visited Auschwitz in December 1989. Referring to Pope John Paul II's visit to the site of the Mathausen concentration camp in Austria in June 1988, where tens of thousands of Jews were put to death, the Pope, in his public address, made no mention of the Jewish victims. After being criticized by a leader of the Austrian Jewish community, the next day the Pope told an audience of eighty thousand people during a prayer service, "Not far

from here is Mathausen, where Christians, Jews and others were persecuted for many reasons, including their religion. Their suffering was a
gift to the world." Rubenstein comments that the idea of the suffering
of those in the camps as a gift is consistent with the image of Christ of-
fering himself for the sins of the world; it is completely understandable
within the Pope's tradition. "It was, however, a symbolism altogether
foreign to Jews, who cannot see the greatest catastrophe in their history
as a gift of any sort whatsoever." In that same speech the Pope also
stated that it would be unjust and untrue to charge Christianity with
the crime of mass death. To this Rubenstein responds that the Pope is
correct up to a point. "Nevertheless, he failed to address the question
whether the Christian identification of the Jews as deicides created a
moral climate in which millions of Europeans could, at least during
wartime, regard extermination as a legitimate enterprise. Nor did the
Pope consider the fact that many of the major war criminals, such as
Franz Stangl, the S.S. commandant at the Treblinka death camp, were
assisted in their flight from justice by Vatican and other Church officials."[6]

Elie Wiesel, in an interview several months earlier, was even
stronger in his words than Rubenstein, a reversal of earlier years. On
the convent Wiesel remarked, "To build a convent on the invisible
graves of the Jewish people who were murdered in Auschwitz is wrong
and offensive. Auschwitz is not the place for the convent. Convents
should be among the living, not the dead." Later in the interview
Wiesel was asked to respond to recent comments by the Pope that were
interpreted as meaning that the covenant had been broken by the Jews
and superseded by the Christian covenant. "Really what does the Pope
want? Does he want us to convert? Then let him say so, but he will be
disappointed. We will remain Jewish. . . . As far as the Pope's idea that
the prophets of Israel came to preach conversion to the new covenant,
that is totally wrong, and baffling. Do you think that Jeremiah, Amos,
Habakkuk, or others want us to convert to Christianity? They wanted
us to become *more Jewish,* not less Jewish. This Pope wants us to be less
Jewish, or to stop being Jewish."[7]

The controversy over the convent is in some ways reminiscent of the
controversy surrounding Ronald Reagan's visit to the Bitburg cemetery
in 1985. Once announced, with the concomitant discovery that S.S. men
were buried there, a storm of protest broke loose in the West, led by
Jews but also including prominent Christians. Forty years after the conclusion of World War II, Reagan's visit was seen, at least by his advis-
ers, as a way of finally burying the tragedy of the war. Instead, it
reopened its wounds. At Bitburg, the reconciliation was posed in
purely political terms, for in their commerce and military exchange

over the years America and Germany had in fact come together. The Bitburg ceremony was to commemorate that fact. However, the outpouring over Bitburg demonstrated an inability to close in a symbolic way that which had already closed in a worldly way. This was the strength of Wiesel's words when in accepting the Congressional Gold Medal of Achievement on national television, with Reagan sitting by his side, he remarked:

> May I, Mr. President, if it's possible at all, implore you to do something else, to find a way, to find another site? That place, Mr. President, is not your place. Your place is with the victims of the S.S.
>
> Oh, we know there are political and strategic reasons, but this issue, as all issues related to that awesome event, transcends politics and diplomacy.
>
> The issue here is not politics, but good and evil. And we must never confuse them.
>
> For I have seen the S.S. at work. And I have seen their victims. They were my friends. They were my parents.
>
> Mr. President, there was a degree of suffering and loneliness in the concentration camps that defies imagination. Cut off from the world with no refuge anywhere, sons watched helplessly their fathers being beaten to death. Mothers watched their children die of hunger. And then there was Mengele and his selections. Terror, fear, isolation, torture, gas chambers, flames, flames rising to the heavens.[8]

This public expression of the Jewish liturgy of destruction after the Holocaust was at the time of Bitburg already familiar to the Jewish community, and at least to portions of the public in Europe and America. But even then the question arose as to how long that liturgy could be recited, given the passage of years and the behavior of the Israelis, which introduced conflicting symbols to people who were reciting and hearing of Jewish suffering and innocence. The convent controversy called forth this liturgy again as the context shifted from a political closure to a religious one.

Whatever the feelings of individual Jews, agreements were reached shortly after World War II and expanded over the years by those who had suffered under the Nazis in Europe and those who had mobilized their nations against the German state. There was little in the way of organized protest by the Jewish community over compensation for war crimes or the normalization of relations. In fact, Israel was and remains today a central benefactor of the reintroduction of Germany into the world of nations, including the billions of dollars that have been paid to Jewish survivors living in Israel and that in the 1950s and 1960s helped fuel a new and struggling Israeli economy. Still, the shift to the religious arena presented a difficulty, for commerce and compensation could happen as an exchange, whereas religious symbols of closure suggested an assent. This is what took Reagan by surprise; even a purely political closure could be seen by the Jewish community as a religious one. The convent controversy was of course more obvious: to raise the cross at the site of Auschwitz was to many Jews to seal the fate of the Jewish dead with the symbol of the historic oppression of the Jewish people. Rubenstein was correct in his assessment: no matter the Christian interpretation, Jews could experience it on one level as another example of the triumphant Church—this despite the fact that a number of Christian leaders and theologians confronted Cardinal Glemp and spoke of the need to relocate the convent, or even the need for silence in face of the suffering at Auschwitz.[9]

We as a delegation were part of an evolving tradition of this public expression of the Jewish liturgy of destruction. Unlike the behavior of Rabbi Weiss, however, or even some officials of Jewish organizations, ours was for the most part circumspect. We asked our questions of the museum staff and even at the new Catholic Interfaith Center (the place further from the site where the nuns were supposed to be transferred) in a polite manner. Our follow-up questions were mostly satisfied, and the responses that evoked anguish were allowed to remain as they were stated. Still it seemed that the mere presence of Christianity and Christian symbols caused offense; their presence rather than their active content threatened the dead and us. We understood this as we drove by the convent, when we were shown Kolbe's cell at Auschwitz, when we stopped at the plaque commemorating Edith Stein at Auschwitz-Birkenau, and when, in an open field beyond the Stein memorial, we noticed a series of four-foot crosses designed and built by European high school students to remember, no doubt in an innocent way, the dead.

But were these crosses left by the teenagers the same as the cross that was placed atop the convent? And should we see in the presentation given by the Catholic priest at the Catholic Interfaith Center simply a more nuanced description of a faith that had encircled our people and given at least symbolic permission for their ghettoization and death? Could it be that despite the rhetoric of Jewish and Christian organizations, something had changed between Jews and Christians—*because of Auschwitz*—a change these leaders participated in and ultimately fought? Has the notion of what it means to be a Jew and a Christian after Auschwitz changed so radically that the Jewish establishment and the Christian establishment defend faith in understandings that are already receding into the past? And could it be that these arguments from the perspective of two religious establishments also mask the collaboration and the collapse of both establishments into one; and that despite Auschwitz and this merger, and despite Auschwitz and Jewish protests over the Christian presence there, we as Jews have in fact joined the Christian establishment in the West? Perhaps our protests increase as the differences between us decrease. After all, we have survived a hostile Christian world and now succeed in a more accepting one. Surely our delegation attested to this very fact: we came to Auschwitz very differently than did the previous generation of Jews.

Christians as Enemy

The ambivalence within the delegation concerning Christians was bound up with the feelings some had about my presence at Auschwitz. When the invitation first came, I thought my presence would be controversial because of my writings about Jewish theology and Palestinians. Although my apprehension turned out to be accurate, I did not realize that it was also tied with my teaching and traveling with Christians. That is, the level of wariness engendered by breaking with the Jewish consensus on Israel was increased tremendously by my association with the Christian community.

I came to realize that I was thought to be in dialogue with our two "enemies," Palestinians and Christians; the fear was that I had crossed over to those enemies and thus become a traitor to Jewish history. When in a discussion with three members of the delegation at breakfast our first day in Krakow, the question arose as to who had funded our respective travel to Auschwitz, I thought my response to be interesting and even important—Maryknoll. Because the invitation had come after our annual budget approval, I approached the president of the school to see if even partial funding was possible. Though Maryknoll had generously funded my travels to Latin America, Africa, Asia, and the Middle East to learn more about Christianity in non-Western settings, this request bore no direct relevance to the teaching mission of Maryknoll. I was pleased when informed immediately that my trip would be completely funded, that it was essential to my growth as a Jewish person and scholar. To me this was an example of how much the existential situation of Jew and Christian had changed since Auschwitz. Rather than provide discussion, however, my story was greeted with a disapproving silence.

Similarly, when we discussed where we were traveling after Poland, I told them I was to visit Rome before going home. To this a delegate assumed that I was to be received there by the Pope. Actually, my trip was far more modest, for I had been asked by a secular socialist group who published my work in their journal to consult with them and lecture at the University of Rome. Still another time, a delegate speaking to me at a reception told me that he would like to see me drunk. Because he himself seemed the height of sobriety, I wondered for a moment what this might mean. It became clear to me later, for he spoke to an age-old Jewish understanding: working for the "gentiles," I had to mask my feelings and my background. He wanted to see me let go of my mask, let my Jewishness surface, and thus, in recovering my true self, return to the Jewish fold.

The intensity of our work together and the myriad of feelings evoked at Auschwitz highlighted our personal commitments and situations. Yet it was precisely my own journey that was so difficult for me to speak about. It was true that the path I had chosen—a path among Christians—was to some extent circumstantial: meeting Dorothy Day of the Catholic Worker in my senior year of university; being invited to teach at Maryknoll because one of the Maryknoll Fathers had read the book I had written on my experience at the Catholic Worker. But to rely solely on the accident of circumstance was to deny motivation. As a teenager and then a young adult, I was determined to understand this foreign, at first *extremely* foreign phenomenon called Christianity, which had had such an adverse impact on my own people. To the Catholic Worker at twenty-one years of age, I brought the question of what a committed life might be like, as well as the question of whether or not a group that fed and housed the poor would hide me and other Jews if America took on the sinister aspect of Nazi Germany. The larger question also had personal ramifications: I wanted to know, beyond books and the classroom, if the Christian tradition, hostile to Jews in the past, would always be hostile, or whether an authentic change had occurred. I remember this, to non-Jews a seemingly ridiculous question in an America that has welcomed us, as a burning question of a young person born the first generation after the Holocaust. In short, my fear and nightmare were typically Jewish—being rounded up in a city or town with other Jews and fleeing those who were persecuting us.

How could I share with the delegates who feared such a journey that after almost twenty years among Christians I had profoundly ambivalent feelings about the tradition and people who were once so foreign and now in some ways were so close to me? One critic of my work among the delegation had written some months earlier of my "mentors at Maryknoll," indicating, as I interpreted it, that I was a "court" Jew among Christians. Perhaps it was difficult to understand how I could be employed within a church setting and remain independent. But rather than a "court" Jew, I was known at Maryknoll for being profoundly critical of the Christian and Catholic tradition, for some far too critical.

And yet I had learned much from the renewal of the Christian community I experienced at Maryknoll, and the Christian world that opened beyond it provided diverse ways for a Jew to teach and to work out his own Jewishness. Along with my nightmares, I had realized this, too, at a young age: it would be impossible for me to understand my journey as a Jew only within the Jewish community. The expected conformity masked an emptiness, and among your own you could do little except follow. If the Christian environment was an ambivalent one for me, so was the Jewish environment; not being mine, the Christian environment offered a challenge of understanding it without the requisites of membership. In short, the fact that it was not mine offered me personal and intellectual freedom.

It also offered an expansion of my world. From the beginning and especially with my university studies, I recognized that the questions of our time were religious ones and that I was interested in what it means to be Jewish after Auschwitz and what it means to be religious in the broader sense as well. Did not this broader religiosity at the same time influence the possibility of being Jewish after the Holocaust? It is interesting to note that it was Richard Rubenstein again who encouraged this search, for in his lectures I encountered the likes of Paul Tillich, Reinhold Niebuhr, and Albert Camus. The broader currents of religious questions intrigued me. At Maryknoll, of course, what I had thought a rather broad consideration of the world seemed, after my arrival, Eurocentric and narrow. My subsequent travels to different parts of the world expanded my realities and pushed my own parameters of experience even further. Soon Tillich and Niebuhr receded and theologians like Gustavo Gutiérrez, Pablo Richard, and Elsa Tamez from Latin America, Samuel Ryan, Emmanuel Asi, and Marianne Katoppo, from Asia, loomed larger. Though sometimes seen as faddish, these theologians were in their context doing what Tillich and Niebuhr had done in their own milieu, that is, struggling to be faithful in the history and context in which they live, balancing the questions of peoplehood and faith. Over the years of reading, meeting, and traveling with these theologians, their struggles ceased to be ones in which I simply observed from a distance. In a strange way they became a part of me and reminded me of my responsibility to my own people.[10]

I was also becoming aware that not all Christians were dominant or even safe. In fact, I began to realize that a majority of Christians in the world were poor and oppressed, and that part of their oppression was intimately tied to this very religion they carried forth. Seeing our Jewish travails as intimately tied to the power of Christianity, I found it difficult at first to understand what this was that I was experiencing. If we as Jews had suffered under and nearly been annihilated by the Christian gospel, the Christians I heard and met had also suffered under the Western Christian onslaught. We had both survived Christianity: Jews with a disoriented religion and culture; they with their religions and cultures very nearly destroyed. Though Christian themselves, most non-European Christians had in fact been conquered by the gospel.

This is what crystallized for me in conjunction with teaching my course at Maryknoll, "The Future of Religious Resistance and Affirmation." At the time I was teaching this course, I was also preparing to leave for Auschwitz. The course began with a study of Columbus, the expansion of Europe and spread of Christianity to the Americas. From the start, the expansion and consolidation of Ferdinand and Isabella's power in what later became Spain was tied to the expansion and consolidation of Catholicism within that country. A two-track system was in place from the beginning: the elements of state and Church worked together, imposing a uniformity on all they touched—political, cultural, and religious. The thrust outward to the Americas for wealth and conversions was matched within by the Inquisition and the cleansing of Jews and Moors from Spanish soil. Violence was projected outward and inward at the same time. The enduring violence and its legacy of empires extended the Columbus event far beyond the Americas geographically and propelled it in time considerably longer than the years of the voyages. 1492 is then and now, even to the present.

As I looked around my class, with non-European Christians from the Philippines, Pakistan, India, Malaysia, Japan, China, Tanzania, Malawi, and Kenya, I considered that these were people heavily touched by the events of 1492. For in 1492 began the dichotomy of first world/third world; that is, the rise of Europe from poverty and disease and the loss in large parts of the globe of settled and vibrant cultures. Surely the African slave trade, which saw the transportation of millions of Africans to the Americas, and the colonization of the Americas and large areas of Africa and Asia were part and parcel of the continuation of 1492. The spread of Western Christianity was intimately linked to the power that confronted and in many cases subdued entire areas of the world; the destruction of culture and religion, along with the protection of the empire, allowed Christian missionaries an open field. I was conscious of this each day when I entered Maryknoll, for above the doorway is the figure of Jesus as the Christ with cross above him, holding the world in his hands. If it was important to preach Christ to the "pagans," it was, to be sure, much more easily accomplished with the backing of empire.[11]

I witnessed this in my class. The Christianity my non-European students carried and in some cases had converted to in their lifetime was hardly indigenous or ancient. Most of it was thoroughly Western in teaching and life-style. And I saw them struggle with the uprooting that the European empire and European Christianity had brought. By adopting Christianity they had been elevated above others in their societies, even within their families; often they were separated physically from their villages and culturally and spiritually by their internalization of Christian values. They were even taught to look down on their own people who had not converted. But through our readings on Columbus and 1492 these students recognized that the privilege of being Christian also masked the violence of being Christianized and that their Christianization was in many cases a thin layer of experience and values that separated them from their own people and from themselves. Over the years this was the realization that many of my students struggled toward, the dual alienation that Christianity imposed from their own culture and from the deepest memories and intuition of self. If Christianity had urbanized, educated, and spiritualized my African, Asian, and Latin American students at a very young age—and even allowed them to come to Maryknoll—as they matured, they embarked on a journey that is almost impossible to complete—to return to their people and themselves.

The problem of religious and cultural identity is historical and ongoing in the aftermath of 1492, especially as that event was and is today a Western and Christian enterprise. The turmoil introduced created and over time re-creates communal and personal suffering. For example, some of my students had been tortured and raped as political prisoners; others were in jail even as I left for Auschwitz. Still others had "disappeared" in Latin America. This is why they understood my discussion of the Holocaust; from their perspective the Jewish Holocaust afforded them insight into their past and present. In some cases, lacking specific knowledge of Jews or Jewish history, they nonetheless identified very much with the Jewish experience because it was at one and the same time foreign *and* intimate to their own experience.

Midway through the course, as my journey to Auschwitz drew near, I realized something that I had experienced in my travels and with my students, but had yet to articulate. It was simply this: we as Jews spend much time and thought explaining the singularity of Jewish suffering, especially in the Holocaust. However, looking at the violence accompanying 1492 into the present, I wondered whether this was the proper emphasis. Although understanding the singularity of every event and people, it seemed to me rather that 1492 and Auschwitz stand in continuity and are in fact concrete examples of the progression of external and internal violence accompanying the rise of Europe and Western Christianity. Were we Jews the victims of the same gospels under which the Native Americans, the African slaves, and the Filipinos suffered?

This common suffering is what James Cone understood when he wrote in his *A Black Theology of Liberation*, published in 1970, of the "death of six million Jews, the genocide of Amerindians, the enslavement and lynching of blacks" as a continuity and the responsibility of the white "Christian" churches. Because of this oppression, Cone characterized white, Western Christianity as the anti-Christ, "the enemy of Christ." This was also the point of Stanislaw Krajewski, a Polish Jewish member of our delegation, when he wrote, "As far as Auschwitz is concerned, Poles perceive their bond of common suffering with Jews to be stronger than their bond of common Christianity with Germans."[12]

A Jewish-Christian Solidarity

The experience of the suffering of Jews and Christians at the hands of a dominant Christian culture introduces a complexity to the discussion of the singularity of Jewish suffering under Christian power. It also introduces a bond. At first, to my surprise, and then with increasing regularity, I heard stories of suffering from my students that were like the ones I had recited to them from the Jewish past. And I also began to hear the kind of testimony that I knew well from Jewish history.

In March of 1985, a Maryknoll priest wrote of the experience of a student of mine, Brother Marty Shea, who works in Guatemala:

> Like mushrooms in a dark forest, new camps for Guatemalan refugees sprang up almost overnight in heavily wooded areas of Campeche and Quintana Roo, states in Mexico's Yucatan peninsula. Early in 1984, Mexican authorities, for political and national security reasons, abruptly decided to move the refugees from two-year-old camps in the state of Chiapas along the Guatemalan border to areas deeper in Mexican territory. Currently some 14,000 refugees have been relocated in Campeche with more arriving every week. The plan is to eventually move 40,000 refugees into the new areas. Presently there are 80,000 to 100,000 Guatemalans still in Chiapas.
>
> Taking only a few possessions they can carry, the refugees are herded by Mexican authorities into box cars and buses and transported hundreds of miles to muddy clearings hacked out of tropical vegetation. The new camps are long rows of rickety shelters made of sticks loosely bound with thin wire and covered with tar paper roofs. At first glance, the huts look more like giant bird cages than housing for families.
>
> The refugees in Campeche are Guatemalan Indians, descendants of the Maya nation, forced to flee their ancestral villages and farms two years ago because of widespread massacres carried out by the Guatemalan

army. "The Indians say that [they] are caught between two fires," explained Brother Martin Shea, 54, with whom I visited a camp in Campeche. "They are caught between the fire of guerrillas and the fire of the army."

According to Brother Marty, Guatemalan troops resorted to "Vietnam-type tactics" to control the countryside: "The guerrillas are the fish and the people are the lake, and the government decided to win the war by draining the lake." Men, women and children were killed indiscriminately, villages burned to the ground, crops destroyed. "Rape and torture are also a part of this process," said Brother Marty. "It's a form of genocide."[13]

By the end of 1992, the situation was little better. As Brother Marty reported, members of the Pueblo Nuevo community, displaced in the 1980s by just such government action, were prevented from returning to their village by the government.[14]

These same struggles are heard in the testimony of a Maryknoll priest who, as a student of mine in 1982, recalled his own horrible journey in Guatemala. One night he received a phone call from a convent in Guatemala City asking if he could come immediately. A woman who knew him well had arrived at the convent, crying hysterically. Her story is unfortunately too familiar. In the week preceding, her son was taken away by the military, then brought back the following day and dumped on her doorstep. He had been shot through the head. The next few days saw her daughter and husband similarly kidnapped and murdered. When the priest approached the woman and heard her story, he had every desire to function as he was taught: to console the grieving, to affirm the deceased's presence in God's care, to speak of what her family had given to the world. Yet as he stood in front of her, his role faded away and so did his words. Nothing he had learned, nothing he had brought with him could speak to this horror. After twenty-two years as a priest he could do little but weep.

Their tears were a form of solidarity framed by a solitude that is haunting and could not disappear. We might say that this solidarity came within solitude and held forth either the prospect of destruction or of a renewed commitment. It did not speak of grace or redemption. The question posed was, What would follow? More senseless death or a movement toward justice that affirms life?

Over the years I have come to know another Maryknoll priest, Roy Bourgeois, who has experienced the poor of Latin America and brought the message back home to the United States. In September 1990 he, with ten others, began a water-only fast at the entrance of Fort Benning, Georgia, to protest the training of Salvadoran soldiers there. On the first anniversary of the killing of six Jesuits in El Salvador, Bourgeois returned to Fort Benning, entered the post, and placed the photos of the martyrs at the entrance of the training school. He poured blood in one of the school's main halls as a reminder that "we cannot wash our hands of the blood of innocent people killed in El Salvador by soldiers trained in the United States." He and his companions were arrested and sentenced to sixteen months in jail. To those who ask Bourgeois if the action he took was difficult, he replies: "Prison is hard and very lonely at times, even with the support of family and friends, who also suffer. My dad cried when I called home to tell him of my sentencing. Yet I did what my faith and the poor called me to do in the face of such violence. As a Christian I feel I must try to relieve the suffering of the poor and integrate my faith in a loving God with action." In 1993, after his release from prison, Bourgeois wrote an open letter to President Bill Clinton arguing that the Fort Benning training center should be closed immediately.[15]

Still, in the face of all of this witness and testimony, my ambivalence about Christianity remains. In its dominant form, most peoples, including Jews, experience Christianity as relentless and triumphal. The preaching of the risen Jesus as Christ, as King, as Lord of all, to which every head shall bow, has an imperialist ring and effect; even Christ among the poor, a theological assertion by many liberation theologians, can be triumphal as well, another certainty, though this time in behalf of the oppressed. Did not most Christians, even those who protest some of the excesses of the missionary work after Columbus, agree with John Paul II in his homily at Higüey in the Dominican Republic, on October 12, 1992, celebrating the fifth centenary of Columbus's voyage, when he spoke the following: "Since that far off 1514, the watchful and loving presence of Our Lady of Altagracia has continuously accompanied the beloved children of this whole nation causing the *immense wealth of Christian life* to flourish in their hearts through the light and grace of her divine son." The Pope continued: "We are celebrating, dear brothers and sisters, *the arrival of the message of salvation on this continent.*"[16]

In a message to indigenous people later that same day, the Pope affirmed that before the arrival of the gospel the living and true God was present in indigenous cultures, "even though no one suspected it." The "seeds of the Word" were present, preparing the way in their ancestors for a revelation of the "Good News" that would include yet lift them beyond their celebration of the natural world. This was the revelation initiated in the life and death of Jesus Christ, which enlightened the indigenous peoples: "In the light of the Good News, they discovered that all the wonders of creation were but a pale reflection of their Author and that the human person, because he is the image and likeness of the Creator, is much higher than the material world and is called to eternal, transcendent destiny." To the excesses of the colonial venture and some of the missionaries, John Paul II asked the people to forgive those who had committed those trespasses and to see them within the broader aspect of the Church's "love" for the people. The previous day, in a visit to Santo Domingo's new missionary seminary, Redemptoris Mater, the Pope encouraged the seminarians to continue the missionary work started five hundred years earlier; on the threshold of the third millennium the seminary would send out the "new evangelists who will bring the whole world to Jesus Christ, 'the Way, the Truth and the Life.' "[17]

As I faced the students at Maryknoll and the dead at Auschwitz, I wondered what this "immense wealth of Christian life" was really about; the "message of salvation" was even more elusive. Can one say in truthfulness that the arrival of the gospel in the Americas had elevated the indigenous people or in some way fulfilled their destiny? And if the gospel message has merit, can one simply assert its importance and brush aside the massive destruction it brought along with the command to forgive? I wondered why the penchant for Christian forgiveness is almost always an afterthought to victory, rather than a humility that precedes, indeed may forestall, the conquest. Why did Christians feel that the goodness they found in their faith was something that all people had to experience to be fully human? To my students at Maryknoll I have often posed this literal dilemma, which might impact their external thrust: if it is true that belief in Jesus Christ sets one free, why is it that so many Christians I meet are so unfree? And why is it that the people Christians want to free often need to be coerced into accepting that "freedom"? Of course, both these queries elicit a denial and an explanation: the truth is above the individual and is separate from the concrete history in which it is carried forth. This was the thrust of John Paul II: the Christian message is above history.

But other than a dominant Christian, who could assert such notions, especially at the site of Columbus's landing? In fact, this was promoted by some Christians at Auschwitz as well. In light of 1492 and Auschwitz, in light of this continuity, it is still argued that the message of Jesus Christ transcends the bitter history that his followers created. This transcendence is challenged by Rabbi Irving Greenberg's statement in 1974 concerning the Holocaust: "After the Holocaust, no statement, theological or otherwise, should be made that would not be credible in the presence of the burning children." If this is taken seriously, then the cross at Auschwitz should be removed and the Pope's homily in Santo Domingo radically revised. Did not the history of Christianity render its message suspect, if not invalid? At Mathausen, where the Pope talked of suffering as a gift, and in Santo Domingo, where he exhorted further evangelization, he asserted a Christian hope in salvation and the future. Greenberg, however, challenges the future with the dead and calls upon such assertions to justify themselves in the face of burning children. Could the call for forgiveness overcome the burning children of 1492 and Auschwitz? Or the slave trade and the witch burnings that also came within Christian history? Could Christians renew their faith by jettisoning their own history? Could they reclaim what Jews have in a different way sought to maintain for themselves, that is, a posture of innocence and redemption?[18]

The Gospel of Columbus and I. G. Farben

It is difficult to analyze 1492 and Auschwitz without coming to the conclusion that more is needed than the mere reform of Christianity. In fact, it has become clear to me in the experiences of Maryknoll and Auschwitz that the gospels spoken about in Christian circles—that is, the canonical gospels of Matthew, Mark, Luke, and John—often function as theological cover for the gospels Christians actually live out in the world—what might be called the historical gospels of Constantine, Columbus, Luther, and I. G. Farben. The church in its liturgical life recites stories of justice and love and in its life in the world acts to the contrary. It is this duality that people experience as violence. Did the indigenous people of the Americas experience the beatitudes or Columbus? Did the Jews experience the Christian call to love one another or the brunt of I. G. Farben, the German chemical conglomerate that built slave labor camps within Auschwitz?

The neat division between the canonical gospels and history, so important for Christian renewal, is, from the perspective of the victim, difficult to articulate. The victims of 1492 and Auschwitz experienced the true face and character of Christian faith and culture in Columbus and I. G. Farben. In history, the cry of Christianity is less "love one another" than "onward Christian soldiers." The Pope was disingenuous at Mathausen and Santo Domingo; instead of commenting on the reading of the canonical gospels as the center of the liturgy, perhaps he should have read from the historical gospels, the Gospel of Columbus in this case, to be relevant to the event. Rather than raising Maxmilian Kolbe to sainthood at Auschwitz, thereby confirming the essence of Christianity as sacrifice of self, John Paul II should have emphasized how Auschwitz and the entire Nazi ethos had arisen in a thoroughly evangelized Europe. The Pope further should have emphasized not the salvation of Christ, but that the banishment of the Jews to oblivion was in some ways a fulfillment of Christian theology. Rather than evasion, then, the choice would be clearly placed before the audience: this has been the Christian way; shall we affirm it or choose another path?

In such a scenario, Christians are confronted with the choice of continuing Auschwitz, although in a quite different way than the Jewish choice, or of ending it. In relation to 1492, the choice is the same—to continue 1492 by emphasizing the triumph of the "Good News" or to end 1492 through a fundamental reevaluation of the entire Christian enterprise. For if to continue Auschwitz from the Jewish perspective is essential to the Jewish community, it is equally true that to continue 1492, albeit with different rhetoric, is essential to the growth and prosperity of Christianity. The joint task of Jew and Christian, therefore, is seen in its opposite, that is, the need to end Auschwitz and 1492. Though obviously a political and cultural challenge, perhaps this goal should be seen as well as a religious task, indeed the central religious task at the close of the twentieth century.

The experience of 1492 and Auschwitz raises the specter of Christian complicity with empire. Guardians of tradition like John Paul II, when mentioning at all the history of suffering, see it as peripheral; the imperfections of the Church cannot compromise its essential and more important mission. Religious reformers also posit a central and unchangeable aspect of Christian faith that has to their mind too often been incorrectly translated into history. Hence "faith beyond history" needs a better translation into present-day circumstances. In the Catholic community, the Vatican II Council represents simultaneously these somewhat divergent approaches. And so we experienced conflicting signals at Auschwitz: sometimes the triumphant Church; other times the repentant Church.

I have experienced this also at Maryknoll over the years and even in the class I was conducting as I left for Auschwitz. Over against those who were experiencing the gospel as a reality that conquered them, others sought to guard the faith. Still others, perhaps the majority, simply hoped for reform and renewal. Is the mission of the Church, and thus of Maryknoll, to evangelize *ad gentes* or to promote the development of peoples? Do these two aspects come together or contradict each other? Endless discussions on this topic provide little clarity; and if truth be stated, the argument almost always ends suspended in silence. One answer may be feared as too explosive, either reinforcing a framework of faith that cannot be maintained or introducing a dynamic that is ongoing and may end up outside the known framework of Christianity.

Certainly, after sixteen hundred years of the historical gospels, it is difficult to argue that the Christian message is found only in the canonical gospels or that by jettisoning the historical gospels the purity of the former can be reclaimed. It is too easy to say that uniting Christianity and empire in Constantine and the extension of Christianity in Columbus violate the Christian message. Without claiming that Luther led to Auschwitz, it is more than coincidence that the heartland of Christian reform also produced some centuries later the Nazi attempt to create a world without Jews. If the Nazis were anti-Christian, as many have claimed, they were also thoroughly imbued with Christianity; rebels against Christianity, they were involved in a cycle introduced or at least joined by Christianity. As Raul Hilberg points out, the Nazis simply took the churches' actions toward the Jews a step further: conversion, ghettoization, expulsion, and now annihilation. Although the Gospel of Luther needed a chastised Jewry to prove the triumph of Christianity, the Gospel of I. G. Farben could dispense with Jews altogether. The modern incarnation of the gospel took the final step without, it appears, much reflection; continuity suggested the next step as logical, perhaps even inevitable.[19]

It is difficult to deny the Christian inspiration of Constantine, Columbus, and Luther, for in their words at least, and in their vision, inspiration lay in an experience of Jesus the Christ. Describing the results of his first voyage to the Americas in 1492, Columbus wrote to his sponsors, King Ferdinand and Queen Isabella:

> And thus the eternal God, Our Lord, gives to all those who walk in His way triumph over things which appear to be impossible, and this was notably one. For, although men have talked or have written of these lands, all was conjectural, without ocular evidence, but amounted only to this, that those who heard for the most part listened and judged rather by hearsay than from even a small something tangible. So that, since Our Redeemer has given the victory to our most illustrious King and Queen, and to their renowned kingdoms, in so great a matter, for this all Christendom ought to feel delight and make great feasts and give solemn thanks to the Holy Trinity, with many solemn prayers for the great exaltation which they shall have in the turning of so many peoples to our holy faith, and afterwards for the temporal benefits, because not only Spain but all Christendom will have hence refreshment and gain.[20]

This is part and parcel of a Christian worldview and theology that Kirkpatrick Sale describes in his book *The Conquest of Paradise: Christopher Columbus and the Columbian Legacy*. The essential argument that Columbus makes with biblical quotation and medieval theology is simple: "Cristóbal Colón was chosen by the Lord as the divine instrument to fulfill the ancient prophecies that would rescue Christianity before the Apocalypse—and that was only 155 years away, as we remember—

namely, to spread Christianity to the unblessed heathen populations around the world, and to provide the gold for financing the crusade to recapture the Holy Sepulcher from the infidels. That was why He led Colón, His Christ-bearer, to the new lands, the *Otro Mundo*, where by divine coincidence there existed both so many heathens and so much gold."[21]

If you follow the description that Columbus himself writes of the people he found in the Americas, it reminds one, paradoxically, of the Christianity now sought in renewal: "It is true that, after they have been reassured and have lost their fear, they are so guileless and so generous with all they possess, that no one would believe it who has not seen it. They refuse nothing that they possess, if it be asked of them; on the contrary, they invite any one to share it and display as much love as if they would give their hearts." Still Columbus saw the need to bring the people to the Christian faith and so be "inclined to the love and service of Your Highness and of the whole Castilian nation." Columbus thus saw a beauty in need of refinement and service to a larger force, that is, empire. The discipline of hospitality that the indigenous peoples practiced was obviously not enough, nor was the fact that they were not, according to Columbus, "idolaters; but they all believe that power and good are in the heavens." The mission of Columbus and Christianity overrides the obvious beauty of the native culture; the hospitality of the natives is to be harvested for a greater good.[22]

The Gospel of I. G. Farben is perhaps more difficult for Christians to accept as rooted within their history because the language of Farben is shorn of Christian inspiration and symbolism. If Columbus's vision can be dismissed as eccentric or a perversion of Christianity by some, I. G. Farben can be seen as completely secular and in its actions anti-Christian. Unfortunately, this is too easy. Modernity itself is to a large extent an extension of Christianity, and the secularization of Western culture over the last centuries is both in conflict with and a fulfillment of the Christian West. The link between Christianity and empire, forged in the gospels of Constantine, Columbus, and Luther, gave birth to a Nazi empire with an internal dynamic that is difficult to disassociate from Christian inspiration. As Richard Rubenstein pointed out in *After Auschwitz*, the German fascination, indeed obsession, with the Jews came from Christianity.[23]

In his later work, *The Cunning of History*, Rubenstein cites the need to distinguish between the manifest values a tradition asserts to be binding and the ethos generated by that same tradition. The Judeo-Christian tradition is thought to proclaim an ethic in which human dignity is emphasized. However, Rubenstein writes that "beyond all conscious intent, it has produced a secularization of consciousness involving an abstract, dehumanized, calculating rationality that can eradicate every vestige of that same human dignity in all areas of human interchange." For Rubenstein, it is the biblical tradition that leads to the "secularization of consciousness, disenchantment of the world, methodical conduct (as in both Protestantism and capitalism) and finally, bureaucratic objectivity." Thus, in Rubenstein's view, the culture that made the death camps possible was not only indigenous to the West but an unforeseen and unintended outcome of its fundamental religious traditions. Indeed, it is more than coincidence that the "land of the Reformation" bore the seeds of death camps:

> It was the land of the Reformation that became the land in which bureaucracy was first perfected in its most completely objective form. The land of the Reformation was also the land where bureaucracy was able to create its most thoroughly secularized, rationalized, and dehumanized "achievement," the death camp. Before men could acquire the "dehumanized" attitude of bureaucracy in which love, hatred, and all purely personal, irrational, and emotional elements are eliminated in one's dealings with one's fellowmen, the disenchantment process had to become culturally predominant; God and the world had to be so radically disjoined that it became possible to treat both the political and natural order with an uncompromisingly dispassionate objectivity.
>
> When one contrasts the attitude of the savage who cannot leave the battlefield until he performs some kind of appeasement ritual to his slain enemy with the assembly-line manufacture of corpses by the millions at Auschwitz, we get an idea of the enormous religious and cultural distance Western man has traversed in order to create so unique a social and political institution as the death camp.[24]

Though Auschwitz was primarily a concentration camp and Auschwitz-Birkenau primarily a death camp, as World War II continued both encompassed an even larger mission that included, among other things, the slave labor camps erected by I. G. Farben. The first of these slave labor camps is known as Auschwitz III, which the company designated I. G. Auschwitz. This camp was constructed in 1941 and initially included a rubber and a gasoline plant, both of which were to become the largest such installations in the world. As Joseph Borkin details the history in his book *The Crime and Punishment of I. G. Farben*, the workers were inmates from Auschwitz; after Heinrich Himmler's first inspection tour of the project, he guaranteed I. G. Auschwitz an immediate labor supply of ten thousand concentration camp inmates. Though profits promised to be tremendous, there were impediments to full implementation of this plan, including limited housing and transportation snafus. For example, the railroad station carrying thousands of Jews a day to Auschwitz was "overburdened." One report sent from I. G. Auschwitz to I. G. Farben headquarters in Frankfurt cited other difficulties: "We have drawn the attention of the officials of the concentration camp to the fact that in the last few weeks the inmates are being severely flogged on the construction site by the capos in increasing measure, and this always applies to the weakest inmates who really cannot work harder. The exceedingly unpleasant scenes that occur on the construction site because of this are beginning to have a demoralizing effect on the free workers [Poles], as well as on the Germans. We have therefore asked that they should refrain from carrying out this flogging on the construction site and transfer it to the concentration camp." A few months later there was a greater appreciation for the difficulties faced by the S.S.: "The work, particularly of the Poles and inmates, continues to leave much room for improvement. Our experience so far has shown that only brute force has any effect on these people. As is known, the Commandant always argues that as far as the treatment of inmates is concerned, it is impossible to get any work done without corporal punishment."[25]

These and other difficulties eventually led to the creation of Auschwitz IV, Monowitz. In this camp the company was responsible for the housing, feeding, and health of the inmates; to the S.S. belonged the task of security, punishment, and supply of inmates. As Borkin relates it, although it belonged to I. G. Farben, Monowitz had all the equipment of the typical Nazi concentration camp: watchtowers with searchlights, warning sirens, poised machine guns, armed guards, and trained police dogs. "The entire camp was encircled with electrically charged barbed wire. There was a 'standing cell' in which the victim could neither stand upright, kneel, nor lie down. There was also a gallows, often with a body or two hanging from it as a grim example to the rest of the inmates. Across the arched entrance was the Auschwitz motto, 'Work Makes One Free.'" The treatment of the inmates became notorious:

Starvation was a permanent guest at Auschwitz. The diet fed to I. G. Auschwitz inmates, which included the famous "Buna soup"—a nutritional aid not available to other prisoners—resulted in an average weight loss for each individual of about six and a half to nine pounds a week. At the end of a month, the change in the prisoner's appearance was marked; at the end of two months, the inmates were not recognizable except as caricatures formed of skin, bones, and practically no flesh; after three months, they were either dead or so unfit for work that they were marked for release to the gas chambers at Birkenau. Two physicians who studied

the effect of the I. G. diet on the inmates noticed that the normally nour-
ished prisoner at Buna could make up the deficiency by his own body for
a period of three months. The prisoners were condemned to burn up their
own body weight while working and, providing no infections occurred,
finally died of exhaustion.[26]

As for shelter at Monowitz, the inmates slept in three tiers of wooden
cubicles. Each slot, barely large enough for one person to lie down, actually held three, thereby making it practically impossible to sleep,
since if one man was in a reclining position, the others would have to
sit up or lie over him. The simplest comforts were denied; even tables
and chairs were almost unknown. Hygienic conditions were subhu-
man. In the summer the heat was oppressive, almost beyond en-
durance, and in the winter there was no heat at all.[27]

As Borkin notes, however, life at Auschwitz had other aspects, at
least for the managers of the enterprise. Just four months after Commandant Rudolf Hoess introduced Zyklon B in the airtight chambers of
Auschwitz-Birkenau: an asphyxiating agent whose traditional, com-
mercial use was as an insecticide, the patent and distribution of which
was owned by I. G. Farben and which was now to be used to kill over a
million Jews, representatives of I. G. Auschwitz took part in a Christmas party with the S.S. high command. According to the company reports, the party "was very festive and . . . ended up alcoholically gay."[28]

Before leaving for Auschwitz, I was certainly familiar with the distinctions that reform-minded Christians make between real and nominal
Christians, that is, between professed Christians and those born of Christian parents but nonpracticing. The presumption is that believing
Christians could never participate in the practices of I. G. Farben, and
indeed some Christians did refuse, even to the point of sacrificing their
lives. The more important point, however, is the impetus behind such
activity, which was at least partially Christian, and the culture out of
which this activity grew, a thoroughly Christian one. Germany did not
have a Buddhist religious background; none of the directors of I. G. Farben were Hindu, nor were any of the commandants followers of Islam.
The enterprise was envisioned, directed, and run by people born in and
living within a Christian culture.

Indeed, this was Dietrich Bonhoeffer's great concern as a committed
Christian. Jailed for his part in a conspiracy to assassinate Hitler, Bonhoeffer found his fellow political prisoners to be atheists rather than
Christians. They needed to separate from the churches and the God of
the churches in order to practice what Bonhoeffer considered to be
Christianity. As he contemplated his own execution, Bonhoeffer wrote
of the inability to celebrate or even to speak about the Christian faith

after the fall of the Third Reich. Christianity had been thoroughly discredited; what was left was the secret discipline, an unannounced Christianity at the end of Christendom.[29]

Still, Bonhoeffer underestimated the survival of Christendom. In Latin America, for example, Pablo Richard, the Chilean biblical scholar and historian of Christianity, wrote in 1987 not only of the colonial Christendom of 1492–1808 and the new Christendom of 1808–1960, but a continuation of Christendom into the 1980s. On a trip to South Africa, just six months after leaving Auschwitz, I witnessed the crumbling of a distant yet powerful outpost of Christendom, one legitimized for years by what might be called the Gospel of Apartheid, a gospel only fully instituted after Auschwitz. In the United States, the S.D.I. defense system proposed by Ronald Reagan in the 1980s and the Persian Gulf War in 1991 are still justified in essentially Christian terms. Though the Episcopal Bishop of Washington refused an invitation to the White House on the night the Persian Gulf War began, Rev. Billy Graham graciously accepted one. The Armageddon theology preached by Rev. Jerry Falwell and Rev. Pat Robertson, seen as ludicrous and even blasphemous by my students at Maryknoll, represents in many ways the authentic successor to the historical gospels of Constantine, Columbus, Luther, and I. G. Farben. And they emanate from the same culture—European Christian culture—now moved westward.[30]

So the question of the historical gospels is not past; it is thoroughly embodied and promoted in the United States. The global power of the United States should be seen within the context of European empire and Christianity, as its continuation and expansion. Freedom of religion can hardly mask the Christian inspiration and domination of American culture. This was true, for instance, with Thomas Jefferson, who helped articulate the separation of church and state and who considered himself a Christian. Jefferson had a lifelong interest in Jesus culminating in a book he wrote titled *The Life and Morals of Jesus of Nazareth*. This book remained in his family until 1904, when it was published by the Fifty-Seventh Congress and a copy was given to each member of the House and Senate. When Rev. Daniel Berrigan commented that, rest assured, if United States nuclear weapons were fired, the person pushing the button would consider it a religious act, this was a reference to Christianity, a type of Christianity he opposed. To state the obvious, it is unlikely that Berrigan was referring to a Buddhist or Hindu act; to push the button would be seen as the final victorious act of the Christian world against the Soviet atheistic world. If this were not enough, in the 1990s with the collapse of communism, John Paul II has been calling for the reintegration of Europe within the context of the revival of European Christian culture.[31]

Thus it seems impossible, if after this long history we are to be honest, to disentangle the canonical and historical gospels or even to declare the primacy of the former over the latter. The renewal movements within Christian history that assert the canonical over the historical gospels simply end up contributing a new historical gospel. An example would be the Protestant Reformation, which sought to distance itself from the historical "perversions" instituted by the Catholic Church. Instead, it resulted in a new wave of violence against Jews and others in the sixteenth century and beyond. From the millenarian preacher Thomas Münzer to the Puritan settlers of New England, the Gospel of Luther (and Calvin as well) has also unleashed a dynamic in history that is often to be regretted, if not actively opposed. After this long history, is the dynamic of Christianity itself, rather than being redemptive, actually destructive? Is the Christian foundation of Western society itself part of the problem rather than a part of the solution? And did I not witness this destruction at Auschwitz and in my students—victims of the triumph of Christianity? Here the next difficult question poses itself: If ending 1492 and Auschwitz are the preeminent religious acts of our time, is this intimately tied to the task of ending Christianity?[32]

The Limits of Christian Reform

In the 1960s and 1970s, reflections on the Holocaust sparked a variety of critiques of Christian history by Christians. In regard to the Holocaust, one thinks of the American Catholic theologian Rosemary Radford Ruether's work *Faith and Fratricide*, published in 1974, which details the anti-Jewish aspects of Christianity from its origins. In Ruether's view, anti-Jewishness is less an aberration within Christianity than it is foundational to it. This anti-Jewishness needs to be rooted out both for its own sake and because it leads to Christian attempts to define anything different or other as outside the good, subject to abolition. Ruether's later work demonstrates this clearly; for example, anti-Jewishness in the Christian tradition is linked with Christianity's patriarchal bias against women. One also thinks of the German Catholic theologian Johann Baptist Metz, who explores the future of Jews and Christians after the Holocaust. For Metz, the post-Holocaust era means a new relationship between Christians and Jews, whom Christians have persecuted, and a new effort to journey together. Christians cannot avoid the Holocaust, pretending that it did not happen, nor move on in history without facing in a concrete way the memory of the Holocaust and its victims. I have often recited Metz's writing on this subject, and a particular passage of his was with me at Auschwitz: "We Christians can never go back beyond Auschwitz; to go beyond Auschwitz, if we see clearly, is impossible for us by ourselves. It is possible only together with the victims of Auschwitz."[33]

Recognizing the victims and traveling with them is also a theme of Christian protests regarding the quincentenary of Columbus's voyage. Like Ruether and Metz with regard to the Holocaust, many Christians see this as a time of repentance rather than celebration. Thus the National Council of Churches of Christ in the U.S.A. labels the arrival of Columbus an invasion, inappropriate to celebrate. The Council's resolution of May 17, 1990, details the atrocities committed by the invaders:

> For the indigenous people of the Caribbean islands, Christopher Columbus's invasion marked the beginning of slavery and their eventual genocide.

> For the indigenous people of Central America, the result was slavery, genocide, and exploitation leading to the present struggle for liberation.

> For the indigenous people of South America, the result was slavery, genocide, and the exploitation of their mineral and natural resources, fostering the early accumulation of capital by the European countries.

> For the indigenous people of Mexico, the result was slavery, genocide, rape of mineral as well as natural resources, and a decline of their civilization.

> For the peoples of modern Puerto Rico, Hawaii, and the Philippines, the result was the eventual grabbing of the land, genocide, and the present economic captivity.

> For the indigenous peoples of North America, it brought slavery, genocide, and theft and exploitation of the land which has led to their descendants' impoverished lives.

> For the peoples of the African Diaspora, the result was slavery, an evil and immoral system steeped in racism, economic exploitation, rape of mineral as well as human resources, and national divisiveness along the lines of the colonizing nations.

> For the peoples from Asia brought to work the land, torn from their families and culture by false promises of economic prosperity, the result was labor camps, discrimination, and today's victimization of the descendants facing anti-Asian racism.

> For the descendants of the European conquerors, the subsequent

legacy has been the perpetuation of paternalism and racism into our cultures and times.[34]

The resolution continues with respect to the Christian aspect of this invasion: "The Church with few exceptions, accompanied and legitimized this conquest and exploitation. Theological justifications for destroying native religious beliefs while forcing conversion to European forms of Christianity demanded a submission from the newly converted that facilitated their total conquest and exploitation." For the National Council of Churches, the history of 1492 is past *and* present, and prompts a call to church members to review current missiologies as to whether they perpetuate the exploitation of the descendants of those who suffered the original invasion.[35]

Still, with all the confession of Christian complicity and the need to reevaluate the Christian tradition and Christian theology in light of 1492 and Auschwitz, the dilemma continues for dominant Christians and the victims of Christianity. Metz's haunting phrase "together with the victims of Auschwitz" is almost mystical. To what destination are the victims of Auschwitz brought? And if the destination is obscure, in what way do the victims and victors travel together? If a minority of Christians will consider both the destination and the travel together, how will they interact with the majority of Christians in a Christian culture who often choose a different path? Can the understanding by Christians of the victimization they have caused halt the dynamic and even the development of historical gospels in the future?

Because of the suffering and the dynamic of Christian culture—which is part of the "victory" of Christianity, at least in the West—the recognition of victimization by Christians can be used to rescue and revive Christianity. Clearly, an instrumental use of the victims of 1492 and Auschwitz to reconstruct the Christian agenda is a continuation of triumphalism in another guise. I often think of this in relation to Vatican II: a church buffeted by external and internal critique jettisons, at least to some extent, the sense that those outside the Church live in darkness. Instead they adopt a theology of service to the world. The Church once triumphant is now to become the servant of all. However, to the people of the world this is a proclamation rather than a response to a specific request. And despite the beauty of Vatican II, it becomes an avenue for the renewal and survival of Catholicism in the West *and* expansion around the world.

Thus 1492 and Auschwitz are places of recognition of both the power of Christianity and its continuation, in unrenewed and renewed ways. They are also places of profound reckoning, where the critique needs still to be pushed farther. If it is true that Christianity now will continue

into the future with a dialectical critique revolving around the suffering
it has caused and its mission in light of that suffering—and that Christian culture in the West, now almost thoroughly disguised in modernity,
will also continue—does this end the discussion, thus fating us to live
within and out of this dynamic forever? Or can we see even in this
Christian discussion a level of abstraction and self-reference that ob-
scures other paths? Surely, the continuation of the debate is essential, as
it is a confrontation with power; at the same time it must go deeper. Do
not the victims of Auschwitz and 1492 ask for this deeper probe of this
religion than simply a dialogue between two aspects of the same reality?

Of all the Christian theologians, Mary Daly, a professor of theology
at Boston College, has taken the question of suffering and Christianity
to its farthest limits, and in her later work has rejected Christianity altogether. Though her emphasis is on the suffering caused to women by
Christianity's patriarchal aspects, she is aware of other victims, including Jews. Naming the historical gospel of patriarchy as embedded in
the churches and in their christological formulae, Daly, in her book *Beyond God the Father*, published in 1973, encourages women to go beyond
the plausibility of these formulae that "reflect and encourage idolatry in
relation to the person of Jesus." In fact, it is this idolatry that for Daly
demands silence about women's historical existence and promulgates
against women and others the "Most Unholy Trinity" of rape, genocide,
and war. As it becomes clear in her later works, the "Most Holy and
Whole Trinity"—power, justice, and love—cannot be pursued within
patriarchal Christianity or within a Christianity beyond patriarchy, if
such were even possible. In *Gyn/Ecology, Pure Lust*, and her autobiography *Outercourse*, patriarchy and Christianity are intimately tied together. Moving beyond God the father is moving beyond Christianity
and even beyond a language thoroughly imbued with Christian and
patriarchal values and concepts.[36]

In *Beyond God the Father*, Daly begins to deal with the distancing by
Christians interested in reform of the historical and canonical gospels.
Daly finds several strategies to pursue in relation to patriarchy and
Christianity. To the question of whether a male savior can save women,
one response is to look forward to the second coming, which may be in
the form of a woman. To the charge that Christianity as it developed is
patriarchal but is not inherently so, Daly cites Leonard Swidler's essay,
which attempts to claim Jesus as a feminist. Her initial response to Swidler is strong: "Jesus was a feminist, but so what?" Such a comment
does not mean that Daly is negative to Jesus; in fact, she seems to assent
to the possibility that as a person on the boundary, Jesus exemplified
and encouraged others to be free. However, for Daly the point is hardly
a blind imitation of Jesus' actions and views: "If reading the Gospels—

or anything else—sparks this freedom, this is hardly to be disparaged. But then Jesus or any other liberated person who has this effect functions as model precisely in the sense of being a model-breaker, pointing beyond his or her own limitations to the potential for further liberation." Still Daly warns against a kind of "continuum thinking" that is comfortable for Christians to assume because it enables us "to call ourselves Christians without putting any great strain upon conscience." It is this kind of thinking which for Daly dulls perception and inhibits women from developing the insights of radical feminism.[37]

In her later work, Daly leaves behind her grappling with Christianity, or so it seems. One wonders if her movement beyond patriarchal Christianity, the bedazzling voyage that Daly names as "outercourse"—that is, a "Voyage of Spiralling Paths moving out from the State of Bondage"— is itself a tribute to the power of patriarchy and Christianity. Paradoxically, in her voyage as a Pirate, recovering the lost story and power of women, Daly, with all of us, is caught in Christian culture. Thus it seems that Rosemary Radford Ruether, in her recent book *Gaia and God*, states it correctly when she comments on the two reasons for her concentration on the Western Christian tradition: "First because that is my tradition and therefore it is the culture for which I must be accountable. Second, it is a culture that has shaped and continues to shape (particularly in its secularized, scientific form) the rest of the world, through imperialism colonialism and neo-colonialism. It is the major culture and system of domination that has pressed humans and the earth into the crises of ecological unsustainability, poverty, and militarism we now experience." Ruether's analysis is verified in Daly's "post-Christian" autobiography, for large portions of it are consumed with her travels to Ireland, a place paradoxically imbued with patriarchal Christianity and holding immense treasures of prepatriarchal life. The latter can only be found within the former. Both Daly and Ruether struggle within the dynamic that Rabbi Irving Greenberg suggested in light of Auschwitz: searching out that which would be credible in the presence of burning children.[38]

The end of Christianity witnessed in its triumph of 1492 and Auschwitz is paradoxically found within its own critique—that is, found together with the victims of 1492 and Auschwitz. Thus Metz, quoted earlier, may be paraphrased as follows: We Christians can never go back behind 1492 and Auschwitz; to go beyond 1492 and Auschwitz, if we see clearly, is impossible for us by ourselves. It is possible only with the victims of 1492 and Auschwitz. Unfortunately, this paraphrase could extend almost indefinitely, including, as we have seen, women, African-Americans, and indigenous people around the world.

Carrying all these victims in the present makes reform, however necessary, a near impossibility. Nor can we simply remain in the dialectic of Ruether and Daly. Rather, the memory of the victims calls Christians to, among other things, differentiate between the Christian religion as it came into being and extended itself through time, and the initial discipline as proposed by Jesus. That is, while investigating the historical gospels and analyzing the canonical gospels, it is crucial, at least as a first step, to go back behind history and canon to retrieve the discipline offered by Jesus and see whether this moves the discussion forward or backward. Does the historical Jesus lead to the canonical Jesus? Do the canonical gospels lead to the Constantinian Christ? Does the historical Jesus subvert or promote a Christianity that is renewed or triumphant? Does this discipline of Jesus say anything to the victims of the religion that carries his name, including among its primary victims the Jewish people? It is this question that is foundational to the attempt to move forward in Christianity and in Christian culture.

5

Auschwitz and the Brokerless Kingdom of God

The Christian struggle to "end 1492" is a struggle against the mainstream of Christianity, its theological triumphalism and its links with the violence of empire, and against many of the symbols and dogmas which characterize that mainstream. If it is true that we as Jews must now jettison our sense of Jewish innocence and redemption through Israel, dominant European and North American Christians must also leave behind their sense of innocence as well as their belief that to affirm Jesus Christ as the savior of all is somehow redemptive for the world. In actual fact, this "redemption" is covered with the blood of many peoples, including the majority of the world's Christians. Of course, it is possible to be a Christian, conquered and oppressed by the gospels, and still hold fast to innocence and redemption, thus a triumphalism from the left as well as the right. As we have seen, however, Christians outside of Europe and America and Christians within the empire are waking up to the fact that redemption played out in the world for one person or people is a disaster for the other.

Interestingly enough, those Christians who seek to move beyond innocence and redemption, like many Jews, find themselves in an awkward and ambivalent place. If Christian history is not innocent and the Christian sense of redemption is covered with blood, what does it mean to be a Christian? And what if the canonical gospels, those to which chastised Christians typically retreat, are found to be problematic—on the one hand representing a polemic that eventually leads to empire, while on the other preserving some traces and obscuring salient aspects of Jesus himself? The Christian establishment, like its Jewish counterpart, proffers its various orthodoxies, enlarging or trimming them when necessary. But they are undermined by the history of Auschwitz and 1492. To many third-world Christians, their overriding existential and even philosophical concern is simply "ending 1492," or at least mitigating its effects. Perhaps the essential task of both Jew and Christian is "ending Auschwitz" in the sense of "never again," and "ending 1492" with the critical understanding of Jew and Christian in Europe and America that we are now participating together in the continuation of 1492. If this is so, it could be that the essential division between Jew and Christian in the West, the figure of Jesus, was then and is today a false dividing point, one that covers over the contemporary essential solidarity of dominant European and American Christians and Jews over against much of the world.

That solidarity is expressed in many ways, including, primarily, in maintaining the power of the West built on the military, economics, and race. This is what Herbert Edwards, an African-American theologian, meant when he wrote in 1976 that historically "the faith that bound together Protestant, Catholic, Jew, rich and poor, educated and illiterate, liberal and conservative, laissez-faire capitalist and New Dealer, high churchmen and low, pious and irreverent, Republican and Democrat, was white racism. Racism has been the only ecumenical faith that America has consistently subscribed to."[1]

This is one way of defining the ecumenical dialogue, which can be characterized as the "ecumenical deal"—the discussion of the Jewish-Christian establishment on how to keep intact its own self-definition and institutional arrangement against the onslaught of history and critical thought coming from dissenters both outside and within the empire. Jewish and Christian participants agree to the old intertribal warfare—whether there are one or two covenants, whether Jesus came for the Jews or the Gentiles—so that both can survive the new challenge of ending Auschwitz and 1492, which they recognize to have profound political, cultural, *and* religious ramifications. It struck me at Auschwitz that the ecumenical dialogue has outlived its purpose of reconciling Jews and Christians after the Holocaust. It serves now instead as a camouflage, deflecting the deeper questions posed by Auschwitz and 1492.[2]

With the failure of Judaism and Christianity in our time, the task before us can be seen either as a need to resurrect the moral bases that are failing or as an opportunity to raise foundational questions as to the viability and importance of both traditions. Thus a full commitment to "ending Auschwitz" and "ending 1492" may bring us closer to the traditions we inherit, or it may distance us further from them. In the final analysis, should our commitment be defined within the parameters of either rescuing or abandoning these traditions? It may even be possible that Judaism and Christianity, whatever their rhetoric, need to continue these events of Auschwitz and 1492 to survive. The example that comes to mind is the institutional churches' desire to speak of justice, even to renounce their previous methods of missionary work, while continuing to evangelize, with new methods and renewed energy, the peoples of Latin America, Africa, and Asia. As in 1492, the internal decay of Christianity in Europe, rather than evoking fundamental discussions about the Christian enterprise itself, increases evangelization outside of Europe. Christianity within the empire diminishes at the same time that it uses empire to expand outside those boundaries. On this issue the ecumenical deal holds: Jews force Christians to renounce their desire to convert Jews as Jews remain silent, even at times give "permission" for Christians to continue to evangelize the world.[3]

Despite these contemporary issues, one cannot help but feel that a series of tragic errors were made centuries ago that either intentionally or inadvertently led to the present impasse. From the Christian side, the most obvious error was the movement from the canonical gospels to the gospels of Constantine and Columbus. Yet it seems that this error came perhaps from an earlier decision—the movement from the Jesus of history to Jesus the Christ. In the beginning, this shift was internal and therefore one of perspective. It represented a choice of direction rather than the founding of an institutional religion. However, the internal choice of direction to see Jesus as the savior soon was projected onto the world, thereby becoming one of objectives and demands. The internal understanding of redemption that an outsider might find compelling, provocative, repulsive, or to which one might remain indifferent was replaced by the "fact" of redemption, which people had to affirm under penalty of ghettoization, exile, or death. One might say that the movement from the Jesus of history to the Christ of faith made it almost inevitable that the historical gospels would develop. Did the proclamation of the risen Christ imbue Christianity with a tendency to link with empire?

As we have seen, the canonical gospels and the historical gospels are difficult to disentangle. The most obvious example is a contemporary Catholic parish built and staffed in the way of empire (the architecture, the separation of cleric and lay person, the substitution of the communion wafer for a substantive meal, the formal codified liturgy rather than the informal recollection of stories related to Jesus). The parish may still discuss how the gathered community should oppose a particular aspect of empire which the Church originally blessed and from which it still benefits. More difficult is the separation of the canonical gospels—which in Christian renewal are seen as wholly good and function to avoid the historical gospels within which Christians have lived—from the life, background, and teachings of Jesus. In this setting the canonical gospels are seen as representing the life of Jesus, and the variance from the historical to the interpretive stories is ignored. But what would Christian renewal look like if the historical Jesus essentially challenges much of the canonical literature, indeed is at odds with it and thus undermines the foundations of Christian religion as it was and is communicated?

On the Jewish side, the questions are somewhat different in history and scope, though no less challenging. By the end of the first century, Judaism was a defeated political and religious movement. As Paula Fredriksen, a New Testament scholar, points out in her book *From Jesus to Christ: The Origins of the New Testament Image of Jesus*, during the first century Judaism at times demonstrated its propensity toward empire and conversion; the rise of the Roman and then Christian empires ended these possibilities. Thus, with very few exceptions the Jewish internal discussion of religiosity was played out in the confines of a small, defeated, and persecuted community. Outsiders were spared any proselytizing by Judaism, only to face a powerful and relentless Christian evangelism.[4]

The internal Jewish discussion was heated both because of the external pressure of the Roman and Christian empires and the internal pressure of conforming to an emerging orthodoxy, which we now know as rabbinic Judaism. It is important to note that just as Christians pursue renewal through an attempt to jettison the historical for the canonical gospels—presuming that the more basic question of Jesus is thereby answered—so, too, Jewish renewal is often pursued by returning to these rabbinic sources developed over a thousand years ago. In doing so, Jews bypass a critical engagement with our own current history of displacing another people in Palestine while ignoring our role in the present empires. Returning to rabbinic sources functions in an ahistorical way and also closes off more radical questioning of the rabbinic system itself. An example is the congregation in a plush synagogue whose rabbi emphasizes Jewish suffering, pledges unequivocal support for Israel, and proceeds to read from the prophet Isaiah. Another example is the current spate of books on Jewish mysticism. The most recent publication within this genre occurred during the spring of 1992 as I prepared for my travels to Auschwitz. Written by Rabbi Arthur Green, president of the Reconstructionist Rabbinical College and titled *Seek My Face, Speak My Name: A Contemporary Jewish Theology*, this work avoids the issues of the Holocaust, Israel, and the oppression of the Palestinian people.[5]

Crucial to understanding the synagogue setting is the fact that few Jews live within the rabbinic framework other than the rabbi, whom one might call a professional Jew, trained and paid to live within that system. How the rabbinic system and the combination of rabbinical and Jewish particularism came into being is unasked and, out of ignorance, is almost impossible to ask. What is before and behind this system, which is promulgated as Judaism and which most Jews in their every-day life essentially reject? Like the question of Christian renewal, Jewish renewal is haunted by its prehistory—interestingly enough, the same prehistory that haunts Christianity, that is, the time preceding and including the era of Jesus. It is here that the fundamentals of Christian and Jewish life as we know them today begin to take shape and the separation of both faiths becomes definitive.

So often the essential division of Judaism and Christianity is assumed to revolve around Jesus. Yet this conclusion is simplistic, for as we know, some Jews rejected Jesus as messiah whereas other Jews accepted Jesus as the Christ. Still others lived and worked with Jesus as a fellow Jew or met him in his travels and no doubt admired his insights and methods as a Jewish thinker and actor. To most Jews, Jesus was simply unknown. After the tumult of the first century, Judaism and Christianity went their separate ways. But the question of Jesus seen in his historical setting actually challenges the rejection/acceptance model of Judaism and Christianity and subverts both of these religions in the forms that they assumed historically. Could the renewed discussion of Jesus function to undermine the Jewish and Christian establishments, thereby promoting the end of Auschwitz and 1492? As we have seen, the Jewish and Christian establishments have in fact, with Jewish success and empowerment, become one establishment, with the separation of Jew and Christian by way of Jesus actually masking our essential and joint projects.

The suggestion of a revived discussion of Jesus—discussion of a historical Jesus that subverts the Jewish-Christian establishment—is fraught with dangers. The first danger is the probability of offending Christian *and* Jewish sensibilities, the former by asserting that Jesus is not the messiah for Jews *or* Christians, the latter by suggesting that Jesus is somehow important for both Jews *and* Christians. At the same time, by challenging the prevailing orthodoxy put forth by the ecumenical dialogue, one is in danger of being disciplined simultaneously by the guardians of both traditions. The ecumenical dialogue states its orthodoxy boldly, for each tradition defines itself and each is accorded its own beliefs and structures. Outside of these parameters no critical thought is allowed. And after the Holocaust, who would dare raise the question of Jesus to Jews who have suffered so much in his name? Yet it is also true that hundreds of millions of others, many of them Christians, have likewise suffered in his name, once again linking Auschwitz and 1492. Perhaps the deeper question is whether it should be prohibited even to raise again the question of Jesus to Jews or Christians because of what has been done in his name.[6]

Jesus and the Jewish-Christian Establishment

Of course, Jesus is often mentioned in the ecumenical dialogue. Some of the great Jewish theologians of the twentieth century have carried on a spirited dialogue with Christianity. These include among others Leo Baeck (1873–1956), Martin Buber (1878–1965), Franz Rosenzweig (1886–1929), Will Herberg (1901–1977), and Abraham Heschel (1907–1972). As Fritz Rothschild, a professor of Jewish philosophy at Jewish Theological Seminary, points out, the central themes of these authors revolve around four topics: the person and significance of Jesus; the issue of law and gospel; the place of the Hebrew Bible in Christianity; the role of the old and new covenants. Not surprisingly, these are also some of the major themes of Richard Rubenstein's *My Brother Paul.*[7]

In the contemporary ecumenical discussion, Jewish participants attempt to link the witness of Jews and Christians. That is, both traditions, although clearly distinct, share foundational principles and aspirations, including the assertion that Christianity cannot fulfill its mission without its Judaic heritage and a living vibrant Jewish community. How could a Christian understand Jesus without understanding him first and foremost as a Jew? Instead of Jews and Christians fighting with one another, their recognition of a common heritage presupposes the real fight in the modern world against which they can join forces: secular pagan influence that denies the transcendent and the inherent dignity of humankind. At certain moments the recognition of a common heritage can jointly boost the theological work or the renewal movement in each community. Heschel's essays "A Hebrew Evaluation of Reinhold Niebuhr," published in 1956, and "The Jewish Notion of God and Christian Renewal," published in 1967, are two examples that come to mind. Another is found in Will Herberg's essay "A Jew Looks at Jesus," published in 1966, in which Jesus is hailed as a great moral teacher and a prophet in Israel, and Christians and Jews are coworkers in the vineyard of the Lord.[8]

Herberg's essay on Jesus is interesting to analyze both for its affirmation of Jesus and the limits of that affirmation, for it is typical of Jewish reflections on Jesus. To begin with, Herberg affirms Jesus as a "great and incomparable moral teacher." In the Sermon on the Mount, for example, Jesus reached the "high-water mark of moral vision and ethical teaching." For Herberg, this teaching is directly in line with the rabbinical tradition, and thus Jesus should be considered among the rabbis of Judaism. But Jesus is also more than a rabbi; he has a clear affinity with the Jewish prophets. As a God-possessed man bringing God's word of judgment and promise, Herberg's Jesus is a prophet of Israel, in the succession of Amos, Hosea, Isaiah, and Jeremiah.[9]

Jesus as moral teacher and prophet is not a problem for Herberg, nor should it be for Jews in general. For Herberg the problem lies elsewhere, in Peter's confession of Jesus as the Christ, a savior who has come to redeem his people and was rejected. When, however, Jesus is interpreted as embarking on a mission to the Gentiles to bring them to the God of Israel, Herberg is able to assent. Jews can thus affirm the ongoing reality of the Church as an institution that seeks not to supplant the old, but to extend and enlarge it. For Herberg, the corruption of the Church is linked historically with its confusion over its own mission, attempting to replace the Jewish covenant rather than broaden it. The survival of the Jews and the continuation of the Church validates a double covenant, each in need of the other. Herberg relies on the work of the German Jewish theologian Franz Rosenzweig when he writes: "Yes, each needs the other: Judaism needs Christianity, and Christianity needs Judaism. The vocation of both can be defined in common terms: to bear witness to the living God amidst the idolatries of the world."[10]

In fact, the religious vocation has been split into two parts, with the Jew fulfilling his or her vocation by staying with God for as long as the world remains unredeemed, and the Christian by going out to the Gentiles to bring the world closer to God. The two religions in Herberg's view relate to the same truth and are equal before God; the world is divided between Jew and Christian on the one hand and pagans on the other. In different ways both Jews and Christians are fighting for the same goal, the kingdom of God, and both are part of God's plan. As Herberg writes:

> The witness of Christianity against the legalistic, moralistic tendencies in Judaism is a witness for which the Jew must always be grateful. And the Christian, too, it seems to me, ought to see the value of the Jewish word in this dialogue. The Christian who tends to be impatient with the Jew for refusing to see in Jesus the fulfillment and completion of God's redemptive work might pause a moment to consider whether this Jewish "obstinancy" was not itself important as an indispensable reminder of the very incompleteness of this completion, of a redemption which may indeed have come but is nevertheless yet to come. The heart of each, Jew and

Christian alike, may ache, perhaps, that the other is not in his camp, seeing things his way and fighting side by side with him on his sector of the front; but he ought also to recognize that though the other fights on a different sector, he is also fighting the same battle for the same God, and that it is perhaps by the providence of God that they are thus separated.[11]

If Will Herberg's analysis of Jesus exemplifies the coming together of Judaism and Christianity from the Jewish perspective, the United Church of Christ Theological Panel on Jewish/Christian Relations statement of May 1990 is a good example from the Christian side. The members of the panel were drawn from a wide variety of perspectives, including Jay Rock from the Office for Christian-Jewish Relations of the National Council of the Churches of Christ, Dr. Gabriel Fackre of Andover Newton Theological School, and a Jewish theologian, Dr. Michael Wyschogrod, representing the American Jewish Congress. Not surprisingly, the questions posed to the panel involved the following: covenant-land-supersession; Christology-atonement-supersession; suffering-Holocaust-anti-Semitism; ethical consequences.[12]

In some ways the panel's affirmations are similar to Herberg's. As Christians they seek to understand the coexistence of the Jewish people and the churches after the death and resurrection of Jesus. They affirm with Paul that the gifts and the call of God are irrevocable; thus the Jewish covenant stands alongside the Christian covenant. Jesus stands in the tradition of the Torah and the prophets and yet expresses a new revelation. This "singular deed" that God has accomplished through Jesus Christ is done for the redemption of the whole world. Rather than causing contempt for Jews, the redemptive event presses Christians to be in solidarity with Jews and all others in their suffering and in their struggle for self-determination. The panel recognized that although the affirmation of the dual covenant of God might seem to be a paradox, it is this affirmation that calls for a deeper probing of the Christian faith. On the question of the state of Israel and Palestinians, the panel was split, stating in its conclusion, "In the land called Holy, prophets heard the word of God and, Christians believe, the incarnation of God's love took place. Can not the Holy Land become for our time a symbol of hope, a community of all believers, a wellspring of peace for the whole world?" The introductory affirmation raises the question of the Christian faith "After Auschwitz," noting that the "Holocaust has sent Christians back to their texts and traditions and to re-examine their theology and to ask about their complicity in the anti-semitism that gave rise to that horror."[13]

From the Jewish side is the desire to join with the dominant Christian ethos and hence stand indispensible to the mission of Christianity in the modern world. Clearly, the agenda of Jews in this dialogue is more than simple survival, for the link with Christianity is also an avenue to respectability in a Christian culture. Since 1967 it also lends itself to the creation of a united front on the question of Israel. At the same time, the pairing of Judaism and Christianity after the Holocaust attempts to forge an establishment that once and for all banishes the questions that Christians ask of Jews and Jews of Christians. In the moral warfare against secular paganism, it is the good Jew and Christian battling the bad pagans. Of course, in the 1950s and early 1960s neither the Christian nor Jewish establishments anticipated the outbreak of radical Jewish and Christian theologies, theologies of the death of God and theologies of liberation, against which they later effectively united. Suffice it to say that the union of the Jewish establishment with the Christian establishment, *to become one establishment,* makes it even more difficult from both sides to explore in a radical way the issues before us. In burying the differences between Judaism and Christianity as they have been lived out, or by accentuating the rhetorical differences, which mean little or nothing as they are lived out, the foundational questions are declared closed. So a Christian critique of Judaism is now impossible, at least in the public discourse of the religious establishment.[14]

From the Christian side, the acceptance of the Jewish covenant as promised by a God who does not break promises is a guarantee that its covenant is not revoked, despite the history of Christianity. Christian repentance is thus accomplished through Christian acceptance of Judaism's validity, which obligates Jews likewise to accept Christianity's validity. The bargain is sealed, and both traditions can continue essentially untouched. A Jewish critique of Christian history vis-à-vis the Jews is allowed so long as the messiah question is left alone and contemporary Christianity is affirmed. And we should also note that this establishment, far from conservative, is filled with liberal Jews and Christians who actually set the limits of public discourse and indeed, as Noam Chomsky has pointed out, the limits of thinkable thought.

Distorting Jesus

Certainly no figure in Western history has been the subject of such intense discussion as Jesus. And the discussion has over the centuries emphasized different aspects of Jesus, indeed has created different Jesuses, each responding to a cultural context and time period. As Jaroslav Pelikan, a historian of Christianity at Yale University, has written in *Jesus Through the Centuries,* Jesus was seen as a teacher and a prophet within the setting of first-century Judaism, as the turning point of history by Christians in the first and second centuries, as a light unto the Gentiles in the Christian evangelization of the Greco-Roman world of the second and third centuries, and as the King of Kings in the rise of Constantinian Christianity in the fourth century. The images of Jesus proliferate as the centuries progress. Jesus becomes the Cosmic Christ in Christianized Platonic philosophy of the third and fourth centuries; the monk who rules the world in medieval Western society of the eleventh and twelfth centuries; and the universal man in the Renaissance of the fifteenth and sixteenth centuries. More recently, Jesus has been seen as the teacher of common sense in the eighteenth-century enlightenment and as the liberator through the nineteenth and twentieth centuries. Throughout his book, Pelikan emphasizes that Jesus is created as much by particular cultures as he is by the facts of his own life. Even belief is secondary to cultural realities, or rather belief comes within culture. Cultures see Jesus in the only way they can see, through their specific cultural lens, which varies in time and place.[15]

Since the late nineteenth and early twentieth century, there has been renewed emphasis on understanding who the Jesus of history was in his own time and culture. According to Pelikan, this inquiry has led to a rethinking of the relation between Christianity and Judaism, a rethinking that accelerated as a consequence of the Holocaust. Ironically, it was in the years of the Holocaust that Christians furthered their awareness of the Jewishness of Jesus, the apostles and the New Testament, an awareness that later came to expression in the language of Vatican II. For instance, Pelikan cites the year 1933, the beginning of the Nazi era in Germany, when there appeared in that country the first volume of the multivolume *Theological Dictionary of the New Testament* edited by Gerhard Kittel, a German biblicist. One of its major themes was that the teaching and language of the New Testament and of Jesus himself could only be understood within the context of first-century Judaism.[16]

Though the Jewishness of Jesus is taken for granted today, this Jewishness remains within a broad formulation. Most often, at least in the renewal movements of Christianity, Jesus' Jewishness is thought to be found in the canonical gospels. But what images of Jesus and the Jewishness of his time are actually found there? For Paula Fredriksen, these images are bound to particular gospels. In John, Jesus is the stranger from heaven; in Luke-Acts, Jesus is the messiah to the Gentiles; to Matthew, Jesus is the Christ of scriptures; and to Mark, Jesus is the secret messiah. Perhaps of most importance, at least for the spread of Christianity, is Paul's understanding of Jesus as the Christ of the Parousia.[17]

Fredriksen's analysis is detailed, her conclusions fascinating. The early apostles are struggling for a place in the Jewish and Greco-Roman world. To them, the end of the world is imminent. Accordingly, they struggle as Jews with acceptance and rejection by other Jews of the message of Jesus as they interpret it. They argue over the place of the Gentiles in relation to this message and search for signs in history to validate their claims. The destruction of the Second Temple in 70 C.E., for example, causes a crisis of belief, for neither the Parousia nor the end of Judaism come to pass. According to Fredriksen, these diverse groups of followers of Jesus develop a "polemic against a perceived opponent who would not go away—whose presence, indeed confronted them from within the very scriptures to which they now laid claim."[18]

Because of this crisis of belief, the canonical gospel understanding of Judaism, the historical setting drawn for Judaism, actually originates from the canonical authors' own day rather than Jesus'. As Fredriksen sees it, the canonical gospel authors had Jesus confront not early first-century Jews but a caricature of the evangelists' own opposition, the Pharisees of the late first-century synagogue. Thus the canonical gospel understanding of Judaism is essentially without historical value; what develops is a series of theological speculations needed to justify a message in the wake of eschatological disappointments. At the same time, Judaism challenged the younger community's identity, and it also was competitive in the mission field. By receiving Gentiles into the Jewish fold and by being extremely attractive to Gentiles in search of monotheism, antiquity, a prestigious sacred text, and a community oriented around ethics, Judaism offered strong competition for converts to this new community, a competition that ended only when Constantine made conversion to Judaism a criminal offense.[19]

The most obvious example of the distortion that is fundamental to the canonical and later historical gospels is the portrayal of Judaism and, in particular, Jesus' relationship to it. Far from separating himself from his people, Jesus in fact was deeply immersed in the struggle of Jews and the Judaism of his time. To Fredriksen, Jesus was an apocalyptic preacher who was political and nationalist. This apocalyptic was part of a Jewish restoration theology that partook of the broad Jewish consensus on what was religiously important: the people, the land, Jerusalem, the Temple, and Torah. According to Fredriksen, Jesus preached a kingdom contemporary Jewish audiences understood, exalting Israel and precluding imperial domination. Even the gospels preserve traces of Jesus' participation in this consensus: "His calling twelve disciples to represent all the tribes of eschatological Israel; his intensification of ethical norms embodied in Torah; his journey to Jerusalem to greet the coming kingdom; his prophetic gesture at the Temple, in anticipation of a Temple not made by hands; his prophecy of the imminent fulfillment of God's promises to Israel fulfilled in Torah." The conjecture that Jesus would have offended his listeners, in preaching a loving and merciful God who forgave repentant sinners and preferred mercy to sacrifice, is rejected by

Fredriksen. "Such a message simply would not have come as news to Jesus' Jewish audience, whose people had been preserving scriptures and creating liturgies stating as much for at least half a millennium." Hence Fredriksen sees the death of Jesus in the context of his apocalyptic worldview: convinced that the end was at hand, Jesus goes up to Jerusalem for the Passover. Because Jesus is attracting crowds, the Jewish priestly authorities fear the indiscriminate use of Roman force. In collaboration with Pilate's troops they arrange to arrest Jesus by night. After his arrest, the High Priest interrogates him briefly. He is turned over to Pilate and condemned to death as a messianic pretender together with other enemies of the empire. Jesus is crucified in the world of politics, not religion.[20]

The canonical gospels, then, misrepresent Jews and Judaism and to a large extent Jesus himself, and it is these views that are enshrined in the sacred book of the West as Christianity joins the empire. With this union of Christianity and empire in Constantine, the diversity of Christians and Christian beliefs is also challenged, including the beliefs of the Docetists and Ebionites. By the end of the second century, in this situation of inter-Christian and Christian-Jewish competition and controversy, the collection of writings we know as the New Testament is first brought together. Fredriksen writes that by the middle of the fourth century, the work of recreating the past was complete. "The Christian canon included the Septuagint but the New Testament superseded it; Christian imperial law made Judaism and various Christian groups pariah; and Orthodoxy could trace its genealogy directly from God's cursing the snake in Genesis to the courts of Constantinople." It is here in the ever-lengthening interim between the resurrection and the Parousia that the christological function of the second coming passes to the Church, an imperial church linked to an imperial state that canonizes and interprets the texts of the gospels. As Robert Grant, professor at the University of Chicago Divinity School, points out, the "unity of the Christian movement was to be maintained by the power of empire." In fact, the Church actually sacralized that which promoted its own unity. This is the conclusion of Averil Cameron, Professor of Late Antiquity and Byzantine Studies at the University of London, when she writes: "The Church developed its own way of sacralizing the non-Christian emperors: one of them was the evolution of Christian political discourse, a theory, or rather a theology, of imperial rule."[21]

Within the context of the analysis of Fredriksen, Grant, and Cameron, it seems more and more difficult to separate the historical and canonical gospels. The gospels as they are written in fact become canonical and lead toward the gospel of Constantine. Anti-Jewishness and the persecution of other Christians may be many things, but they are not anti-Christian. Rather, they are involved in the very formation of Christianity.

At the same time the canon develops, the world Jesus knew and acted within is left behind. By the time of Paul, the man from rural Galilee is interpreted in the urban environment of Antioch, Rome, and other Hellenistic cities such as Petra, Gerasa, Philadelphia, and Bostra. Within a decade of the crucifixion of Jesus, the Greco-Roman world becomes the dominant environment of the Christian movement, with results that Wayne Meeks of Yale University analyzes in his book *The First Urban Christians: The Social World of the Apostle Paul*. Meeks finds Paul to be a city person, with the city breathing through his language. "Jesus' parables of sowers and weeds, sharecroppers, and mud-roofed cottages call forth smells of manure and earth, and the Aramaic of the Palestinian villages often echoes in the Greek. When Paul constructs a metaphor of olive trees or gardens, on the other hand, the Greek is fluent and evokes schoolroom more than farm; he seems more at home with the cliches of Greek rhetoric, drawn from gymnasium, stadium or workshop." As Meeks points out, the transformation is almost complete with Paul; he divides the world into city, wilderness, and sea, and the productive countryside is absent. Outside the city there is nothing. As urban Pauline Christianity makes inroads into the empire and Greek becomes the dominant language of Christian writings, it returns to village cultures in need of translation to indigenous languages, including, ironically, Aramaic, the language of Jesus and those who gathered around him. Soon a further linguistic and cultural translation is needed: the vision of an apocalyptic, rural teacher that included the restoration of Israel, and a critique of empire, returns to the villages in the language of a new age emphasizing the Gentiles, and in the language of empire.[22]

If, as Fredriksen and Meeks point out, the canonical gospels and the Pauline letters, indeed the New Testament itself, are by the end of the first century already removed from the context of Jesus, his culture, geography, and ultimately his religion, who, then, was this Jesus and what was he about? As do most scholars writing of this period, Fredriksen and Meeks emphasize the real and imagined strains of Judaism of the period in which Jesus lived. But if Jesus was Jewish, what kind of Jew was he in thought and practice? How does the recovery of the Jesus of history impact the crisis of a Christianity involved in the last fifteen hundred years in one historical gospel after another? Does the Jesus of history speak to the religious tasks of our day, ending Auschwitz and 1492? And, paradoxically, after this long and bloody history, does the Jesus of history speak to contemporary Christianity and Judaism?

Just before I left for Auschwitz, John Dominic Crossan's book *The Historical Jesus: The Life of a Mediterranean Jewish Peasant* was featured in the *New York Times Book Review*. Incorporating insights from Fredriksen and Meeks, Crossan moves beyond both. In a sense, though this was hardly his aim, Crossan undermines the foundations of the Jewish-Christian establishment by analyzing the identity and historical milieu of Jesus. As the title indicates, there are two foci of Jesus' identity, as a Jew and as a Mediterranean peasant. Unlike other authors who have recovered the Jewishness of Jesus in relation to the varieties of Jewish belief and groupings, like E. P. Sanders in his book *Jesus and Judaism*, Crossan, by emphasizing the locality and social class of Jesus, sees Jesus in a broader context.[23]

Crossan's Jesus emphasizes less his dialogue with Jewish authorities than his assimilation of and confrontation with Mediterranean peasant culture and Hellenistic ideas, both of which permeate the world Jesus was born into and acted within. For Crossan, Jesus is a peasant Jewish cynic whose practice includes a "combination of free healing and common eating, a religious and economic egalitarianism that negated alike and at once the hierarchical and patronal normalcies of Jewish religion and Roman power." Thus Jesus never settles down or forms a group that sees him as a broker or mediator of God. Rather, he sees himself as an announcer proclaiming that neither a brokered nor mediated relationship should exist between humanity and divinity or between humanity and itself. Crossan analyzes Jesus' combination of miracle and parable, free healing and common eating as "calculated to force individuals into unmediated physical and spiritual contact with one another." This is why, according to Crossan, Jesus announces the "brokerless kingdom of God."[24]

In this announcement, Crossan's Jesus opts for an inclusive Judaism over against an exclusive Judaism. That is, Jesus was close to a form of Hellenistic Judaism, which Crossan defines as Judaism "responding with all its antiquity and tradition to a Greco-Roman culture undergirded by both armed power and imperial ambition." The point that Crossan is making here is critical: with other Jews, Jesus rejects an exclusive Judaism that seeks only to distance itself from Hellenistic culture. Instead, Jesus seeks to adopt his ancient tradition as liberally as possible with aspects of Hellenism that he, along with other Jews, finds intriguing and beneficial. Jesus is seen within a dialectical relationship—approving and critical—with his own inheritance, which was Jewish *and* Hellenistic, Mediterranean *and* peasant. However, this dialectical reality that Jesus embodied and struggled within was soon obscured by the events of 70 and 135 C.E., when Jews rose against Rome and were systematically defeated.[25]

According to Crossan, the Roman victories produced two results: first, the destruction of the temple and Jewish exclusion from Judea, and second, the destruction of Egyptian Judaism, which "facilitated the move from levitical to rabbinical Judaism and also the ascendancy of exclusive over inclusive Judaism." This meant that both Jesus and the Jewish-Hellenistic dialectic, and later the emerging Christian movement, would be judged in Jewish circles by those who emerged as leaders of the new Jewish religious framework—that is, by the rabbis. On the Christian side, Jesus was interpreted by a Constantinian Christianity, which likewise placed its own interpretation on a Jewish Mediterranean peasant it was incapable of understanding. Christianity, then, early in its history, could not or did not wish to understand that the early followers of Jesus inherited an inclusive Judaism that the Church, culminating with Constantine, systematically betrayed. Considered historically then, the religious disputes of the following two thousand years were between a rabbinic exclusive Judaism with internal power only, and an inclusive Judaism, now Christian and exclusive, and carried by the likes of Constantine and Columbus.[26]

The point here is that as they became institutionalized, both the rabbinic and Christian movements distorted their prehistory as a way of legitimizing their ascendancy. Early on, Jesus and the Judaism of his day—as well as his cultural and social base—were lost to a Judaism and Christianity operating in a new social, political, cultural, and religious world. The rise of imperial Christianity profoundly impacted the Christian understanding of Jews and Judaism as it reshaped its own identity. The rise of the rabbis also had a profound effect on Judaism and the identity of the Jewish people. With the distortion and rejection of Jesus by the Jewish establishment, the consolidation of the exclusive tradition accelerated. Because of this, much of Jewish history came to be interpreted as a defiance of outside influences, as if "the other" threatened self-definition rather than enhanced it. No doubt, the rise of the Roman and Christian empire did much to reinforce or even create this understanding, for it stifled what seems to be a dialectic in Jewish history typified by Crossan's Jesus—on the one hand a people profoundly conservative, tribal, and sometimes militant; on the other, liberal, open, and subversive of establishment power.

To fix attention solely on Jesus was probably the first mistake of the early Christian movement, for by the time of Constantine it had become a form of idolatry that in large measure continues today. At this moment in history, it would likewise be a monumental mistake to suggest that Jews should take as central the life of Jesus. Crossan avoids this partly because so little can be attributed to Jesus directly and partly because the overall sensibility exhibited by Jesus and other Jews in that peasant Mediterranean culture seems to be the message. The drama being played out is less one against others, or even one as unique; rather, at a particular moment in history, at the intersection of empire and community, a small group of people explored a different path. By focusing on the path taken rather than simply on Jesus, ancient Palestine is opened again to Christian and Jew without either needing beforehand to be for or against. In doing so, a history is revealed that takes us beyond the ahistorical canonical gospels and rabbinic framework.

A deep history often subverts accepted religious dogma and practice. As a Jewish Mediterranean peasant, Jesus and those around him seemed to give all to the present and invite all to share in that present—hence the centrality of the shared table with commensality, as Crossan interprets it. Jesus' sense of the kingdom as one filled with "nobodies and undesirables" subverted a variety of distinctions—sexual and social, political and religious—and this, too, is central to Jesus' understanding of what Crossan names as the brokerless kingdom of God. Or perhaps it would be better stated that Jesus and those around him felt that the brokerless kingdom arrived in the shared meal *and* the subversion of political, social, cultural, and religious hierarchy. Pursuing this brokerless kingdom by acting to bring it about, Crossan's Jesus reflects little about what religious authorities see as the important questions: whether one is acting within the tradition or transgressing the tradition's boundaries; on what basis is one acting and what are the consequences for those whose function it is to carry forth the tradition; will the thought and action further advance or at least safeguard the place of the tradition in society. Instead, Jesus and his followers delight in simply moving in history—radicalizing the teachings, taking the opening to cross boundaries and through expressive activities forcing the questions to new levels.

That these understandings of Jesus can be considered as a "break with law" or as an "adversarial position" with regard to his own people is pure retrospection from the Jewish-Christian establishment. Crossan's Jesus is simply acting to do what needs to be done. In an era that speaks of the confines of tradition, this may be the central message of Crossan's book: Jesus and his followers were Jewish Mediterranean peasants; they did what they felt needed to be done. They acted the way they traveled, as themselves, without guards or luggage, nor were they defending, exhorting, or expanding. They were neither brokers nor builders. But they broke all sorts of deals, including the ancient ecumenical, social, political, and cultural deals. In short, as Crossan analyzes it, Jesus and his followers were simply being faithful within their history as they saw it. That they would be caught up in a two-thousand-year debate, used as ideological instruments to prove or disprove salvation, and most horribly to legitimate Auschwitz and 1492, is, to understate the obvious, totally beyond their imagination. Within a short time, every deal that Jesus and his followers broke was literally resurrected, and in his name.

Hospitality and Healing

Reading Fredriksen, Meeks, and Crossan just after returning from Auschwitz raised obvious questions. How did the brokerless kingdom of God that Jesus announced become the Other Kingdom of Auschwitz? How did those who suffered the Other Kingdom come to legitimate the expansive policies of the state of Israel? How did the peasant ministry of Jesus become housed in imperial churches, and how did those who rejected those imperial churches come to worship in plush suburban synagogues? How did the religious leaders of both traditions become so smug, so filled with illusion that their brokering has become *the* brokering?

These questions were present to me at Auschwitz, again in the person of Richard Rubenstein. Before embarking for Auschwitz, half-expecting that Rubenstein would be there, I went through a period of reviewing his books. After first re-reading his autobiography, pondering the similarities of our experience with Jewish leadership, I looked once more at *My Brother Paul*, a work that is largely neglected today. As an undergraduate student, I endeavored to read everything my teachers published, though the timing of their publication, like the writing of a book, was to me a mystery. It was only in once more reading *My Brother Paul* that I realized that Rubenstein wrote the book as I was attending his classes. At that point in my life, having been raised in a completely Jewish neighborhood, having never been in a church or even knowing the distinction between Protestant and Catholic, let alone the foundations or nuances of Christian theology, Rubenstein's discussion of Paul in class was for me *ex nihilo*. It is clear now that Rubenstein named for me not only the Holocaust, but helped initiate me into a dialogue with Christianity.[27]

Rubenstein's own dialogue with Paul of Tarsus as a brother is fascinating. As a nonobservant Jewish youth, Rubenstein went through a phase of attraction to Christianity only to later become an orthodox Jew. Yet in becoming orthodox and ultimately a rabbi, Rubenstein began to see the limits of the law. With the death of his infant son on the morning before Yom Kippur in 1950, Rubenstein's faith in God and the law broke down. In the end, Rubenstein found his way forward through psychoanalysis as midwife to his rebirth.[28]

Throughout the ordeal and culminating in his book, Rubenstein finds Paul to be a fellow traveler. Like Paul, Rubenstein finds himself in conflict with the law; both Paul and Rubenstein are reborn, having undergone a conversion experience of death and resurrection. Rubenstein parts company with Paul over the content of their conversions:

"Paul's conversion took place when he became convinced that Christ had defeated death; mine began when I finally gave up all hope that God would in the end redeem me from death." However, Rubenstein and Paul share the same existential choice; both resolve the conflict between experience and tradition in favor of their own experience.[29]

Rubenstein's *Paul* is filled with interesting and provocative insights, but as one Pauline scholar noted, the book is much more about Rubenstein than it is about Paul and certainly much more about the modern Jewish religious predicament than it is about a first-century follower of Jesus. Rather, it is Rubenstein's understandings after Auschwitz and in the midst of an inadequate religiosity that startle and control here. As Rubenstein writes in his introduction, "I do not reject Paul's solution because he was a Christian and I am Jewish. *I find the normative Jewish and Christian solutions equally unacceptable.*" Commenting on his reliance on psychoanalysis as a way of rebirth, Rubenstein writes, "The fact that I came to see my conflicts as psychological was not unrelated to the fact that I grew up in an urban middle-class Jewish environment. Had my parents been rural peasants, it is not likely that I would have ever seen my conflicts as psychological." For Rubenstein, neither the law nor Christ sufficed: psychoanalysis was the only path to healing.[30]

It is to the possibility of healing that we return. Although some may find it arrogant that Rubenstein compares himself to Paul, the great interpreter of Jesus and doctor/saint of the Church, Rubenstein goes further by naming him as brother. The continuity, the collapse of a distance that both traditions now assert with reference to Paul, is reasserted by Rubenstein because they share a similar predicament as Jews. Across the centuries and in spite of the religious establishment, Rubenstein faces similar questions within a common communal framework. That is, Rubenstein analyzes Paul as one who is breaking with the normative religiosity as a way of healing a break that cannot be healed within the normative. For Rubenstein, Paul is in process and as yet uncanonized, a Jew in search of healing rather than a dogmatized saint.

Across the divide and with due attention to the ravages of Auschwitz, indeed to the entire history of Christian anti-Jewishness, Rubenstein simply accepts the search of a religiously Jewish Paul. According to Rubenstein, this is why Jewish scholars have found it impossible to appreciate or understand Paul. "The greatest single failing of Jewish attempts to understand Paul has been a persistent refusal to take Paul seriously as both a loyal Jew and a theologian of extraordinary competence." In a sense, Jewish scholars are too busy trying to debate whether Paul's position was correct or not. But, as Rubenstein writes, "We are more likely to account for the differences between Paul and the rabbis by considering the differences in their experience than by attempting to establish whether Paul's religious position or that of his adversaries was the 'true' one." Rubenstein might well address the same comment to Christian scholars who miss much of Paul because they use him to reinforce their own sense of what is true. Therefore Paul, like Jesus, is taken up in a new communal debate that very early on has little to do with the world he lived in. Even the attempt to investigate the historical world of Paul, with its tensions and possibilities, is limited, consciously or not, by the fact of fifteen hundred years of Christian hegemony in the West.[31]

Perhaps this is one of the reasons why Rubenstein chooses to describe Paul, not Jesus, as his brother. Although controversial in the Jewish community, Paul is the interpreter of the end of normative Judaism rather than the initiator of that end, usually thought to be Jesus. And though Paul has been used against the Jewish community, the actual call to arms has been under the banner of Jesus the Christ. Furthermore, and this I think is crucial, Rubenstein identifies with Paul because Paul wrestles with the experience of death and rebirth and because Rubenstein can identify a continuity of this kind of Jewish wrestling into the twentieth century. At the conclusion of his introduction, Rubenstein writes, "*Under the impact of the Christian religious revolution, which was at least initially an internal Jewish revolution, Paul came to understand, as did later Jewish mystics, that reality as apprehended by common sense offers only hints of the deeper and truer meaning of the human world.* Paul thus prepares the way for and anticipates the work of the twentieth century's most important secularized Jewish mystic, Sigmund Freud." Rubenstein, having broken with normative Judaism, identifies Paul and his journey as a precursor of a new Jewish religiosity, psychoanalysis, which holds out the possibility of a healing that traditional Judaism can no longer deliver.[32]

Rubenstein's Paul is a healer of the individual rather than a healer of a people. In fact, Rubenstein's Paul breaks with the normative Jewish religiosity and has to break with it in order to be healed. Paul is Rubenstein's brother, then, because reluctantly, and with great anguish, they both choose the same path. The connection of Paul and Freud for Rubenstein is the same, for they choose the art of healing over religious norms. Another connecting link between the three is that they are powerful Jewish religious thinkers attempting to probe the times in which they live. By identifying with Paul and Freud, Rubenstein is placing himself in their provocative tradition, predicting the end of the Jewish tradition even as they reinterpret it and, paradoxically, provide a new framework for its continued vitality. Thus if Paul was a Jewish Christian and Freud a godless Jew, Rubenstein is a post-Holocaust Jew.[33]

Richard Rubenstein's presence at Auschwitz echoed by extension the presence of the other Holocaust theologians, Elie Wiesel, Emil Fackenheim, and Rabbi Irving Greenberg. Other guardians of the normative tradition, professors and rabbis, were also present. The brilliance of European Jewish thinkers—some who perished in the Holocaust; others, like Freud, who escaped it—was remembered. Paul, too, while unnamed of course, was there, in the Polish Catholic intellectuals who joined us for discussion and at the Catholic center, whose convent and cross had become so controversial. Had this history so concentrated and omnipresent at Auschwitz brought us as individuals or as a people to a true healing? Could the discussion of Paul from a thousand different angles, or even the continued reading of his letters in Christian liturgies, lead to anything but a transient individualized coming to grips with a broken history, Jewish and Christian? Was not this constant re-reading ultimately to give sanction to the continuation of Auschwitz and 1492?

What was missing at Auschwitz was Crossan's Jesus and those with him who simply gave all to the present without rejecting the present or being burdened by the past. There seemed to be little or no ulterior motives in this Jesus movement—certainly not fame, wealth, or a religion to be pursued in one's name. The method—the shared meal, egalitarian living—represented also a vision: the brokerless kingdom subverted the powers who pursued then, and pursue now, the Other Kingdom, realized in 1492 and Auschwitz. As Crossan analyzes it, the Jesus movement centering on the shared table, with commensality, *was* the healing: the missionaries "share a miracle and a Kingdom, and they receive in return a table and a house," thus initiating a shared egalitarianism of spiritual and material resources. Crossan insists that the mission he is talking about is not, "like Paul's, a dramatic thrust along major trade routes to urban centers hundreds of miles apart. Yet it concerns the longest journey in the Greco-Roman world, maybe in any world, the step across the threshold of a peasant stranger's home." Reading this passage, I could not help but think of our kosher meals and how they were seen as a boundary, a symbolic gesture to say that we had survived. At the same time it also symbolized a brokenness and a lack of vision. Despite the title of our delegation, our summons was remembrance rather than a future.[34]

What was this longest journey in the Jewish and Greco-Roman world, then, and what is it in the Jewish-Christian-secular world today? Does this journey speak to Auschwitz and 1492? It seems that, in the final analysis, crossing the threshold of a stranger's home was for Jesus and his followers a discipline wrought from their Jewish inheritance and culture in contact with Hellenism and the Greco-Roman Empire. It was a discipline that constantly clarified the social, political, cultural, and religious differences as it confronted the injustices of the Jewish and Greco-Roman establishments. This discipline was based on neither rejection nor acceptance. In itself it established a freedom of movement and invitation; that is, the discipline was the freedom and the healing, at one and the same time. It was born in the "broken middle," as the Jewish philosopher Gillian Rose, a member of our delegation, has named it; that is, the discipline was forged in the mix of history, at the depth of a historical moment, rather than transcending history by pretending to go backward to a golden past or forward to a glorious future. Crossan's Jesus is neither a romantic nor a utopian. Rather, the longest journey is a practice that opens the person and the community to the world in all its dimensions. Unlike the individualized healing that psychoanalysis promised Rubenstein, Jesus' discipline sought a communal healing. Rubenstein's discipline helped him feel at home and even participate in the empire. Jesus' discipline was a confrontation with empire.

At Auschwitz, both Jew and Christian inherited a discipline as well—the discipline framed by the rabbis and by the triumphal Church, which, although not completely foreign to the discipline of Jesus and his followers, significantly distorted it. Like Rubenstein and, before him, Paul and Freud, these disciplines formed the backdrop for life in the world—something to be measured against but no longer lived out. For we ourselves are governed more by the discipline of the modern world than by these Jewish and Christian disciplines about which we speak so piously; the discipline of the modern world overwhelmed the ancient disciplines in Auschwitz and 1492.

As became clear at Auschwitz, we cling to these disciplines as the important facts of our life, as if they are important in and of themselves, as if to preserve them is fidelity and to leave them betrayal. We seem trapped in a self-definition of Jew and Christian through the rabbinic and canonical gospels that is increasingly irrelevant in the world. I wondered at Auschwitz, and continue to wonder now, if we remain within these definitions because we fear that in reality they have come to an end.

6

State Religion and the New Discipline

To dwell on a definition of Jew and Christian that has come to an end is to cease traversing boundaries or to be so laden with prior categories that a crossing is symbolic only. In another sense, the boundaries have ceased to be or are defined in such a way that they are irrelevant. A priestly or rabbinic class preserves these with a technical expertise unknown before in history, though their knowledge can be communicated only within their own class of specialists. They produce and reproduce their own religious systems; parishioners and the congregations, while dwindling in numbers, function as consumers. The task of the priests and the rabbis, the scholars and the intellectuals, is to guard the traditions that are threatened with collapse. The discourse of the guardians, once derived from the people, is now specialized and refined. It no longer emanates from the people, but is separate from them. The separation of the people from the primary discourse is derided as ignorance which the specialists through their superior knowledge are supposed to correct.[1]

As the end draws near and becomes more apparent, alliances evolve, even between former enemies. That Jews and Christians come together today is to be lauded, though the function of that togetherness—to survive in a world thought to be hostile to their traditions—is suspect. In a sense, the guardians of tradition are right in their assertion that the world is increasingly hostile to the basic claims of these traditions as inadequate to the history we inherit and continue. That is, the claims of the Jewish and Christian traditions are seen more and more as abstractions to be tolerated when necessary and rejected when the penalties for rejection decrease. They are also seen as forms of oppression from which one seeks liberation. Most of the freedom from tradition remains inarticulate, chosen but unspoken. And much of the freedom is shallow, sometimes even destructive.

This is the point of Christopher Lasch's *The Culture of Narcissism*, in which he defines a narcissist as someone loosed from tradition who seeks freedom from every institution and belief save those that feed the ego and the affluence of the narcissist's world. However, as Lasch also understands, this freedom is illusory, for the narcissist simply allows power free rein. As an isolated person who camouflages this isolation with affluence, when the narcissist turns inward, he or she finds nothing. But is not this camouflage similar to the one employed by Judaism and Christianity? The trappings of dogma and ritual, even the innovative Christian and Jewish liturgies and the Jewish-Christian dialogue, mask an inner emptiness exposed by Auschwitz and 1492.[2]

The question of the historical Jesus confronts this mask and, to some extent, the emptiness as well. To the mask of Christianity, it raises the issue of the canonical and historical gospels and how they fashioned a religion that claims universality from a discipline rooted in a geographic and cultural context. The movement from the Jesus of history to the Christ of faith needs a compelling explanation in light of its subsequent history. This movement from history to faith, when solidified, universalized, and militarized in empire uproots both those who carry that faith and those who have it imposed upon them. One wonders if that which is uprooted and transported across time and geography, until it is hardly recognizable in its original form, can be counted on after Auschwitz and 1492 to restore what has been disrupted. Historically, the cycle of uprootedness is beyond doubt, but can that which engendered the cycle somehow end it simply because it claims to carry the message of redemption?

I witnessed this dilemma concretely in an Australian student at Maryknoll who, in response to my query about uprootedness and Christianity, analyzed aboriginal spirituality as rooted in the land because aborigines are indigenous to it; he, a dual foreigner to Australia as European and Christian, was unprepared for the geography of the land he now lives in. This, of course, was already the problem of Paul; the countryside from which the discipline of Jesus arose was for Paul outside the recognizable boundaries of history. He, with others, "solved" this dilemma by speaking of faith rather than geography, universality rather than particularity. It was this Christianity that had, through many twists and turns, led to Auschwitz. Perhaps in Auschwitz the mask, at least for some Christians, was ripped away; too often, however, the mask is seen as an aberrant history which, once exposed and jettisoned, uncovers the purity of the Christ of faith. In reality, though, it may simply be a new mask that is in place.[3]

For Jews, Jesus raises a dual question of oppression from those carrying his name and a masking of our own deeper history, which we as Jews have left behind. Although we affirm the fact that Jesus was thoroughly within the Jewish fold and that Christianity arose from Judaism, we rarely admit that normative Judaism was developed not simply on its own but in the matrix of Christianity. As it turns out, the Judaism we inherit was formed as much by its confrontation with the rise of Christianity as a state religion in the fourth century as it was by its past. This is the theme developed by Jacob Neusner, the renowned Jewish scholar at the University of South Florida, in his book *Judaism in the Matrix of Christianity*—that both Judaism and Christianity emerge as religions over and against each other. Neusner emphasizes this point: "When Rome became Christian, Judaism as it would flourish in Western civilization reached that familiar form and definition which we know today. Judaism was born in the matrix of Christianity triumphant or, to use theological language of a sort, Christ enthroned dictated not only the dominant faith but also the successful one." The confrontation between the two forced both to redefine their canon, teleology, and defining symbol, so that, according to Neusner, each doctrine in Judaism responds to a point of contention with Christianity. As Neusner writes, "What did Israel's sages have to present as the Torah's answer to the cross? The Torah was defined first in the doctrine of the Mishnah as oral and memorized revelation, and by implication, other rabbinical writings fell into the same category of Torah. The Torah, moreover, was presented as the encompassing symbol of Israel's salvation. Finally, the Torah was embodied in the person of the Messiah who, of course, would be a rabbi. The Torah in all three modes confronted the cross with its doctrine of the triumphant Christ, Messiah and king, ruler now of heaven and earth."[4]

A parallel development occurs for both Jews and Christians as an abstraction from time and place, from geography, as it were, becomes codified into a religion. The rabbinic discipline is canonized in the form of a diaspora religion rather than evolving in the place of its origin. Already uprooted by historical circumstance, the rabbis develop a religion that enshrines that uprootedness. From this moment, the greatest longing of Jewish prayer is for a return to a place and time that fewer and fewer Jews have ever experienced. The present is always a time of exile, awaiting the moment of redemption. In anticipation of the messiah, the community draws more defined barriers, at least symbolically withdrawing from the cultures in which it is present. This is in part a response to the now-empowered and soon to be relentless Christian ethos. Exclusive Judaism becomes enshrined, demanding a separation in order to define a religious way of life.

For Neusner, the evolution of Judaism in the fourth century into a Judaism of the dual Torah—that is, the combination of the revealed word in the Pentateuch and the oral teachings recorded in the Mishnah and the Talmuds of Babylonia and Palestine—is developed within the context of a continuing Jewish community over time. This form of Judaism remained normative until the eighteenth and nineteenth centuries, when the increasing secularization of European life opened civic and political rights for Jews. From that period until today, a proliferation of Judaic systems has unfolded, including socialism and Yiddishism, Zionism, and what Neusner labels the American Judaism of Holocaust and Redemption. Neusner finds the proliferation of these Judaisms understandable, though limited. The first two systems, socialism and Yiddishism, have already been found wanting; responding to their times, they have been overwhelmed by the failure of the socialist state experiment and the elimination of Eastern European Jews in the Holocaust.[5]

As I witnessed at Auschwitz, the fourth system, the American Judaism of Holocaust and Redemption, exists within a dialectic framework—insisted upon and yet facing periods of recession. According to Neusner, this final Judaic system is destined to fail:

> They focus such imaginative energies as they have generated upon the Holocaust as myth, and center their eschatological fantasies on "the beginning of our redemption" in the State of Israel. But they have not gone through the one nor chosen to participate in the other. Not having lived through the mass murder of European Jewry, American Jews restated the problem of evil in unanswerable form—the Holocaust is beyond all speech—and then transformed that problem into an obsession. Not choosing to settle in the State of Israel, moreover, American Jews further defined redemption, the resolution of the problem of evil, in terms remote from their world. One need not look far to find the limitations of the system of American Judaism: its stress on a world other than the one in which the devotees in fact are living.[6]

Neusner affirms that the reason for the failure of the Judaic system based on Holocaust and Israel is because it is alien to the everyday experience of most Jews. And yet, like his Christian counterparts, Neusner seeks the continuation of the Jewish people in a return to the religion enshrined in the fourth century, the Judaism of the dual Torah.

It is the Judaism of the dual Torah that for Neusner provides Jews access to the formative event of Sinai, and therefore functions in a way similar to that of the canonical gospels in providing access to Jesus for Christians. For Jews, the way back to Sinai is the same path back for Christians to Jesus, through the filter of a canon developed more than fifteen hundred years ago. In this view, events of history such as Auschwitz and 1492 divert the attention of these communities, and the limitations of historical response to these events point the communities back to their origins.

The question remains, then, as to how the textual canon represents and interprets the original event, for both the Jewish and Christian commentators are already uprooted from that original history. And here Neusner, chiding American Jews for developing a theology from experiences that they do not live within, proposes a theological system as a future, much further removed and abstracted from Jewish experiences than the Holocaust and Israel. Again like his Christian counterparts, he rails against the ignorance of the living Jewish community, which prefers the "hovel of the present" to the "mansion of the past." Neusner sees the consequence of relying on contemporary experience rather than the study of the Jewish canon as a "strikingly abbreviated agenda of issues, a remarkably one-dimensional program of urgent questions. Left with Israeli nationalism and American Judaism, Jews work only with the raw material made available by contemporary experience—emotions on the one side, politics on the other."[7]

It is interesting to note that Neusner links the decline of Jewish knowledge in and affirmation of the dual Torah—that is, Judaism's inability to persuade Jews of its self-evident truth—with the inability of Christianity to enjoy self-evidence among Christians. Here Neusner refers to the secularization of the West; in our context it expands to the events of Auschwitz and 1492. The crisis of belief found in the Enlightenment certainly distanced the events of Sinai and Jesus, but it is the crisis of contemporary history that confronts both secularization and Jewish/Christian religiosity. Can we say honestly that the Judaism of the dual Torah, or for that matter the Jesus of the canonical gospels, speaks to Auschwitz and 1492? Here Neusner also avoids the more radical discipline of Jesus as a challenge to Judaism and Christianity in light of Auschwitz and 1492.

Neusner also fails to develop a further level of discussion involving tradition, which he initially introduces. The proposition that there is such a thing as a religious tradition that is continuous, has a history, and unfolds in a linear way is for Neusner unsupportable. Communities pick and choose elements within their inheritance and in their particular context. With regard to Judaism, Neusner believes that each

Judaic system begins on its own and then—only then—goes back to the received documents in search of texts and proof texts. For Neusner, this is a testimony to humanity's power of creative genius: "making something out of nothing." Although each Judaism claims to "form the tradition or the natural and historically necessary next step, in fact all pick and choose. Each creates and defines itself."[8]

The discontinuities within Judaism, and for that matter within Christianity, are masked by the canon as interpreted within the context of tradition. The canon itself often contains traces of these fractures, which are later glossed over by religious authorities and communities in search of a usable past. Orthodoxy can be viewed accordingly—the attempt to unify what was diverse and to codify what was once expansive. Reformers can be seen within the context of an orthodoxy that is failing: that which ceases to be self-evident is reconstructed to be made more appealing to a community that refuses orthodoxy. However, reform most often is the unannounced initiation of a new orthodoxy that carries on the old in revised language and symbols. At Auschwitz, for example, the Latin mass seems unsuitable, even archaic, but in light of the victims, would it be so different if the mass were said in Polish or French? Irving Greenberg's statement that any theological proposition must be credible before the burning children collapses orthodoxy and reform into a similar pattern.

Crossing Boundaries

Perhaps it is by uncovering the broken threads, the discontinuities, that a way forward beyond orthodoxy and reform can be found. At the same time, the manner in which these discontinuities disappear can be instructive. The canon as interpreted by tradition may at times be a decision of a particular community, say in the fourth century or today, but it also almost always represents a decision by the religious and politically powerful. This is why the German Jewish philosopher Walter Benjamin, who died in the Holocaust, wrote that traditions have a tendency to conform to power and that the task of every generation is to wrest tradition from a power that is about to overwhelm it.

Benjamin is a good example of this very problem. Already at Auschwitz the hidden tradition of Jewish critical thought, of which Benjamin was a part, was receding in the Jewish understanding of that event. Whereas Benjamin as a Jew focused his writing on analyses of the known and unknown literary figures of Europe and aimed to produce a book of quotations drawn primarily from non-Jewish sources, we of the Auschwitz delegation were narrowing even the experience of those who died there; thus the outburst over the French Jews who returned to Auschwitz on "pilgrimage" and the concern over our separation from other cultures. A new power was exerted at Auschwitz, ostensibly on behalf of the dead but in reality *over* the dead, to build a structure of orthodoxy around the Holocaust.[9]

Historically, the breaks in tradition are many, and recovery of them is important. The Hebrew scriptures, for example, contain many traces of a Jewish culture and religiosity that contravene the traditional teachings of Judaism. One of the deepest memories of my early synagogue education was the story of Abraham and the breaking of the idols. Another was the role of the prophets announcing God's justice. Through simple stories told to young children, the themes of monotheism and justice are still projected by sophisticated Jewish and Christian scholars. And yet they are only part of the truth, subverting important aspects of continuing Jewish polytheism; likewise, the prophets may seek justice, but they also discipline the people and force them to abandon beliefs and rituals indigenous to them. The movement toward monotheism, celebrated by Jews as a fundamental contribution to the world and reinforced by the prophets, was also at times experienced as a form of oppression.[10]

The work of Dartmouth biblical scholar Susan Ackerman, *Under Every Green Tree: Popular Religion in Sixth-Century Judah*, confirms this in her study of five passages from the prophets Jeremiah, Ezekiel, and Isaiah. Of special interest is Ezekiel 8, which relates an event at midpoint between the Babylonian invasions of 597 B.C.E. and 587 B.C.E. Ezekiel, who was exiled to Babylon after the first invasion, is himself transported back to Jerusalem in a divine vision. Finding Jerusalem in a state of religious and moral collapse, Ezekiel experienced a vision that culminates in the departure of Yahweh from the defiled Temple. Ackerman is interested in the first part of this vision in which God shows Ezekiel manifestations of sixth-century popular religion: the image of jealousy, elders burning incense in a room of reliefs, women wailing over Tammuz, and men bowing down to the sun.[11]

This latter aspect of Ezekiel's vision, men bowing down to the sun, is interesting to follow. Found in the inner courtyard of the Temple, this worship of the sun is of extreme importance, as testified to by Ezekiel's anger. As Ackerman points out, there is no consensus on whether the worship of the sun is in origin an Egyptian, Mesopotamian, or native West Semitic cult, though she leans toward the suggestion that this was an Aramaean cult that combined elements of the Mesopotamian and West Semitic. However, for Ackerman the precise nature of the solar cult matters little; rather, what is crucial is that those who practice the sun cult in the courtyard of Yahweh's Temple turn their backs to the Temple as part of their worship. Ezekiel interprets the gesture of turning their backs to the Temple as turning their backs on Yahweh and a rejection of the Israelite national god in favor of another deity. The speculation that these men might be priests, of course, complicates the problem, as Yahweh's priests turn their backs on both God and their designated calling. It is no surprise, then, that Ezekiel finds worship of the sun to be Judah's greatest cultic abomination. As Ackerman points out, later rabbinic edicts see in this manifestation of popular religion a metaphor for faithlessness.[12]

In her study, Ackerman finds that Israelite religious historians who view Josiah's reforms as the major turning point in the development of ancient Yahwistic faith—that is, resolving the struggle between "pure Yahwism" and various pagan syncretistic "abuses"—are incorrect. Rather, she postulates the reform to have been "limited in scope, temporary in effect, and clearly fail[ing] in its goal of impressing a monolithic description of Yahwism on all of Yahweh's devotees." As important is Ackerman's finding that the phenomenon of the popular religion of that time—which is often labeled syncretistic, foreign, pagan, or Canaanite—is instead indigenous to the practice of Yahwistic religion. As Ackerman states:

> Even those Judahites who worshiped the Queen of Heaven and who mourned the death of Tammuz, who dedicated a *marzeah* banquet to a god other than Yahweh and who bowed down to the sun probably considered themselves Yahwists. Certainly those who worshiped Tammuz and the god of the sun used Yahweh's very temple and thus acknowledged the sanctity of at least the cult site of the god of Israel. Moreover, these worshipers are never reported as rejecting Yahweh; they simply believed that it was legitimate in Yahwism to supplement the worship of Yahweh with the worship of other gods. Clearly this belief guided those who participated in the cult of Asherah, for they worshiped this goddess alongside Yahweh as his hypostatized female aspect or even consort.[13]

Ackerman concludes that the definition of what constitutes proper Yahwism in popular religion encompasses far more than the definition of Yahwism proposed by most biblical writers and interpreters. It is also probable that those who deviated from pure Yahwism were in the substantial majority. This is what Isaiah 65:1–7 implies for Ackerman, "that almost the entire nation irrespective of gender and social status worshiped Yahweh along with Asherah at the *bamot* throughout the land."[14]

In the final analysis, the majority is suppressed and the priestly/ Deuteronomistic/prophetic minority wins out; those with nonpriestly, non-Deuteronomistic, and non-prophetic orientation of popular religion are defined as heterodox. But Ackerman understands that heterodoxy and orthodoxy are decided by those who come later and have power. For Ackerman, it was the gradual process of canonization beginning in the post-exilic period that made Deuteronomistic, priestly, and prophetic religion the norm, a norm that condemned the cults Deuteronomists, priests, and prophets denounced.[15]

Hellenistic Judaism also provides a glimpse of discontinuity and the power of later tradition to erase and demean it. By the early third century B.C.E., the language of the Western Jewish community had become Greek; in fact, familiarity with Hebrew had faded to the point where the Torah was translated into Greek so that the scriptures would be accessible to the Jewish community. As Paula Fredriksen points out, the translation of the scriptures from Hebrew to Greek facilitated the translation of ideas from one cultural system to another. "When for example, the Jewish God revealed his name to Moses at the burning bush (Ex. 3:14), the Hebrew *ehyeh* (I am) became in the Greek *ho on* (the Being): anyone with even a rudimentary Hellenistic education would recognize in this designation the High God of philosophy. Similarly, when the Lord established the heavens 'by a word' (Ps 33:6), the Hebrew *davar* became the Greek *logos*: the Creator had suddenly acquired a very Hellenistic factotum." Greek concepts did not need to be read into scripture. By virtue of the new language of the text, they were already present.[16]

In this cultural milieu, Judaism undergoes a transformation that can be seen in the interpretation of Moses. Unlike the Torah view of Moses as a humble servant, he emerges in the Hellenistic world as a vigorous prophet-philosopher-king. A second-century B.C.E. Jewish historian, Artapanus, for example, portrays Moses as an Olympian athlete gracefully grown to maturity. The late rabbi and scholar, Daniel Jeremy Silver, in his book *Images of Moses*, describes Artapanus's Moses as "big boned, of ruddy complexion, with a white beard, a full head of hair, and a commanding presence." In this portrait Moses, who spent most of his life wandering in the countryside and the desert, becomes a city man. Because the Greeks could not imagine a lawgiver unconnected with a city, Moses becomes the founder and lawmaker of Jerusalem, a city in which he never lived nor even viewed from a distance.[17]

Several centuries later, a Greek-speaking, thoroughly Hellenized Jew of Alexandria, Philo Judaeus (20 B.C.E.–50 C.E.), wrote a biography of Moses. Having mastered both the Torah and Greek curriculum of his time, Philo sought to show the correspondence between the Jewish and Greek ways of approaching ethical and metaphysical questions. According to Silver, Philo, as a pious and observant Jew, wrote to praise

Moses and prove to the Jewish and non-Jewish Hellenistic elite that the Torah was a constitutional document of universal importance. Philo emphasizes in Moses' life that which comports to the cardinal virtues lauded by Hellenistic culture: prudence, justice, temperance, and bravery. Philo tirelessly underscores Moses' virtue. Philo's Moses is "free of ambition. Proof: he did not attempt to establish a dynasty by designating his sons as heirs. He was free of greed. Proof: unlike most tyrants, Moses did not levy tolls. There was not greed or avarice or vanity in his nature. Proof: the Bible is silent about Moses' dress or the management of his household." In sum, Philo creates a Moses who is the ultimate philosopher-king, "a law incarnate and made vocal"—a teacher of religious enlightenment.[18]

The interpretations of Moses by Artapanus and Philo suggest attempts by Jews to find a place in the Greco-Roman Empire and to suggest further that Jewish experience is relevant to Jews and non-Jews alike. This precipitated a struggle within the evolving Jewish consciousness of that time between the desire to retain a particular identity and, for reasons of expediency, a strong pressure to conform to the dominant culture. There was an additional complication, for many Jews experienced a powerful attraction to the values of Greco-Roman culture, which in some respects seemed harmonious with the Jewish ethos and biblical traditions. At the same time, non-Jews were attracted to Jewish worship and belief. As Fredriksen writes:

> The boundary between these communities and the outside world was a fluid one, and interested pagans could visit the synagogue as they would. Some, as the Greek magical papyri evince, came simply to acquire some knowledge of a powerful god in whose name they could command demons. Others—like those Gentiles who annually joined Alexandria's Jews in celebrating the miracle of the Torah's translation into Greek—attached themselves as God-fearers, often remaining pagans while assuming as much of the Law as they cared to. But many—including some of the most illustrious names of Hellenistic Judaism—apparently decided to take upon themselves full observance of the Law. They thus became proselytes and, according to Jewish tradition, full Jews.[19]

If the inclusion of popular religion in the cult of Yahweh, or rather the cult of Yahweh as an inclusion in popular religion, is found by the prophets to be an abomination and by the rabbis to be a sign of infidelity, the attraction of Jews to Hellenism is portrayed by the rabbis as assimilationist. The evolution of Chanukkah, a minor religious holy day, exemplifies this condemnation of Hellenism in the story of the defilement of the Temple and the miracle of the untainted oil that fuels the light above the ark for eight days. Within this story is the theme of Jewish resistance to false and "pagan" gods and the importance of maintaining a boundary for the Jewish faith. It also underscores a second theme, one more important at the time of the Maccabees—the conflict between the Hasmoneans, who sought to reclaim the Second Temple in Jerusalem, and the Alexandrian Jews, who had accepted a temple built by Onias IV after the religious persecutions of Antiochus triggered a wave of refugees from Palestine into Egypt. In fact, the miracle of fire, accompanied by the rededication of the Second Temple in 165 B.C.E., was seen at least by the Hasmoneans as proof of the superiority of that temple over against the temple in Alexandria. Thus the Chanukkah story serves two functions in the tradition as it develops: to warn against foreign influence that threatens the purity of Judaism and to counsel Jews that a foreign influence may emerge within by those who are attracted to other cultures and philosophies. It is interesting to note that, because of the relative powerlessness of the Jewish community after the defeat of the Jewish revolts in 70 and 135 C.E., the military aspect of the Hasmoneans vis-à-vis the Greek Syrians and the Hellenistic Jews is downplayed and nearly erased, only to be revived in modern Israel as an attempt to highlight that military aspect of Jewish history.[20]

Despite the revolts and the interpretations, as well as the destruction of the Temple and Jerusalem, these "deviations" continued and Jewish popular religiosity flourished. This can be seen in the third-century synagogue at Dura Europos, an ancient city on the Euphrates discovered in 1932. It has been interpreted by the late Erwin Goodenough, a Yale historian of religion, in a thirteen-volume work titled *Jewish Symbols in the Greco-Roman Period*. In this synagogue, Goodenough found pictorial representations of Jewish figures as well as representations of pagan images; the entire synagogue reflects that the Jews of Dura lived within a diverse pagan city influenced by Syrians, Greeks, Iranians, and Romans, and that the ideas and images of these fellow citizens were in fact incorporated into the building and decoration of the synagogue. Goodenough describes the detail in one part of the synagogue:

> Two temples are on the inside. The Temple of Aaron, at the left, is clearly derived from a stock representation of a pagan mystic shrine, but is cleverly adapted to make room for the instruments of Aaron's cult. Aaron seems to be conducting a worship which centers in the menorah, itself dedicated to the Ark of the Covenant veiled in an inner shrine which, in turn, was topped with figures of the goddess of Victory. Indeed the menorah is painted on the Ark itself. Three doors superimposed upon the outer wall seemed a fresh and arbitrary appearance of the three doorways

which have appeared so often in mystic and eschatological symbolism. The scene could no more be identified with a single biblical incident than the stone temple could be identified with the portable tent shrine of the wilderness, or than Aaron's dress as an Iranian priest could be identified with the robes specified for Aaron in the Bible. . . . Besides this scene at the left the cosmos was again presented in worship as Moses in the checked cloth of priesthood released from the Well of the Wilderness a flow of water to the twelve tribes as the twelve signs of the zodiac. This worship also centered in cult instruments, especially those of incense and the menorah, dedicated to a shrine of mystery at the back. It seemed not a chance that these two scenes adjoined the figure which I called Moses at his death in cosmic worship with the heavenly bodies. If it is Abraham rather than Moses who stands here, still these three scenes strikingly present the notion of a cosmic worship for and in Judaism.[21]

Goodenough then describes yet another section:

At the bottom Ezekiel begins his role as preacher to the dead bones, and, as God's own hand carries him in by the hair, he wears the Persian dress. The pieces of anatomy go through a split mountain, are reassembled, and the four winds as four Psyche figures flutter down to give them the breath of life. Then the men too are restored and appear, ten of them, in the Greek robe of glory. For the two final stages Ezekiel's own garb is changed to that of the white robe. But having accomplished his great mission, he must go back through the mountain, resume his human, Persian dress to be arrested at the Jewish altar by a royal figure in armor, and then beheaded.[22]

What shocked Goodenough in this synagogue and what prompted his reflection was the juxtaposition of this discovery with the received tradition of normative Judaism—the separation of Jewish and pagan influences and the announced absolute prohibition of images in Jewish life. Within the context of rabbinic Judaism, then, the synagogue at Dura Europos was impossible. The task of Goodenough is to ask what this impossible reality means. Somehow the study of the sacred book featured in rabbinic Judaism had at least in the third century exploded into a panoply of diverse images, Jewish and pagan. For Goodenough, the Jews of Dura were utterly loyal to the Jewish tradition and the Torah as they understood them; yet they expressed their loyalty in a building designed to copy the inner shrine of a pagan temple "filled with images of human beings and Greek and Iranian deities and carefully designed to interpret the Torah in a way profoundly mystical." Goodenough comments:

For the Judaism that seems expressed here is a Judaism which finds its meaning in mystic victory, a victory reached by two paths, the cosmic and the abstractly ontological. Yahweh of Hosts, or the Lord of the Powers, reveals himself through his creation, the universe, and also through the abstract values symbolized by the ten and the seven. I suspect that the black and white horses reflect a dualism nearer to Manichaeism, and to Iran in general, than to rabbinical Judaism, dualistic as the rabbis often are. Dionysiac feeling is rampant, but it seems to me no chance that the entrance to the Closed Temple was marked by the symbols most sacred at the time in Pahlavi Iran. The end result might be called a new paganism enlightened by Judaism or a new Judaism made cosmic and mystic-metaphysical by paganism. In any case, the two are deeply interfused. The people in the synagogue, however, would passionately have rejected the suggestion that they were presenting a new paganism, much as such thinking has always seemed a paganizing of Judaism to *halachic* Jews. I can myself see no reason that Jews who want to live by the mystic implications they feel in their traditions should not be free to call their religious ideas and practices Judaism; or that the historian should either belittle the mystic formulation which the Dura art implies, or rule it out of Jewish history.[23]

In the face of this evidence of a Judaism outside the normative, Goodenough posits two paths of Judaism: the vertical path by which Jews climb to God and even share in a divine nature, and the horizontal path by which Jews walk through this world according to God's instructions. The vertical path found at Dura and later in the Kabbalah, a collection of Jewish mystical writings developed after the expulsion of Jews from Spain in 1492, and the Hasidic movements in the eighteenth and nineteenth centuries were consistently fought and ultimately defeated by the rabbis, who followed the horizontal way. Activities and beliefs associated with the mystical path were often repressed; as often, rabbinic instruction simply absorbed aspects of the mystic liturgy, but taught the meaning of those rites from a rabbinic point of view. Its synthesis completed, the new rite seemed to have its "chief value as being part of the horizontal path of conformity to the will of God." As Goodenough's study confirms, some of the most common symbols of contemporary Judaism, such as the menorah and the shofar, originated outside the Jewish world and first entered that world through the vertical rather than the horizontal path.[24]

Goodenough's analysis is controversial. A recent essay by the late Warren Moon, Professor of Classics and Art History at the University of Wisconsin, disputes aspects of Goodenough's analysis of specific story cycles and symbol representation, yet at another level affirms a central point of his work. Noting that the paintings in the synagogue were "not decorative but didactic, the focus of instruction and religious debate," Moon states that the "programmatic nature" of the paintings is Greco-Roman and asks, "Could there have been available to the synagogue artists another set of visual conventions better suited to Jewish representation than the Roman, more authoritative, widely recognized, highly visible and therefore more successful for the purposes of instruction? Certainly not. Roman artistic schemes carried for the congregation levels of meaning that were immediately apprehensible, automatic and spontaneous." Jacob Neusner's appraisal of Goodenough's work would thus no doubt be affirmed by Moon as well: "If the cumulative evidence is inspected as cautiously as possible, it can hardly yield a statement other than the following: At the period between the first and sixth centuries, the manifestations of the Jewish religion were varied and complex, far more varied, indeed, than the extant Talmudic literature would have led us to believe."[25]

Goodenough's analysis moves within and beyond the Jewish world as he attempts to understand the continuation of the mystical path even as it is repressed by the vertical in Greek religion and Christianity as well. Here Goodenough develops the definition of formal state religions, that is, religions that express themselves in fixed laws and observances. According to Goodenough, the official religions of Athens, Rome, and Jerusalem often have a basis other than the symbols they claim and interpret as their own. The symbols that engendered deep emotion and ecstasy—religions directly and consciously centered in the renewal of life and the granting of immortality—were "not to be seen in the forum at Rome, they were everywhere in mystical Pompeii and ecstatic Phrygia and North Africa. Largely absent from official Athens, they were common in the popular Athens of the vases. Never found in the life and teachings of the Pharisees, they became central in Christianity as tokens of its hope of divine life here and hereafter." In Goodenough's analysis, official religion takes over and, as it were, straightens out popular religion. At the same time, the former is intimately tied to the centralization of political and religious power. That is, normative religion, by overcoming, indeed overwhelming the diversity of prior religiosity, too often becomes a tool of empire. Of course, sometimes, as seen in Constantinian Christianity, that which seeks to become normative uses the power of empire to achieve its goals. The pattern of rabbinic Judaism in its quest to become normative is repeated by Christianity as it represses, consumes, and reinterprets symbols it finds in pre-Christian pagan cultures.[26]

Elisabeth Schüssler Fiorenza's *In Memory of Her: A Feminist Theological Reconstruction of Christian Origins* is a book that seeks to find the now-buried story of women as it evolved within the Jesus movement before the formalization of the Christian canon and empire. Schüssler Fiorenza's work is thus similar to the work of Goodenough in that she attempts to deconstruct an official religion—this time Christianity— that masks its own origins and conflicts. Schüssler Fiorenza, a feminist biblical scholar at Harvard Divinity School, also articulates the perspective that the normative understandings that are brought to the study of the past are often inadequate, for "the androcentric scholarly paradigm can thematise the role of women as a societal, historical, philosophical and theological problem but cannot question its own horizon." For Schüssler Fiorenza and Goodenough, women or anyone outside the parameters of the normative are forced to question the interpreters' framework as well as the historical text; it is Schüssler Fiorenza's view that rather than understand the text as a reflection of the history about which it speaks, "we must search for clues and allusions that indicate the reality about which the text is silent."[27]

What Schüssler Fiorenza finds in the study of Jesus and the early Christian movement is an attempt to radicalize cultural and religious relations in general and between women and men in particular. Her Jesus is in line with the prophets *and* wisdom theology, the latter not characterized by the "fear of the goddess in its apologetic defense of monotheism." Instead, Sophia is inspired by an attempt to speak in the "language of its own culture and to integrate elements of its 'goddess cult,' especially of Isis worship, into Jewish monotheism." For Schüssler Fiorenza, this is how the Palestinian Jesus movement understands the ministry and mission of Jesus: "as that of the prophet and child of Sophia sent to announce that God is the God of the poor and heavy laden, of the outcasts and those who suffer injustice." Then and now, most of the poor and heavy laden were women, and thus it is more than coincidence that women were the first non-Jewish members of the Jesus movement. Unfortunately, the insurgent "prophetic Sophialogy" of Jesus was supplanted by a patriarchal ethos soon enshrined in Constantinian Christianity. With this, "Sophia, the God of Jesus, [who] wills the wholeness of humanity of everyone and thereby enables the Jesus movement to become a discipleship of equals" becomes a distant memory. For Schüssler Fiorenza, the early followers of Jesus stood in the succession of Sophia-prophets, announcing shalom to Israel; only later would the normative framers of Christianity attempt to banish women and Jews from its center. In sum, the discipleship of equals that Schüssler Fiorenza finds in the life of Jesus needs to be uncovered—in the same way that the popular religion of Judaism in relation to the prophets and Hellenism in relation to rabbinic Judaism need to be uncovered—beneath the normative, somehow outside the reach of the powerful. This leads Schüssler Fiorenza to understand the Jesus movement as an "inner-Jewish renewal movement that presented *an alternative* option to the dominant patriarchal structures rather than an oppositional formation rejecting the values and praxis of Judaism."[28]

Could it be, for example, that the discipleship of equals promoted by Jesus, confirmed in different ways by Schüssler Fiorenza and John Dominic Crossan, was a popular religious movement ultimately to be denied by the official religions of Judaism and Christianity—that is, by Jerusalem *and* Rome? And that the denial of the Jesus movement is similar to the denial of other subversive movements, both historically and in the present? It is interesting to note that these movements sought and seek today to root communities in a language of equality and passion that they find lacking and abstract in the official traditions.

This rooting seems in the examples we have analyzed to exemplify a give and take with the local environment and geography. In Ezekiel, the priests in the Temple courtyard bowing to the sun are combining elements of their inheritance without, to their own minds, contradicting or betraying it. Jews in the Greco-Roman Empire did this as well, extending their relationships physically and through symbol among those with whom they lived. Jesus replicates this pattern, and the first non-Jews who hear about him do so in the synagogues where they felt welcome. A reciprocal relationship of Jews and non-Jews thus existed at certain points of these discontinuities, which raises the question in a different way: Is that which is portrayed as normative in fact normative for most adherents to a particular religion? Or is the normative actually a minority experience with the power to define? A religious experience at a certain moment in history over time becomes *the* religious experience, that is, orthodoxy. That which crosses boundaries is itself declared outside the newly defined parameters, and all that has crossed before is seen as deviant or even heretical. A division crossed between Jew and Hellenistic Greek, between men and women in the Jewish Jesus movement of renewal, between Jewish belief and pagan rites at Dura Europos, is a division resurrected to last forever.

Ending False Divisions

Yet as we have seen, orthodoxy is continually buffeted by historical events. In the present, Holocaust theology can be seen in at least two lights: as a popular religiosity in response to mass death and as a desire by Jewish elites to create a new orthodoxy. In the first aspect, it is interesting that the remembrance of the Holocaust as the significant memory of the Jewish people was originally opposed by the rabbis, for they realized the threat it posed to the rabbinic religious framework and the religious power structure. Those who articulated the significance of the Holocaust came at least initially from outside this establishment, such as Elie Wiesel, or were banished from it, like Richard Rubenstein. The memory of the Holocaust soon, though, became linked with the centrality of Israel, a link also initially opposed by the Jewish establishment. The religious hierarchy understood quite correctly that new Jewish institutions would grow within this context and that the synagogue and rabbinic leadership would diminish in relevance and hence stature. Holocaust theology as popular religiosity in fact became important so quickly that the divisions in Jewish life that arose in the nineteenth century among Reform, Conservative, and Orthodox soon lost the memory of their own internal quarrel with the centrality of Holocaust and Israel. In a major way, Holocaust and Israel overwhelmed these divisions and reoriented major aspects of each. That the Reform movement declared in its founding platform of 1886 that Jews are no longer a nation and do not look to return to Palestine was forgotten by the 1970s; so, too, was the Orthodox position that a return to Zion was a messianic proposition to be performed by God rather than human action.[29]

The genius of the normative tradition is its ability to handle outbreaks of popular religiosity by channeling and ultimately transforming them back into the system. In a sense, the normative tradition rebuffs insurgencies as long as it can and then takes elements of the insurgency, ideological and leadership, into itself. By subsuming into itself elements of Holocaust and Israel, the events themselves are rendered part of the prevailing normative framework. The leaders of the insurgency are necessary to help protect the shaken but surviving normative framework. In a paradoxical way, then, protests against the inadequacy of a religious framework become affirmations of it in a new configuration. Of course, this means splitting those who articulate the sensibility by virtue of who can be absorbed into the normative framework and who cannot. This paradox explains the rise of Elie Wiesel from survivor of Auschwitz to the most noted spokesperson for contemporary Judaism and his ascension to the Nobel Prize for Literature. It also explains the exile of Richard Rubenstein from a prominent Hillel rabbi to a professor at a southern university with no discernible Jewish population and his reemergence years later on the Auschwitz delegation.

Over time the initial outpouring, the initial crossing of boundaries, within the group or outside of it, is lost as new lines are drawn. And so often the new boundaries are defined by their link to power. If Crossan's and Schüssler Fiorenza's Jesus is difficult to maintain within the canonical gospels as the meaning of Jesus is debated, by the time of Constantine the debate is guarded and directed by a militaristic church and empire. With Christian empire, the boundaries crossed at Dura Europos, for example, become too dangerous, for Jews, Christians, and for pagans. As Fredriksen points out, the attraction of the latter two groups to Judaism continues until it is outlawed by Constantine under the penalty of death. Jewish openness to other cultures also closes down under this threatened penalty. The Holocaust, which in some way brings to an end the closed boundaries erected in Constantine's time and challenges at the deepest level Judaism and Christianity as they formed within that period, *because the end result of that empire and division is Auschwitz*, and which poses again the question of the discipleship of equals and interpenetration of cultures, is quickly turned into another point of division. Although Auschwitz is in many ways an end of the normative traditions of Judaism and Christianity, it is transformed into a reason for the continuation of this history more fervently guarded than ever against the critique that Auschwitz embodies. Ultimately, this transformation of critique is molded into a reason for continuation by a Christian and Jewish community now in league with the power of the United States and Israel.[30]

Thus the explosive questions found in the discontinuities are often defused in relation to religious and political power. Can, for example, we as Jews speak today about the God of history with regard to our suffering as we did before we caused suffering to others? Can we authentically call Christianity to account for its empire as we pursue our own? As often, these questions are not only defused but abused: our suffering can be used to justify the suffering of others in the name of a once questionable but now triumphant God of history. Once the questions are placed in the service of empire, a new dynamic emerges loosed from the event itself. The other side of Elie Wiesel becomes the late Meir Kahane, the proponent of cleansing Israel and Palestine of Palestinians; the pressure on Wiesel is narrowed to declare his support for Yitzhak Rabin, formulator of the "might and beatings" policy after the beginning of the Palestinian uprising, or Yitzhak Shamir, political pursuer of the Greater Land of Israel philosophy. Irving Greenberg, who in 1974 articulated the most radical statement on belief after the Holocaust, by 1988 is authoring an extensive essay on the ethics of Jewish power, calling on Jews to understand that in the "normalization" of the Jewish condition, in our assumption of power, we need to use and will sometimes abuse that power. For Greenberg, the point is to correct the abuse rather than condemn the very use of power, a position Greenberg no doubt would condemn if John Paul II uttered it in respect to Christianity during and after the Holocaust.

And how can Jews raise the question of boundaries if a new excommunicable sin is set in place, namely, questioning the legitimacy of Israel as it is now constituted? Within two decades the insurgents become the guardians of a new orthodoxy, and when Jacob Neusner questions this orthodoxy of Holocaust and Israel, he does so by harkening back to a system that reifies the divisions that mark the dead in Auschwitz. At the same time, the hope of Judah Magnes to live in a mutually beneficial way with Palestinian Arabs and the Arab world in general, thus replicating in some ways the particular and universal thrust of early Jewish history, gives way to A. B. Yehoshua, who seeks only separation. The end result of this, as I witnessed at Auschwitz, is increased isolation and fear exactly at the time in history when these barriers might honestly be bridged.

Why does that which claims to be normative fear the bridge to something beyond itself? Why do contemporary movements look to the past for their own validation, which in reality is a past of their own making? And is this past, constructed by contemporary movements themselves, creating a self-fulfilling reality? It is curious that the normative and non-normative aspects of religious life look to the past for validation; they ultimately seek a religious hegemony that betrays the ground from which they started. It is almost too obvious to cite again the example of Jesus, who has been a captive of Christianity for almost two thousand years. The inclusive becomes exclusive, linked to power and then to death, death of cultures by the dozens and people by the millions. With reference to Jesus, perhaps it is the fear that he belongs outside the Church that claims him that redoubles the attempt to hold him fast within its normative tradition. Or perhaps it is the knowledge that Jesus had little time for the elements of the Jewish hierarchy that have been replicated and extended in Christianity.

For the Jewish community, the fear, at least since the fourth century, has been of decimation and assimilation—in short, of disappearance. Yet it remains that the insights and struggles that brought a diverse group of tribes together some three thousand years ago derived from the necessity to struggle for liberation from oppression rather than the desire to erect a perpetual boundary between these tribes and the other nations of the world. Even here in the origins is a reality that contradicts the present understanding: these tribes, which ultimately became Israel, preserved *and* crossed boundaries in their search for freedom. When centuries later, Ezekiel came upon diverse customs and worship, he was witnessing a reality present from the beginning. Was the member of the Auschwitz delegation who witnessed the French Jewish "pilgrims" performing the "Stations of the Cross" attempting that which Ezekiel failed to accomplish, because Jews have always crossed boundaries, even after Auschwitz? Perhaps we can say after Auschwitz that the barriers are false and that the focus on preserving Judaism, or

Christianity for that matter, itself masks emptiness and dissolution. Perhaps the opposite is the case: to cross barriers without an agenda is itself a way of preserving and expanding that which is precious and good.

The response of the normative, of course, is that the preservation of the community is paramount, for it carries into the future the truth revealed to it. For Jews, the burden of covenant that it carries leads to the messianic age; for Christians, the death and resurrection promise the return of Jesus the Christ as the messiah. Revealed truth comes from outside history and awaits a response. Indeed, these and other aspects of revelation have historically been held for thousands of years, at least by the normative. But revelation is understood differently in each time period, depending on its orientation in culture and its relationship to power. Surely it is difficult to assert that the priests in the Temple whom Ezekiel condemned knew God's revelation less than the rabbi from Peekskill, New York, who once lectured me in Jerusalem as a wayward Jew because of my expressed hope that Palestinians would be included in the vision of the Jewish people. It is equally difficult to argue that a Protestant minister in a Swedish church carefully laying out the argument for a sinful and redeemed humanity is more faithful to revelation than Jesus and his Jewish followers, who invited to hospitality the people they met. And what could the revealed word mean in light of Auschwitz and 1492, when the carriers of that word and the ethos they generated led to mass death?

A New Discipline

What does it portend for the future of Jewish and Christian religiosity if we define the essential religious goal of our time to be to cross boundaries in the struggle to end Auschwitz and 1492? By establishing the criteria of religiosity as resistance to these events, will it mean that in resistance one has also affirmed? Will the maintenance of religious particularity end in a utopia of a freewheeling universality? Are the foundations of Jewish and Christian faith, seen by the normative as Sinai and the Jesus-as-Christ event, to fade into a mythic past and be discarded? How will the faith of Jew and Christian be described and passed on generation to generation and what will the context of affirmation be? After Auschwitz and 1492, what boundaries will be drawn, and who will draw them? In the main, these are questions that the religious establishment asks and I leave to them to answer. My intuition is—my experience tells me—that these issues are of less importance or may even be missing the fundamental questions of our time. And too often they obfuscate the path before us.

At Auschwitz, at least for me, many of these questions reached closure. The brutality of the history concretized at Auschwitz confirmed that the way to the future lies somewhere else. If the cries of the victims were still to be heard at Auschwitz, mingling with the cries of the contemporary world, I realized that Jewish leadership, and dominant Christian leadership too, is totally unprepared for a political, cultural, and religious future worth bequeathing to our children. They are living on borrowed time, time purchased with great suffering, spoken and written about with great eloquence but also increasingly empty of meaning.

And I also realized that I did not want to live in a world as defined by some of these Jewish intellectuals and scholars, or Christian ones for that matter, and that they actually did not live in the world that they articulated either. For the most part, they speak of a suffering experienced by others as they live comfortably and successfully in universities, churches, and synagogues. It appears a facade, a mask to put on and take off at the appropriate time, like attending synagogue on Saturday morning or church on Sunday and pursuing the ways of the world the rest of the week. Who knows this better than these religious professionals, rabbis, priests, ministers, and academics who spend their lives uplifting, defending, exhorting, lamenting, serving (while often building a career) the religious systems dying before them? And who better to define the parameters of thinkable thought than the guardians of tradition, some of whom were present with me at Auschwitz?

For Auschwitz has become a tradition, with its own structure and dogmas from which one can be exiled for unorthodox opinions or language. I thought of two statements I used in my lectures at Maryknoll before leaving for Auschwitz that spoke to me even more powerfully while there in the death camp: "Oppose all orthodoxy" and "Beware the guardians of tradition." For whom and what do they guard, whose questions do they ask, and whose and which questions remain unasked? Do the guardians of the Holocaust guard its victims or themselves? Has the Holocaust become our protection, one that threatens through the counsel of silence to become our prison? Do the heralds of Jesus the Christ speak and act from his discipline or attempt to convert others to a faith simply to reinforce their own belief? Does the Christianity of 1492, dressed in nuanced language, promise liberation to those conquered by the gospel?

After Auschwitz, perhaps we should simply admit that the Holocaust has changed everything and nothing. The world goes on its regular course, combining brutality and beauty, tragedy and possibility. The sun rose and set before and during the Holocaust and while we were at Auschwitz in the same way it did at that horrible time. And the same

Jewish prayers that were chanted in Auschwitz by its inmates were chanted by some in our group, and in the most forbidding of locations, like the guard tower overlooking the railroad tracks at Birkenau. Were these prayers heard then or now? If God did not hear those prayers when first recited, would God hear them today?

Perhaps we should further acknowledge a certain folk wisdom to the choices people make in light of Auschwitz and 1492, even as the theological and intellectual communities continue their search. Auschwitz certainly raises the issue of choice precisely because the victims had no choice. Too often, though, this choice is seen as affiliation or nonaffiliation with an old or new orthodoxy; the setting of Auschwitz demands a deeper probing. After my journey there, I perceived the invocation of the fundamental religious question, indeed fundamental religious choice, of our time: whether as individuals and as a people we pursue community or empire. Auschwitz was total empire, an extension of the empires built in 1492. Why is it that I meet so many Jewish and Christian leaders who support empire, actively or through silence, and so many "unaffiliated" Jews and Christians who, confused, searching, and without the requisite Hebrew training or Christian "faith," resist empire?

It may be that what is called for is a new discipline, a new crossing of boundaries that joins fidelity to the dead and seeks to build a world that protects and encourages life. This discipline would promote community and fight against empire, not so much in search of utopia but a life grounded in hospitality in the broadest sense—personal, cultural, spiritual, and political. The past could be put to use, the discontinuities especially; and even that which has become normative can, when placed properly as an insight rather than an orthodoxy, be seen in a different, more positive light. The division of Jew and Christian, for example, thus takes on a different connotation. Rather than two religions, a common path with varying emphases is seen. Even Judaism and Christianity as defined over the last fifteen hundred years are challenged to include the pagan, which is in fact inside both of these traditions.

The reality of Judaism and Christianity has always been syncretistic, and for good reason: life knows no Jewish and Christian path away from a world filled with geographic and cultural diversity. And it is not only that the pagan is part of our world, it is properly a part of our spirituality. Were not Auschwitz and 1492 attempts to sort out and destroy the other, to impose a uniformity on the other, a uniformity that is not even present in ourselves? Perhaps the normative sense of idolatry as it evolved in Judaism and Christianity is at the root of the problem: the attempt to cleanse the diversity inside leads to an attempt to cleanse the .diversity that is visible outside. But have not Judaism and Christianity, so jealously guarded, become idolatrous of themselves? Could the

constant purification, expansion, and self-concern of both be sympto-
matic of idolatry, reifying a path as *the* path and clinging to certain
forms as if life itself depended on it? In the face of Auschwitz and 1492,
there is little more ridiculous than watching the solemn declarations of
Jewish and Christian leaders who are at the same moment part of a new
structure of empire.

This new discipline also includes the atheist who, like the pagan, is
not only outside Jewish and Christian life, but within as well. In fact,
atheism is often a response to classical theism, a triumphant monotheism that is abstracted from the diversity of reality. Atheism is a rejection
of a strict monotheism and of a particular type of God found wanting in
the travails of history. The atheism of Karl Marx, for example, is thus to
be seen as intimately tied to the monotheism of a repressive Church.
But after Auschwitz and 1492, both atheism and monotheism collapse,
and the victims ask us to go beyond a conflict that often as not leads to
more burning children. This is what Rabbi Irving Greenberg meant
when he wrote that "neither classical theism nor atheism is adequate to
incorporate the incommensurability of the Holocaust; neither produced
a consistently proper response; neither is credible alone—in the presence of the burning children." Instead, Greenberg speaks of moment
faiths, "moments when Redeemer and vision of redemption are present, interspersed with times when the flames of the burning children
blot out faith—though it flickers again."[31]

For Greenberg, the dialectic of moment faiths prompts a response in
the reaffirmation of meaningfulness, worth, and life—through acts of
love that are life-giving: "The act of creating a life, of enhancing its dignity is the counter-testimony to Auschwitz. To talk of love and of a God
who cares in the presence of the burning children is obscene and incredible: to leap in and pull a child out of a pit, to clean its face and heal its
body, is to make the most powerful statement—the only statement that
counts." Now we must add as well the victims of 1492 to Greenberg's
analysis and paraphrase him thusly: neither classical theism nor atheism
is adequate to incorporate the incommensurability of the Holocaust and
1492, neither is credible alone—in the presence of the burning children.
The act of creating a life, of enhancing its dignity, is the countertesti-
mony to Auschwitz and 1492.[32]

7

A Postcard
from Auschwitz

A fter the Holocaust and 1492, is it possible to speak about God? At
Auschwitz I felt the power of Irving Greenberg's words about
burning children. At home I faced the task of speaking of the experience of Auschwitz and the question of God in light of Auschwitz to my
son Aaron, then five years old. After my colleagues and I gave our public presentations, wrote our books, and certified ourselves as authentic
Jewish scholars, was not the passing down of our story and commitment the central and most intimate of our callings? I realized a strange
paradox in my own life: because of Palestinian visitors and the discussions in our home revolving around Israel and Palestine, Aaron was
quite aware of the suffering of the Palestinians; he and I in fact had several discussions on the subject. But I had rarely broached the subject of
Jewish suffering through history, let alone the Holocaust.

To some of the young delegates I inquired how they communicate
the story of the Holocaust to their children. In general they avoided the
subject until their children were older, a reasonable choice to be sure.
But still I felt it was possible to introduce the subject to Aaron, albeit in
a nuanced way. On the last day at Auschwitz, I purchased a postcard
that featured the railroad tracks to Auschwitz-Birkenau, lined by several gas-lit flames commemorating the dead. I sent the card by mail
with the following message: "Dear Aaron, I am sending this postcard
from a place called Auschwitz. It is a place where many Jews died and

yet we are alive today. I hope that this never happens again and that you will help build a world safe from this violence. Love, Daddy."

When I returned home I asked Aaron if he would like to discuss my trip to Auschwitz, and when he nodded, I read him the postcard. For a moment he was silent. Then he asked the most obvious question: Why was this done to Jews? After I responded that some people did not like Jews, but others did, such as his many schoolmates who were Christian, he looked at me and said, "I bet those Jews who are alive really thank God that they are alive." The corollary question of how to inquire about God in relation to the dead went unasked, and I was grateful that it did. What could I answer to Aaron, a child who often wonders about God, that would make sense to him *and* to the burning children? Could I tell Aaron that after Auschwitz we could no longer speak about a God of history? Aaron is a child who in his innocence and goodness speaks to me of this very presence.

There were other contradictions to explain as well: our celebration of Shabbat at home and my difficulty in participating with any integrity in synagogue life; asking God's blessing when we light the Shabbat candles, when the very presence of God is sometimes difficult for me to affirm. When a decade ago our family began to observe the rituals of Shabbat, I realized then that it was more a remembrance of the dead in the present than a celebration. It was several years later that a deepening occurred, with the naming of Aaron after Moses' brother, the one who reintroduced Moses to his people, who spoke for Moses, and who accompanied him on his journey to the desert. But at the moment of that deepening, Passover, which was for me even as a child the center of Jewish life, became, like the synagogue, almost impossible. I could no longer remember our slavery and celebrate our liberation as we enter a new slavery in the oppression of others. Chanukkah similarly became more difficult, but for a different reason: I could no longer side with the Maccabees in more than a symbolic way. I do not, after all, seek a freedom that emphasizes separation, a divorce from cultures which, though ambivalent in themselves and in regard to Jews, are worthy in and of themselves and also enrich the Jewish people. As difficult to explain to Aaron is that some of our Maryknoll guests at Shabbat—priests, sisters, and students—are our historic oppressors, while others are themselves oppressed by the Christianity they affirm. Similarly, it is not easy to explain to Aaron and to others that those Christians who oppose Christendom often carry the same questions as do I, and that some of them indeed share a great solidarity with me. In short, the intermingling of Auschwitz and Maryknoll in my life will prompt equally complex questions for Aaron in his.

The barrier crossed does not always guarantee an easy answer.

In fact, to traverse such limits almost assures a difficulty seemingly avoided through separation. For me, crossing into the Christian arena continues to prompt ambivalent feelings and contradictory signs; it is not my world, nor will it be Aaron's. At Auschwitz, however, I realized that the insular Jewish world was not mine either, nor would it be my son's. The boundary between Jewish and Christian life that also abuts the boundary between paganism and atheism is a relatively unexplored area, at least in normative theological language. However, in exploring Jewish history then and now we have lived on these boundaries seemingly forever. Could we after the Holocaust explore once again the boundaries that many of the victims of the Holocaust themselves explored?

The fact is that Jews have explored these boundaries after the Holocaust, though the exploration is usually unannounced, not remembered. One of the most moving moments of Richard Rubenstein's journey, however, I do recall; namely, his indebtedness to the great Protestant theologian Paul Tillich, with whom he studied at Harvard. It was Tillich whose sympathy for paganism both "shocked and enlightened" Rubenstein. Tillich taught Rubenstein how to express and conceptualize the pagan instincts he had been suppressing during his years of rabbinical study. That is, Tillich freed Rubenstein to accept himself as he really was. "My practical experience as a clergyman had convinced me that in spite of all pretense of serving a male sky god, the religion I and my community were actually practicing was a pagan cult rooted in the vicissitudes of earthly, biological existence. Tillich's lectures taught me to recognize it as such. Although it was hardly his intention, he also helped me to understand that it is possible to be both pagan and Jewish at the same time." Though obviously a coincidence, it was nonetheless symbolic when the news of Tillich's death reached Rubenstein as he concluded his first trip to Auschwitz in 1965. After addressing the Catholic Intellectual Club in Warsaw, he learned the news of Tillich's death. He was upset, though, as he later wrote, "there seemed to be a peculiar appropriateness to learning of his passing the day I visited the Warsaw Ghetto."[1]

Can we forget that the movement of the story of the Holocaust into Western culture was also facilitated by Christians? Thus, when a youthful Elie Wiesel, then living in France, sought to bring his manuscript *Night* to the attention of publishers, it was the Catholic writer François Mauriac whom he approached and who ultimately wrote the introduction to that book. Similarly, the ecumenical discussion, at least historically, has been a forum of mutual learning. An example of this is Will Herberg who, when the ideology of Marxism was failing him, read Reinhold Niebuhr's *Moral Man and Immoral Society*. The book changed the course of his life. "Humanly speaking," Herberg wrote, "it converted

me, for in some manner I cannot describe, I felt my whole being, and
not merely my thinking shifted to a new center." The fruit of this conversion was a renewed engagement with Judaism, a path that Niebuhr
approved. As John Murray Cuddihy notes, "Herberg was converting
to a biblical faith," becoming, in fact, "the Jewish counterpart of
Niebuhr."[2]

The interplay of Niebuhr and contemporary Jewish theology is a
story worth telling. Just a year before his own death, Abraham Joshua
Heschel, a close friend to Niebuhr, presided at Niebuhr's funeral. At the
close of the service Heschel spoke: "He appeared among us like a sublime figure out of the Hebrew Bible. . . . Niebuhr's life was a song in the
form of deeds, a song that will go on forever. Revered, beloved Reinhold: In the words of the Psalmist: 'You are the fairest of the sons of
men, Grace is poured upon your lips, Therefore God has blessed you
forever.'" Niebuhr's influence continues today with reference to the
work of Irving Greenberg. Greenberg's rhetoric in correcting the abuses
of power while maintaining the ability to project it, the discussion of
morality and immorality, all heavily echo Niebuhr's discussion of
moral man and immoral society.[3]

And beyond the Holocaust theologians are other interpretations of
Jewish life—breaks with the normative—that are heavily indebted to
the crossing of boundaries. One thinks of Harold Bloom, Sterling Professor of Humanities at Yale University, who in a long and distin-
guished career has consistently brought the wealth of English literature
to the discussion of the Jewish past and future. A recent work of his,
The Book of J, is delightful in this regard, and his conclusions are daring.
A quotation from his concluding chapter serves to demonstrate the interplay of Jewish and non-Jewish: "J, like Shakespeare, works between
truth and meaning, just as belief does, but neither J nor Shakespeare
seems to me a believer, whether in Yahweh or in Yahweh and Christ, at
least not a believer as most people believe. J and Shakespeare, being
poets upon the heights of the sublime, do not waste their energies by
choosing forms of worship from poetic tales. They work rather to represent reality, but in the urgent mode of compelling a perpetual fresh reality to appear." The Jewish feminist Robin Morgan, especially her
book *The Anatomy of Freedom: Feminism, Physics, and Global Politics*, also
comes to mind. Without overt religious language, she proposes to find
a spirituality for our time combining feminism and physics, thus re-
vealing the interconnectedness of that which has been seen as separate;
gender, race, global politics, family structures, economics, and the environment. It is more than coincidence that her introduction ends with a
quotation from Einstein about God and creation, and that her epigraph
is from Hannah Arendt about the possibility of freedom. The work of

singer/songwriter Bob Dylan and poet/singer Leonard Cohen should also be seen in this light, as Jews who in crossing boundaries have spoken powerfully to the spiritual, political, and cultural crises of our time. The convergences of Cohen's Buddhist practice and his Jewish roots finds expression in his *Book of Mercy*, a collection of fifty prose poems modeled on the Psalms. His poem "The Spice Box of Earth" evokes the spice box blessed and the aroma of which is inhaled at the end of the Sabbath. It is a ritual that separates that holy day from the rest of the week, marking the boundary between the sacred and the profane.[4]

Still, despite the interaction, for many Jews it is this exploration that is proscribed after Auschwitz because those who explored and those who remained separate found a common fate in mass death. An unspoken theme in the works of Holocaust theologians is that the past is also part of the future, and those who explore the boundaries after Auschwitz may bring upon the Jewish people another holocaust. Thus is seen the need in Rubenstein's view to escalate in the present the cost of taking Jewish lives. Greenberg also assents to this when he writes that the critique of Israeli power may in fact lead to what Israel ostensibly prevents, a second holocaust. Still one needs to ask if Rubenstein's and Greenberg's sensibility can enhance Jewish life in the future. Can we honestly say after this long and difficult journey through history that Greenberg's 1988 essay "The Ethics of Jewish Power," with its emphasis on normalization and Jewish power, is the sense of Jewish life we want to bequeath to our children? And what does the newly opened United States Holocaust Memorial Museum in Washington, D.C. mean in the context of normalization and power? Will the continual replaying of the Holocaust narrative, sanctioned and funded by a monied Jewish elite and the United States government, provide a future for the Jewish people? Can we honestly hand this to Aaron as his inheritance?[5]

If the Holocaust will continue to define in part Jewish identity and memory, I would prefer to hand Aaron the diverse stories that follow, all of which took place during the Nazi period. In trying to explain Kiddush Hashem—that is, the sanctification of God's name in martyrdom—Eliezer Berkovits, an Orthodox Jewish theologian, writes that instead of concentrating on the degradation or even the heroic, the true mystery of the ghettos and death camps should be seen within the discipline that subverted the aim of the Nazis. Berkovits recalls a story in Emmanuel Ringelblum's history of the Warsaw Ghetto, when Ringelblum marveled at the way pious Jews continued to wear beards and traditional frock coats even though this exposed them to vicious beatings by the Nazis, or even death. Berkovits quotes Ringelblum: "An elderly Jew passed the guards on Twarda Street and did not—for reasons of piety—take off his hat in salute although the Jewish guards warned him. So [the Nazis] tortured him a long time. An hour later, he acted the same way. 'They can go to hell!' were his words." Berkovits comments that the Jewish action was not an act in fulfillment of any religious duties. According to Jewish law, it was quite permissible for them to shave their beards, to change their traditional garb. "Yet, they refused. And perhaps one should not use that word. They continued in their Jewish 'routine,' living their own life and ignoring the world around them." With reference to a group of Hasidim who continued with their Shabbat observance as they were ordered on the trains that would take them to Treblinka, Berkovits continues: "All of this was done in the tradition of Rabbi Akiba—contempt for a form of reality that does not even deserve a reaction. . . . One is unimpressed by Nazi Germany as one was unimpressed with Hadrian's Rome—one continues in the routine of being a Jew."[6]

If the stories recounted by Berkovits are of identifiably religious Jews, these stories are complemented by Jews who are less traditionally religious or who are on the boundary of Jewish religiosity. David Roskies, in his book *Against the Apocalypse*, recalls the story of Hillel Zeitlin, the religious existentialist who in the Warsaw Ghetto began to translate the psalms into Yiddish. When his building was blockaded, Zeitlin went to the *Umschlagplatz*, the infamous point of roundup for deportation, dressed in prayer shawl and *tefillin* as a sign of the continuity of Jewish history and resistance. It was also a recognition of the fleeting power of the Nazis. So, too, the life of Etty Hillesum, the young Dutch Jew who experienced the world with passion and an almost mystical simplicity, similarly demonstrates nontraditional religiosity. Her spiritual guides were the German poet Rilke and the Russian novelist Dostoevsky, and she explored both the Jewish and Christian scriptures. Imprisoned in the transit camp Westerbork and destined to die in Auschwitz, Hillesum developed an openness to God and to the spirit not often found in reflections on the Holocaust. In one of her last diary entries before her transport to Auschwitz, Hillesum wrote: "All I want to say is this: The misery here is quite terrible, and yet, late at night when the day has slunk away into the depths behind me, I often walk with a spring in my step along the barbed wire. And then time and again, it soars straight from my heart—I can't help it, that's just the way it is, like some elementary force—the feeling that life is glorious and magnificent, and that one day we shall be building a whole new world."[7]

Berkovits understands the story of the Hasidim within the context of faith in a transcendental meaning of existence. "The vaster the degradation and the misery, the more miraculous the manifestation of man's faith in the values and meanings he cherishes. If the evil was unnatural so, too, was the good. Or shall we say super-natural? If the humiliation was inhuman, so was the preservation of man's dignity at all cost too inhuman. Shall we rather say, super-human?" Therefore, for Berkovits the question of faith for the Jew is not to explain the silence of God during the Holocaust, but whether within the Judaic framework it is possible to take "cognizance of the tragedy and promise of existence and whether one may hold on to the promise in spite of the tragedy." But one wonders if the stories cited by Berkovits as well as the image of Zeitlin in *tefillin* and Hillesum's desire to build a new world should be testimony to faith or the continuing relevance or irrelevance of the Judaic religious framework. Rather, they seem testimony to the strength of an inheritance, accepted, rebelled against, expanded, and exhibited in defiance of those who declared total war on Jews and everyone who stood in the way of Nazi ideology and power. Each of these stories becomes a testimony to the development and securing of a discipline that asserts the goodness of humanity—the triumph of the human over death. Here once again the boundary comes into play but in a more complicated way. For the Hasidim, the boundary of the human is asserted in the Jewish routine. The Jewish routine in this situation subverts the ultimate power of the Nazis; it demystifies their power. In a different way this was true with Zeitlin and Hillesum. Having left behind the orthodox way—having crossed the boundaries of language and text—they retain an identity that is sure and specific. Confronted with evil, the stakes are clear, and each living in different situations responds within the matrix of his or her own life and situation.[8]

Who is to say where these people would find themselves after Auschwitz? Would the Hasidic men have reaffirmed their faith or denied it? Would the Jewish routine have continued its meaningfulness to them, or would they have abandoned it? Would Zeitlin have continued his translations into Yiddish or moved away from this language into a literature of another people? Would Hillesum have continued the optimism she held in the darkest of places or lost it in the postwar world? What would she have thought of the founding of the state of Israel? Would she have included Israel as part of the new world being born, or would she have recognized in its creation the displacement of another people and therefore deemed it a hindrance to the world she sought to build? Would they collectively recognize the critique of Richard Rubenstein, the voice of Elie Wiesel, or the faith reconstruction of Eliezer Berkovits? Would they hear their own stories in these theologians? What would they have thought of our delegation, of the work of Joan Ringelheim, or even the idea of ending or continuing Auschwitz?

There is no way of knowing, of course, and, as Neusner suggests, the sense of tradition—of Jewishness in the present—comes from contemporary questions that then reconstruct the past. Already in my own life, the lives of these Holocaust victims are seen through their interpreters, Rubenstein and others, and Aaron will have access to them through my own generation—people like Michael Lerner, A. B. Yehoshua, and Joan Ringelheim. Still, the root experience of lives lived to their fullest remains available, and this can be explored only if the lives themselves are not exploited for other agendas, to prove or disprove God's presence, to support or deny Israel, or even to silence the questions about God or Israel. Could it be that at this moment in history, those who lived during the Holocaust and those who have come after should be seen in the context of their own struggle to be faithful and that their labors should prompt our own struggle to be faithful within the circumstances of our history?

Taken as a whole, then, Jewish history presents a series of affirmations, denials, expansions, contractions, borrowings, singular contributions—that is, a conversation and activity over time about the meaning, triumphs, and tragedies of history that we inherit, interpret, continue, and change.

In this way my early years in the synagogue when I "overheard" the Jewish conversation I was destined to enter is similar to the conversation that Aaron overhears in our home and in my postcard from Auschwitz. Aaron, then, is being presented with a framework that he will enter and from which he will choose his direction. Thus Aaron and his generation will follow Jews who have lived out this initiation and choosing; the priests who bowed to the sun *and* Ezekiel; Jewish Hellenists *and* the Maccabees; those Jews who practiced the discipline of Jesus *and* the rabbis; the Jews of Dura *and* the makers of normative Judaism; the Bundists *and* the Zionists; the Hasidim, Zeitlin, and Hillesum; Holocaust theologians like Rubenstein and Wiesel; as well as the explorers of modern literature and science like Bloom and Morgan.

At the same time, Aaron inherits as part of his history the canonical *and* historical gospels, dominant Christianity *and* the Christianity carried by those who have been conquered by the gospel. He inherits Auschwitz *and* 1492 and the questions that come with both these events. Could it be that the commentary of Gustavo Gutiérrez, the Peruvian liberation theologian, on the past and present holocaust is as germane to Aaron as my postcard from Auschwitz?

Our task here is to find the words with which to talk about God in the midst of the starvation of millions, the humiliation of races regarded as inferior, discrimination against women, especially women who are poor, systematic social injustice, a persistent high rate of infant mortality, those who simply "disappear" or are deprived of their freedom, the sufferings of peoples who are struggling for their right to live, the exiles and the refugees, terrorism of every kind, and the corpse-filled common graves of *Ayacucho*. What we must deal with is not the past but, unfortunately, a cruel present and a dark tunnel with no apparent end.[9]

So too are the words of James Cone in reference to the witness of Martin Luther King Jr. and Malcolm X:

> Racial justice was the area in which Martin and Malcolm made their mark. They gave their lives for America's salvation; but America is not redeemed. Racism is still alive and well operating in every segment of American society. . . . America is a nightmare for the poor of every race. In this land of plenty there are nearly forty million poor people who are trying to survive with little or no resources for their emotional and physical well-being. . . . One does not need a graduate degree in religion, ethics or philosophy to know that America's national and international policies are morally bankrupt.[10]

Rosemary Radford Ruether's words are also important as part of Aaron's inheritance when she writes of the need for a committed life over time, despite the trends or the appearance of victory or defeat. "We also remain clear that life is not made whole 'once and for all,' in some static millennium of the future. It is made whole again and again, in the renewed day born from night and in the new spring that rises from each winter."[11]

Finally, Aaron also inherits the historical Jesus as analyzed by John Dominic Crossan and Elisabeth Schüssler Fiorenza in counterpoint to the Jewish and Christian establishments or, more accurately stated, the Jewish-Christian establishment of our day. He therefore inherits the possibility of crossing boundaries, which those Jews before, during, and after the time of Jesus sought also to do with those Christians after the time of Jesus who have likewise struggled for justice and healing. That is, Aaron's generation has behind it a history flawed and yet with possibility, a history that is open to a future beyond the definitions of the present.

These at least are the thoughts I brought back to Aaron from Auschwitz, one might say, my hope for his future. Of course, in the end I can only bequeath to him my journey. And part of my own journey came to an end at Auschwitz. In a sense, I had been preparing for this journey my entire life and yet in retrospect I seemed hardly ready for it.

It was important for me that Richard Rubenstein, as part of our delegation, was at Auschwitz, the place where his life's work had taken on direction and his exile began. Approaching his seventieth birthday, Rubenstein, the difficult thinker, had returned to the forbidding

ground of his beginning. Over the years, Rubenstein had become a political conservative and a staunch advocate for Israel as a response to
Auschwitz. For this he was granted a stay, a parole if you will, when he
was awarded an honorary doctorate for his contribution to religious
thought by Jewish Theological Seminary. In his early years as a theologian, Rubenstein broke with the old; in his later years he became a
guardian of a tradition that he initially took on at great risk.

We met infrequently over the years since I left university, though we
commented in print on each other's work. Year after year I have used
his book *The Cunning of History* in my classes, including the course I
was teaching when I left for Auschwitz. My students were intrigued
and often moved by his analysis of the twentieth century as a century
of triage and holocaust; third-world Christians especially identified
their own experience with that of the Jewish people. Rubenstein had
written a review of my book *Toward a Jewish Theology of Liberation*,
which was originally published in 1987, coincidentally the same month
in which he received his honorary doctorate. The review was rejected
as too conservative for the progressive journal *Tikkun*, but was received
readily by the neoconservative journal *Commentary*; it was later included in the much-awaited second edition of *After Auschwitz*, published in 1992.[12]

After showing an initial sign of respect in his introductory remarks,
Rubenstein's review is relentlessly critical. Though he affirms my integrity and right to speak as a Jew, Rubenstein sees my theological position as too involved in Christian theologies of liberation and my
political position as possibly endangering the state of Israel. My own
sense is that Rubenstein, in arguing from the perspective of his own
generation and journey, simply missed the point that he himself had
originally made—that after Auschwitz the world is shrouded in darkness, that the Jewish experience of Holocaust is a paradigm for the future
of other peoples, and that the prevention of such events is of paramount importance. Had he not written so prophetically of the future
from which my students emerged, a future I had witnessed through
them?

There is always the danger that Metropolis will become Necropolis. The
city is by nature antinature, antiphysis, and hence, antilife. The world of
the city, *our world*, is the world of human invention and power; it is also
the world of artifice, dreams, charades, and the paper promises we call
money. But even the richest and most powerful city can only survive as
long as the umbilical cord to the countryside is not cut. Whenever men
build cities, they take the chance that their nurturing lifeline to the countryside may someday be severed, as indeed it was in wartime Poland.

One of the most frightful images of the death of civilization envisages a time when the city, deprived of the countryside's surplus food and bloated by the countryside's surplus people, feeds upon its own ever-diminishing self and finally collapses. The starving inmates of Auschwitz, consuming their own substance until they wasted away into nothingness, may offer a prophetic image of urban civilization at the end of its journey from the countryside to Necropolis. Could it be that as the Jews were among the countryside's first exiles and among the pioneer inhabitants of Metropolis, so too they were among the first citizens of Necropolis, but that, unless current economic, social and demographic trends are somehow reversed, there will be other citizens of the city of the dead, many others?[13]

We had parted company less in our concerns than in the paths we chose to take—his neoconservative; my own, at least in his mind, leftist and radical. Yet it is important to me to separate Rubenstein as my teacher and Rubenstein as critic of my work. For along with others, Rubenstein was part of a generation—courageous, outspoken, and defiant—that attempted to be faithful to the experience of Auschwitz. For two days I carried his bag full of cameras and books around Auschwitz as his student, listening to his commentary, understanding that these times together would soon come to an end. I, along with others of my generation, would soon be on our own; for the generation forged at Auschwitz is giving way to a new generation, one that champions and dissents, most often superficially and occasionally with depth. Would we one day, like Rubenstein, find ourselves in the unexpected role as guardians of a tradition we challenged and thereby helped to create? The creation is, of course, not nearly as easy as the critique; nor is living at the end when others are celebrating a rebirth. But what could one hope for after Auschwitz and 1492, except to end those events, thus holding out the promise of a new and unpredictable beginning.

Notes

Chapter I: Preparing for Auschwitz

1. The first meeting of this group took place at Yarnton Manor, Oxford, England, on May 6–8, 1990, in response to a commission established in the fall of 1989 by the Polish prime minister, Tadeusz Mazowiecki, to consider the future of the museum and monuments at Auschwitz. I was invited to this first meeting but due to prior commitments was unable to attend. The invitation I received in the summer of 1991 was for the second meeting, to be held April 6–9, 1992, at Krakow and Auschwitz. The first meeting led to a series of general principles and concrete suggestions that were released to the press on May 8, 1990, under the title "The Yarnton Declaration of Jewish Intellectuals on the Future of Auschwitz."

2. A good overview of the contemporary problems associated with Auschwitz can be found in Jonathan Webber, "The Future of Auschwitz: Some Personal Reflections," Frank Green Lecture Series, published by the Oxford Centre for Postgraduate Hebrew Studies, Oxford, England, 1992.

3. Eliezer Berkovits, a Jewish theologian, expressed the drama and fear of the days leading up to the 1967 war in the foreword to his book *Faith After the Holocaust* (New York: KTAV, 1973) when he wrote: "The main thesis of this volume was worked out during the critical weeks that led up to the Six-Day War between Israel and the Arab nations, and was completed during those drama-filled six days: the last word of its heart was written practically when the last shot was fired in that war. It was written under almost unbearable tension, and against darkest fears and anxieties. The threat of another holocaust was hanging over Jewish people. This destruction would have been final for all Israel the

142

world over, and not only for the Jewish people in Israel. Our generation could not have survived another holocaust and, certainly, not this one"(1).

4. Rubenstein details his journey in his book *Power Struggle: An Autobiographical Confession* (New York: Charles Scribner's Sons, 1974). See also his *After Auschwitz: Radical Theology and Contemporary Judaism* (Indianapolis: Bobbs-Merrill, 1966) and *My Brother Paul* (New York: Harper & Row, 1972).

5. Rubenstein's understanding of God at the time I was a student of his revolved around the theology of the sixteenth-century Jewish Kabbalah scholar Isaac Lucia and is reflected in a passage from Rubenstein's review of Arthur Cohen's *The Natural and the Supernatural Jew*. Rubenstein writes: "*Death is the Messiah. Death is the perfection and completion of life. Life is a system of needs. A system of needs is a want of perfection, whether in God or man. One can perfect a system of needs only through ending need. . . . Death abolishes the needs and instabilities of the organism.*" For Rubenstein, this death leads to the consummation of individuality and history, which can "only be a return of all things to God's Nothingness." See Rubenstein, *Auschwitz*, 184.

6. We read James Cone, *Black Theology and Black Power* (New York: Seabury Press, 1969). William Miller's book on the Catholic Worker deeply influenced me. See Miller, *A Harsh and Dreadful Love: Dorothy Day and the Catholic Worker Movement* (New York: Liveright, 1973).

7. My experiences at the Catholic Worker are related in my first book, *A Year at the Catholic Worker* (New York: Paulist Press, 1978).

8. My first essay on the subject of a Jewish theology of liberation was published under the title "Notes Toward a Jewish Theology of Liberation," in *Doing Theology in the United States in Dialogue with the Indigenous Nations and Traditional Peoples* 1 (Spring/Summer 1985): 5–17. The entire issue revolved around my essay, with responses by Robert McAfee Brown, J. Deotis Roberts, Franklin Woo, Ada María Isasi-Díaz, Rosemary Maxey, and Rafael Cetala. Those responses encouraged me to expand this essay into the book *Toward a Jewish Theology of Liberation* (Maryknoll, N.Y.: Orbis Books, 1987), which was also published by Orbis in a second, expanded edition in 1989 under the title *Toward a Jewish Theology of Liberation: The Uprising and the Future*. The following year I published *Beyond Innocence and Redemption: Confronting the Holocaust and Israeli Power* (San Francisco: HarperCollins, 1990).

Chapter 2: Auschwitz, Israel, and the End of Jewish Innocence

1. See Jonathan Webber, "The Future of Auschwitz: Some Personal Reflections," Frank Green Lecture Series, published by the Oxford Centre for Postgraduate Hebrew Studies, Oxford, England, 1992, 5–6.

2. In "The Krakow Proposals," which evolved from our meeting and were released to the press on April 10, 1992, the question of encouraging visitors to go to Auschwitz-Birkenau was left essentially unresolved. However, problems with the continued deterioration of the physical condition of the Birkenau site were highlighted. Citing the need for substantial funding and sophisticated

techniques of preservation, the proposals suggest, among other things, apply-
ing to UNESCO to help fund and protect the site, a moratorium on the removal
of objects from the jurisdiction of the Auschwitz state museum, and a prohibition against film crews using the site. In relation to the latter issue, see "Jews
Try to Halt Auschwitz Filming: Group Protests Use of Camp for a Movie by
Spielberg," *New York Times*, January 17, 1993. For a review of some of the issues
relating to our discussions at Auschwitz, see James Young, "The Future of
Auschwitz," *Tikkun* 7 (November/December 1992): 31–32, 77. Young was a
member of our delegation.

3. David Roskies, *Against the Apocalypse: Responses to Catastrophe in Modern
Jewish Culture* (Cambridge: Harvard University Press, 1984); Alvin Rosenfeld, *A
Double Dying: Reflections on Holocaust Literature* (Bloomington: Indiana University Press, 1980); Richard Rubenstein, *After Auschwitz: Radical Theology and Contemporary Judaism* (Indianapolis: Bobbs-Merrill, 1966).

4. For an interesting exchange on the question of how distance from the
Holocaust has changed perspectives on it, see the essays of Philip Lopate, "Resistance to the Holocaust," Yehuda Bauer, "Don't Resist," and Deborah Lip-
stadt, "What Is the Meaning of This to You?" as well as Lopate's response in
Tikkun 4 (May/June 1989): 55–70.

5. David Rousset, *The Other Kingdom*, trans. Ramon Guthrie (New York:
Reynal and Hitchcock, 1947); Bruno Bettelheim, *The Informed Heart: Autonomy in
a Mass Age* (New York: Free Press, 1960); Victor Frankl, *Man's Search for Meaning* (Boston: Beacon Press, 1959); Hannah Arendt, *The Origins of Totalitarianism*
(New York: Harcourt, Brace & Co., 1951); idem, *Eichmann in Jerusalem: A Report
on the Banality of Evil* (New York: Viking Press, 1963). This opening of Jewish
suffering to the world was controversial from the beginning. For the controversy regarding Hannah Arendt, see a collection of her essays and responses to
her work in Ron H. Feldman, ed., *The Jew as Pariah: Jewish Identity and Politics in
the Modern Age* (New York: Grove Press, 1978), 225–79.

6. Abraham Joshua Heschel, *Man Is Not Alone: A Philosophy of Religion* (New
York: Farrar, Straus & Giroux, 1951); idem, *God in Search of Man: A Philosophy of
Judaism* (New York: Farrar, Straus & Giroux, 1955).

7. Rubenstein, *Auschwitz*, ix–x. For an interesting discussion of Heschel, see
Rubenstein, *Power Struggle: An Autobiographical Confession* (New York: Charles
Scribner's Sons, 1974), 72–73, 125–28.

8. Rubenstein makes this point in a response to Harvey Cox's *The Secular
City*, which he titles "Judaism and 'The Secular City'": "Cox," writes Rubenstein, "is deeply influenced by Dietrich Bonhoeffer's question of April 30, 1944,
'. . . how do we speak of God without religion?' As I have suggested, I believe
the real question should be *not how we speak of God without religion, but how we
speak of religion in the time of the death of God.* . . . What the death of God theologians depict is an indubitable *cultural fact* in our times: God is totally unavailable as a source of meaning or value." See Rubenstein, *Auschwitz*, 205.

9. On the subject of Jewish powerlessness, see Richard Rubenstein, *The Cunning of History: Mass Death and the American Future* (New York: Harper & Row,
1975), 68–77.

10. Rubenstein, *Auschwitz*, 13.

11. Elie Wiesel, "Talking and Writing and Keeping Silent," in John K. Roth and Michael Berenbaum, eds., *Holocaust: Religious and Philosophical Implications* (New York: Paragon House, 1989), 364.

12. Ibid., 367.

13. Richard Rubenstein, "Some Perspectives on Religious Faith After Auschwitz," in ibid., 361, 356. On the issue of escalating the cost of Jewish lives, Rubenstein is clear: "For years there have been persistent rumors of Israeli nuclear weapons. . . . Faced with the destruction of the only political entity they can trust to defend their existence and dignity, the state of Israel, they would unleash their bombs on Cairo, Alexandria, Amman and Damascus in the certain knowledge that the extinction of Haifa, Tel Aviv and Jerusalem would swiftly follow. Should the Israelis become convinced that once again the world will consent to the extermination of Jews . . . [the] Israelis will not depart from history alone." See Rubenstein, *Power*, 193. For Rubenstein's discussion of Israel after the 1967 war, see "Homeland and Holocaust: Issues in the Jewish Religious Situation," in Donald Cutler, ed., *The Religious Situation, 1968* (Boston: Beacon Press, 1968), 39–64. Also see the responses of Milton Himmelfarb, Zalman Schachter, Arthur Cohen, and Irving Greenberg in ibid., 64–111.

14. Wiesel, *"Talking,"* in Roth and Berenbaum, eds., *Holocaust*, 369, 364. For Wiesel's sense of this miracle, including the innocence of the Israeli soldiers, see Wiesel, "A Moral Victory," in Irving Abrahamson, ed., *Against Silence: The Voice and Vision of Elie Wiesel*, vol. 2 (New York: Holocaust Library, 1985), 187.

15. "The Krakow Proposals," 1–5. Also see Young, "Future."

16. For Jewish Israeli historians analyzing the founding of Israel, see Benny Morris, *The Birth of the Palestinian Refugee Problem, 1947–1949* (Cambridge: Cambridge University Press, 1987); Tom Segev, *1949: The First Israelis* (New York: Free Press, 1986).

17. On the Holocaust and unaccountability, see Boaz Evron, "The Holocaust: Learning the Wrong Lessons," *Journal of Palestine Studies* 10 (Spring 1981): 16–26.

18. Ari Shavit, "On Gaza Beach," *New York Review of Books* 38 (July 18, 1991): 10. Referring to the torture of a Palestinian prisoner whose screams he heard, Shavit continues: "And now, as the screams grow weaker, as they change to a kind of sobbing, wailing, you know that from this moment on nothing will ever again be as it was. Because a person who has heard the screams of another person being tortured is already a different person. Whether he does anything about it or not, a person who has heard the screams of another person being tortured incurs an obligation" (p. 11). For a detailed discussion of torture in Israel, see Stanley Cohen, "Talking About Torture in Israel," *Tikkun* 6 (November/December 1991): 23–30, 89–90.

19. Jacobo Timerman, *The Longest War: Israel in Lebanon*, trans. Ina Friedman (New York: Simon & Schuster, 1984), 7.

20. Quoted in *Ha'aretz*, August 11, 1982.

21. Segev, *1949*, 88–89.

22. Ibid., 89. Segev reports that the eventual resettlement of Deir Yassin with Jewish Israelis and with the new name Givat Shaul Bet caused little or no embarrassment. "Several hundred guests came to the opening ceremony,

including Ministers Kaplan and Shapira, as well as the Chief Rabbi and the Mayor of Jerusalem. President Haim Weizmann sent written congratulations. The band of the school for the blind played and refreshments were served" (89–90).

23. For a discussion of the reversal of Israel as functioning for American Jewry, see John Murray Cuddihy, *No Offense: Civil Religion and Protestant Taste* (New York: Seabury Press, 1978), 101–56.

24. John Murray Cuddihy, "The Elephant and the Angels: or, The Incivil Irritatingness of Jewish Theodicy," in Robert Bellah and Frederick Greenspahn, eds., *Uncivil Religion: Interreligious Hostility in America* (New York: Crossroad, 1987), 28.

25. Ibid., 25, 26. Cuddihy continues: "And yet the New York pundit and critic John Leonard announces, 'If we stop reading [Wiesel]—if we stop listening—we will lose our souls'"(26). For an extended discussion of how the Holocaust is carrier of increased status for Jews, see John Murray Cuddihy, "The Holocaust: The Latent Issue in the Uniqueness Debate," in Philip Gallagher, ed., *Christians, Jews, and Other Worlds: Patterns of Conflict and Accommodation* (Lanham, Md.: University Press of America, 1988), 62–79.

Chapter 3: Auschwitz and Palestine in the Jewish Imagination

1. From the book by Tom Segev, *The Seventh Million: The Israelis and the Holocaust*, trans. Haim Wotzman (New York: Hill & Wang, 1993), 488. For Segev, the inability to deal with the Holocaust except in emotional terms is related to the "demonization of Nazi evil [which] frees the textbooks of the need to explain Nazi crimes and, most importantly, it frees them of the need to face the possibility that this horror was born in a normal human environment."

2. Joan Ringelheim, "Women and the Holocaust," *The Jewish Quarterly* 39 (Autumn 1992): 19, 20. For the importance of connections during the Holocaust, see Helen Fein, *Accounting for Genocide: National Responses and Jewish Victimization During the Holocaust* (Chicago: University of Chicago Press, 1984).

3. Henry Schwarzschild, "On Withdrawing from Sh'ma," *Sh'ma*, September 6, 1982, 159.

4. Ibid. Schwarzschild continues, "The price of the millennial survival of the Jewish people has been high; I do not think the point was to make others pay it."

5. Gadi Gofbarg, "Divorcing Zionism," unpublished essay (ND).

6. Ibid.

7. Michael Lerner, "The Occupation: Immoral and Stupid," *Tikkun* 3 (March/April 1988): 7; idem, "Israel's Choice: Either Transfer a Million Palestinians or Get Out of Gaza," *Tikkun* 8 (January/February 1993): 7.

8. Amos Oz, "Off the Reservation," in Haim Chertok, *We Are All Close: Conversations with Israeli Writers* (New York: Fordham University Press, 1989), 161. For his dissent in the Lebanon War, see idem, *The Slopes of Lebanon*, trans. Maurie Goldberg-Bartura (New York: Harcourt Brace Jovanovich, 1989).

9. A. B. Yehoshua, *Between Right and Right: Israel, Problem or Solution?* (Garden City, N.Y.: Doubleday & Co., 1981), 8. Also see idem, "No Autonomy Without Civil Rights," *Yediot Ahronot* (April 21, 1991), in which Yehoshua writes: "There cannot be permanent autonomy without full civil rights for all the people living in the autonomous region. And those who think they can avoid paying this price are fooling themselves, in the same way that after the Six Day War people naively asked: Are there Palestinians?"

10. Yehoshua, *Between Right and Right,* 9.

11. For an analysis of the biblical literature, see Abraham Halkin, "Zion in Biblical Literature," in Abraham Halkin, ed., *Zion in Jewish Literature* (New York: Herzl Press, 1961), 18–37. For an analysis of the rabbinic literature, see Gerson Cohen, "Zion in Rabbinic Literature," in ibid., 38–64.

12. Tudor Parfitt, *The Jews in Palestine, 1800–1882* (London: Boydell Press, 1991).

13. For an extended discussion of the Jewish bi-nationalist idea in Palestine, see Susan Lee Hattis, *The Bi-national Idea in Palestine During the Mandatory Times* (Haifa: Shikmona, 1970). It is important to note that even those who abandoned the bi-nationalist idea did so from a solely Jewish perspective. See Hans Kohn's letter to Berthold Feiwei and copied to Martin Buber, written in Jerusalem on November 21, 1929, in Paul Mendes-Flohr, ed., *A Land of Two Peoples: Martin Buber on Jews and Arabs* (Oxford: Oxford University Press, 1983), 97–100.

14. Arthur A. Goren, ed., *Dissenter in Zion: From the Writings of Judah L. Magnes* (Cambridge: Harvard University Press, 1982), 276.

15. Ibid.

16. Ibid., 279.

17. Ibid. An extended analysis of these views can be found in Judah L. Magnes, *Like All the Nations?* (Jerusalem, 1930).

18. Ibid., 389–98.

19. Ibid., 389–90.

20. Ibid., 393.

21. Ibid., 393–94.

22. Ibid., 397. Also see M. Buber, J. L. Magnes, and E. Simon, eds., *Towards Union in Palestine: Essays on Zionism and Jewish-Arab Cooperation* (Jerusalem: IHUD, 1947).

23. Ibid., 492, 493. In June 1948, Magnes responded to the unfolding developments in the Middle East, which included the declaration of Israeli statehood, by drafting a detailed plan titled "United States of Palestine: A Confederation of Two Independent States." Here he outlined the structures of a political union with particular reference to foreign affairs, defense, international loans, federal courts, and the protection of religious shrines, historical monuments, and collections of cultural, artistic, and scientific importance. It is interesting to note that this plan was published in the October 1948 issue of *Commentary* as a response to Major Abba Eban's article in the September *Commentary* criticizing the discussion of Palestine as put forth by bi-nationalists. Of course, Abba Eban was at this moment taking his place as the authentic and progressive Jewish spokesperson on the issue of Israel and the Middle East, a place he has reserved until the present. By the time this letter to the editor was published, Magnes

had died, and the U.N. representative for whom Magnes had argued, Count Bernadotte, had been assassinated by Jewish terrorists. Magnes praised Bernadotte as the person "who had come closer than any other man to bringing Jews and Arabs to an understanding" and lamented his murder "as a tragedy of historical importance for both peoples." See ibid., 511–18.

24. With regard to a Western colonial vision, Martin Buber can also be cited. See Buber's letter to Mohandas Gandhi written from Jerusalem on February 24, 1939, in which he argues that what appears to be a colonial venture really is not one. To prove this point, Buber cites the lack of productivity in Arab agriculture compared to Jewish productivity. Buber writes: "Ask the soil what the Arabs have done for her in 1300 years and what we have done for her in 50! Would her answer not be weighty testimony in a just discussion as to whom this land 'belongs'?" See Mendes-Flohr, ed., *A Land of Two Peoples*, 122. Obviously, Magnes, Buber, and Arendt were participating in what Edward Said has termed orientalism, an issue that deserves serious analysis. See Edward Said, *Orientalism* (New York: Random House, 1978).

25. Amos Elon, *Jerusalem: City of Mirrors* (Boston: Little, Brown & Co., 1989); Avishai Margalit, "The Myth of Jerusalem," *New York Review of Books* 38 (December 19, 1991): 61–66; Yehoshafat Harkabi, *Israel's Fateful Hour* (New York: Harper & Row, 1988); Mark Heller and Sari Nusseibeh, *No Trumpets, No Drums: A Two-State Settlement of the Israeli-Palestinian Conflict* (New York: Hill & Wang, 1991). Heller fulfills the analysis of Edward Said when Said cites the paradox of Jews arguing and internalizing Orientalist positions with the backing of Western and Israeli state power. See Said, *Orientalism*, 306–12. Contrast the above with Hannah Arendt, "To Save the Jewish Homeland: There Is Still Time," in Ron Feldman, ed., *Hannah Arendt: The Jew as Pariah* (New York: Grove Press, 1978), 178–92, and Muhammed Hallaj, "The Palestinian Dream: The Democratic Secular State," in Rosemary Radford Ruether and Marc H. Ellis, eds., *Beyond Occupation: American Jewish, Christian, and Palestinian Voices for Peace* (Boston: Beacon Press, 1990), 222–30.

26. Robert Fisk, "Arafat's Road to Gaza Is Graveyard of the Palestinians," *The Independent*, September 6, 1993.

27. Maxim Ghilan, "Accounting," *Israel and Palestine Political Report*, no. 185 (September 1993): 3, 4. Palestinian-American Professor Edward Said seems to agree with this sentiment when he writes: "The 'historical breakthrough' announced recently by the PLO and the Israeli government is a joint decision to signal a new phase of reconciliation between two enemies, but it also leaves Palestinians very much the subordinates, with Israel still in charge of East Jerusalem, settlements, sovereignty and the economy" (Edward Said, "Arafat's Deal," *The Nation* 257 [September 20, 1993]: 269–70). Uri Avnery, the Israeli peace activist, takes a more optimistic approach: "I do not wish to belittle the concessions made, the matters postponed, the conditions accepted. This is an historic compromise, the beginning of the end of an 111-year-old conflict, into which a fifth generation has been born on both sides. But if one views the achievement without ideological blinders, one sees its greatness. . . . Old ideas, old slogans, old dogmas have to be reexamined so that we can continue the effective struggle until the state of Palestine will take its place alongside the state of Israel, in a new united Middle East" (Uri Avnery, "A Giant Step," *Israel and Palestine Political Report*, no. 185 [September 1993]: 19).

Chapter 4: Jews and Christians after Auschwitz

1. The following chronology of events is summarized in Carol Rittner and John K. Roth, *Memory Offended: The Auschwitz Convent Controversy* (New York: Frederick A. Praeger, 1991), 1–26.

2. Joseph Glemp, "We Trust in the Capital of Wisdom," in ibid., 224, 222–23.

3. For Shamir's comments, see ibid., 6. For an interesting account of the entire controversy from a Jewish Polish perspective, see Stanislaw Krajewski, "The Controversy Over Carmel at Auschwitz: A Personal Polish-Jewish Chronology," in ibid., 117–33.

4. Jonathan Webber, "The Future of Auschwitz: Some Personal Reflections," Frank Green Lecture Series, published by the Oxford Centre for Postgraduate Hebrew Studies, Oxford, England, 9. For a Polish Catholic interpretation of the meaning of Auschwitz for the Polish people, see Wladyslaw Bartoszewski, *The Convent at Auschwitz* (New York: George Braziller, 1991).

5. See Rittner and Roth, *Memory*, 20.

6. Richard Rubenstein, "The Convent at Auschwitz and the Imperatives of Pluralism in the Global Electronic Village," in ibid., 42, 43.

7. Elie Wiesel, "An Interview, August 29, 1989," in ibid., 115. To the question of whether he would support the establishment of a synagogue at Auschwitz, Wiesel replied, "I am against it. No religion should build religious institutions at Auschwitz" (114).

8. Elie Wiesel, "Your Place Is with the Victims," in Ilya Levkov, *Bitburg and Beyond: Encounters in American, German and Jewish History* (New York: Shapolsky Publishers, 1987), 44.

9. See Mary Jo Leddy, "Auschwitz: Where Only Silence Becomes Prayer," in Rittner and Roth, *Memory*, 169–76. Leddy writes: "I respect the Jewish view that we should not attempt to give any meaning, Christian or Jewish, to what happened at Auschwitz. It is a place that has become a black hole of meaning, a hole of oblivion for human faith and understanding" (175).

10. This journey culminated in 1988 when I organized a seminar featuring liberation theologians from around the world. From that seminar I edited with Otto Maduro *The Future of Liberation Theology: Essays in Honor of Gustavo Gutiérrez* (Maryknoll, N.Y.: Orbis Books, 1989).

11. For a book-length treatment of the voyages of Columbus and their consequences, see Kirkpatrick Sale, *The Conquest of Paradise: Christopher Columbus and the Columbian Legacy* (New York: Penguin Books, 1991). Also see David Stannard, *American Holocaust: Columbus and the Conquest of the New World* (Oxford: Oxford University Press, 1992).

12. James Cone, *A Black Theology of Liberation: Twentieth Anniversary Edition* (Maryknoll, N.Y.: Orbis Books, 1990), 80; Krajewski, "Controversy" in Rittner and Roth, *Memory*, 121.

13. Stephen DeMott, "It's a Form of Genocide," *Maryknoll Magazine* 79 (March 1985): 20–21. I remember during the semester he was taking my course that Brother Marty traveled several hours by car to hear Elie Wiesel speak. He was profoundly influenced by Wiesel's book *Night*, which I had assigned.

14. Martin Shea, "Christmas Came Late," *Maryknoll Magazine* 87 (July/August 1993): 38–43.

15. Roy Bourgeois, "School of Terror," *Channel: A Newsletter for Missioners in Latin America* (January 1993): 7. Also see "Open Letter to Bill Clinton," *Maryknoll Magazine* 87 (July/August 1993): 34–36.

16. John Paul II, "The Almighty Has Done Great Things," *L'Osservatore Romano*, October 21, 1992, 1.

17. John Paul II, "Forgive All Who Wronged You," ibid.; John Paul II, "Spread This Message of Peace and Love," ibid.

18. Irving Greenberg, "Cloud of Smoke, Pillar of Fire: Judaism, Christianity and Modernity After the Holocaust," in Eva Fleischner, ed., *Auschwitz: Beginning of a New Era?* (New York: KTAV, 1977), 23.

19. Raul Hilberg, *The Destruction of the European Jews* (New York: Harper & Row, 1961), 3–4. See also his discussion of Luther in ibid., 9.

20. Sale, *Conquest*, 127.

21. Ibid., 189.

22. Ibid., 124.

23. Richard Rubenstein, *After Auschwitz: Radical Theology and Contemporary Judaism* (Indianapolis: Bobbs-Merrill, 1966), 19. Rubenstein writes: "*Nazism is the product of a negative reaction to the Judaeo-Christian world*. As much as the nineteenth and twentieth-century Teutonists wanted to rid themselves of Christianity, they were far more influenced by it than they imagined. In the end, the Nazis were able to *negate* Christianity and its values while using the Christian myth of Jewish villainy to their own purposes"(19).

24. Richard Rubenstein, *The Cunning of History: Mass Death and the American Future* (New York: Harper & Row, 1975), 29–30, 31.

25. Joseph Borkin, *The Crime and Punishment of I. G. Farben* (New York: Free Press, 1978), 118–19.

26. Ibid., 125, 121.

27. Ibid., 125.

28. Ibid., 119. For an equally troubling discussion of Christian ritual and counseling in relation to the commandant of Treblinka, Franz Stangl, see Gitta Sereny, *Into That Darkness: An Examination of Conscience* (New York: Vintage Press, 1974), 233–235.

29. For an extended discussion of Bonhoeffer's witness, see Eberhard Bethge, *Dietrich Bonhoeffer: Man of Vision, Man of Courage* (New York: Harper & Row, 1970).

30. For the continuation of Christendom, see Pablo Richard, *Death of Christendoms, Birth of the Church* (Maryknoll, N.Y.: Orbis Books, 1987). In an address on January 27, 1992, to the National Religious Broadcasters, a group of Christian radio and television station officials, President Bush commended the broadcasters for their support of the Gulf War. "I want to thank you for helping America, as Christ ordained, to be a light unto the world." See "In a Speech, President Returns to Religious Themes," *New York Times*, January 28, 1992. Of course, Bush did not discuss how the Western world, including America, delivered arms for profit to what later became the satanic state of Iraq. For an important discussion of this theme, see Kenneth Timmerman, *The Death Lobby: How the West Armed Iraq* (Boston: Houghton Mifflin, 1992).

31. For Jefferson's fascination with Jesus, see Stephen Mitchell, *The Gospel According to Jesus* (New York: HarperCollins, 1991), 3–5.

32. Rosemary Radford Ruether sees Calvinism as dismantling the sacramental cosmos of medieval Christianity while maintaining and reinforcing its "demonic universe. . . . Everything 'pagan' including Roman Catholics as well as unconverted Indians and Africans, was the playground of demonic powers." According to Ruether, those who carried the Gospel of Calvin became the primary witchhunters and the "major formulators of the new understanding of the patriarchal family as the key institution for both church and state." See Rosemary Radford Ruether, *Gaia and God: An Ecofeminist Theology of Earth Healing* (San Francisco: HarperCollins, 1992), 193.

33. Rosemary Radford Ruether, *Faith and Fratricide: The Theological Roots of Anti-Semitism* (New York: Seabury Press, 1974); Johann Baptist Metz, *The Emergent Church: The Future of Christianity in a Postbourgeois World*, trans. Peter Mann (New York: Crossroad, 1981), 19.

34. National Council of the Churches of Christ in the U.S.A., "A Faithful Response to the 500th Anniversary of the Arrival of Christopher Columbus," *Church and Society* 82 (January/February 1992): 111–12.

35. Ibid. Also see the 1990 statement by the Presbyterian Church (U.S.A) in ibid., 109–110.

36. Mary Daly, *Beyond God the Father: Toward a Philosophy of Women's Liberation* (Boston: Beacon Press, 1973), 69, 93, 114–15. Also see idem, *Gyn/Ecology: The Metaethics of Radical Feminism* (Boston: Beacon Press, 1978); idem, *Pure Lust: Elemental Feminist Philosophy* (Boston: Beacon Press, 1984); and idem, *Outercourse: The Be-Dazzling Voyage* (San Francisco: HarperCollins, 1992).

37. Daly, *Beyond God the Father*, 73, 75, 73.

38. Ruether, *Gaia*, 10. Also see Daly, *Outercourse*, especially with regard to her trips to Ireland, 65–66, 280–84, 347–55, 358–71, 378–79, 402–3. For Ruether's discussion of Daly, see *Gaia*, 147–48, 171. Also see a critique of Daly from an African-American perspective found in Audre Lorde, *Sister Outsider* (Freedom, Calif.: The Crossing Press, 1984), 66–71.

Chapter 5: Auschwitz and the Brokerless Kingdom of God

1. Herbert Edwards, "Black Theology and Liberation Theology," in Sergio Torres and John Eagleson, eds., *Theology in the Americas* (Maryknoll, N.Y.: Orbis Books, 1976), 190. This solidarity of dominant Christians and Jews in the West was recognized years ago by those who raised the question of black liberation. The Black Manifesto presented by James Forman at the Riverside Church, New York City, on May 4, 1969, specifically links "white Christian churches and Jewish synagogues" to the capitalist system that has exploited African-Americans; therefore both are obligated to "pay reparations to Black people in this country." See Gayraud Wilmore and James Cone, eds., *Black Theology: A Documentary History, 1966–1979* (Maryknoll, N.Y.: Orbis Books, 1979), 84. For my own analysis of some of the dynamics between the African-American and Jewish

community, see Marc H. Ellis, "Weak Jews/Tough Jews: A Jewish Reflection on Suffering, Empowerment and the Crisis of the Black Male," in Lawrence Carter, ed., *The Crisis of the Black Male* (Washington, D.C.: Beckham House, 1993), 200–245.

2. For an extended discussion of the ecumenical deal, see Marc H. Ellis, "Beyond the Ecumenical Dialogue: Jews, Christians and the Challenge of the Palestinian People," in Clark Williamson, ed., *A Mutual Witness: Toward Critical Solidarity Between Jews and Christians* (St. Louis: Chalice Press, 1992), 83–118. For a fascinating discussion from a Latin American perspective on how Christians and Jews might move beyond their mutual understanding of innocence and redemption, see Pablo Richard, "Jewish and Christian Liberation Theology," in Otto Maduro, ed., *Judaism, Christianity and Liberation: An Agenda for Dialogue* (Maryknoll, N.Y.: Orbis Books, 1991), 33–39. Also in the same volume, see Julio de Santa Ana, "The Holocaust and Liberation," 40–54, and my concluding remarks, "Postscript: Jews, Christians and Liberation Theology: A Response," 141–50. For a Palestinian Christian perspective of the ecumenical deal, see Naim Ateek, Marc H. Ellis, and Rosemary Radford Ruether, eds., *Faith and the Intifada: Palestinian Christian Voices* (Maryknoll, N.Y.: Orbis Books, 1992).

3. For a discussion of Christian mission to the Jews and the continuing evangelization of large areas of the globe, see Eugene Fisher, "Is There a Christian Mission to the Jews? A Catholic Response," in Williamson, ed., *Witness*, 15–32. Also see my response on pp. 51–55 and a further response by an African-American attending the conference on 55–56.

4. Paula Fredriksen, *From Jesus to Christ: The Origins of the New Testament Images of Jesus* (New Haven: Yale University Press, 1988), 212.

5. Arthur Green, *Seek My Face, Speak My Name: A Contemporary Jewish Theology* (Northvale, N.J.: Jason Aronson, 1992). In relation to Jewish renewal, see also Sara Bershtel and Allen Graubard, *Saving Remnants: Feeling Jewish in America* (New York: Free Press, 1992) and a review of that book by the leading proponent of Jewish renewal, Arthur Waskow, "Sewing Jewish Remnants into a New Tallit," *Tikkun* 7 (March/April 1992): 69–74.

6. For a succinct statement of the "rules" of the ecumenical dialogue, see Leonard Swidler, "The Dialogical Decalogue," *Journal of Ecumenical Studies* 20 (Winter 1983): 15–18.

7. Fritz Rothschild, ed., *Jewish Perspectives on Christianity* (New York: Crossroad, 1990), 15, 16; Richard Rubenstein, *My Brother Paul* (New York: Harper & Row, 1972).

8. For Heschel's essays, see Rothschild, ed., *Perspectives*, 283–300, 325–40. For Herberg's essay, see ibid., 256–66. As Rothschild points out, not all of the public affirmation of Christianity made by these authors reflected their private opinions. See ibid., 10–11.

9. Will Herberg, "A Jew Looks at Jesus," in ibid., 256–57.

10. Ibid., 257–258.

11. Ibid., 262.

12. "God's Unbroken Covenant with the Jews," *New Conversations* 12 (Summer 1990): 9.

13. Ibid., 7, 5.

14. For a fascinating discussion on the discourse of unification of the Jewish-Christian establishment and the hidden questions within it, see John Murray Cuddihy, *No Offense: Civil Religion and Protestant Taste* (New York: Seabury Press, 1978).

15. Jaroslav Pelikan, *Jesus Through the Centuries: His Place in the History of Culture* (New Haven: Yale University Press, 1985).

16. Ibid., 232.

17. Fredriksen, *Jesus*, 18–61.

18. Ibid., 211.

19. Ibid.

20. Ibid., 125, 108, 130. For a variety of perspectives on the Jewishness of Jesus, see James H. Charlesworth, ed., *Jesus' Jewishness: Exploring the Place of Jesus Within Early Judaism* (New York: Crossroad, 1991).

21. Ibid., 213–214; Robert M. Grant, *Augustus to Constantine: The Rise and Triumph of Christianity in the Roman World* (San Francisco: Harper & Row, 1990), 249. As Grant points out, the Gospel of Constantine was rigorous as Constantine "proceeded to treat heretics just as his predecessors had treated Christians. . . . He spoke of the poison, the pollution, and the disease produced by Novatianists, Valentinians (Gnostics), Marionites, Paulianists (followers of Paul of Samosata), and Cataphrygians (Montanists), and forbade their assemblies. All public meeting houses were to be surrendered to the Catholic Church, while private houses used for meetings were to be confiscated by the state" (249). See also Averil Cameron, *Christianity and the Rhetoric of Empire: The Development of Christian Discourse* (Berkeley: University of California Press, 1991) 125.

22. Wayne Meeks, *The First Urban Christians: The Social World of the Apostle Paul* (New Haven: Yale University Press, 1983), 9, 15.

23. John Dominic Crossan, *The Historical Jesus: The Life of a Mediterranean Jewish Peasant* (San Francisco: HarperCollins, 1991), 421–22. Also see E. P. Sanders, *Jesus and Judaism* (Philadelphia: Fortress Press, 1985).

24. Ibid., 420–21.

25. Ibid., 422. Other works that help probe the Judaism and the world Jesus was born into include Martin Hengel, *Judaism and Hellenism: Studies in Their Encounter in Palestine During the Early Hellenistic Period* (Minneapolis: Fortress Press, 1974), and Richard Horsley and John Hanson, *Bandits, Prophets and Messiahs: Popular Movements in the Time of Jesus* (Minneapolis: Winston Press, 1985).

26. Ibid., 420–21. Crossan walks a fine line with reference to Jesus and the Church. He points out that the ultimate betrayal of Jesus was the movement from Christ to Constantine, but finds "no contradiction between the historical Jesus and the defined Christ, no betrayal whatsoever in the move from Jesus to Christ." See Crossan, *Jesus*, 424. To me, Crossan's entire book undermines the movement toward both Christ and Constantine.

27. My other teachers in the religious studies department also participated in this education, especially Leo Sandon, Lawrence Cunningham, and Charles Swain.

28. This story is related in Rubenstein, *Paul*, 1–22.

29. Ibid., 6.

30. Ibid., 20.

31. Ibid., 4.

32. Ibid., 22.

33. For a fascinating study of provocative Jewish thinkers that helps place the work of Rubenstein in a broader perspective, see Susan Handelman, *The Slayers of Moses: The Emergence of Rabbinic Interpretation in Modern Literary Theory* (Albany: State University of New York Press, 1982).

34. Crossan, *Jesus*, 341.

Chapter 6: State Religion and the New Discipline

1. For a fascinating discussion of religion, production, and consumption, see Otto Maduro, *Religion and Social Conflicts* (Maryknoll, N.Y.: Orbis Books, 1982), 85–105.

2. Christopher Lasch, *The Culture of Narcissism: American Life in an Age of Diminishing Expectations* (New York: W. W. Norton, 1978).

3. If the foreign quality of Christianity may be difficult for the foreigner, it is often fatal for the indigenous people. As Tony Swain, an Australian anthropologist has argued, an invasion of an idea may be as devastating as a military invasion, in this case, the idea of Christian love. Swain writes: "I am going to suggest that genocide was replaced by an idea which might yet have the effect of destroying the genius of Aboriginal cultures. And that idea is the Christian concept of love" (68). See Tony Swain, "Love and Other Bullets," *Religious Traditions: A Journal in the Study of Religion* 13 (1990): 68–87.

4. Jacob Neusner, *Judaism in the Matrix of Christianity* (Philadelphia: Fortress Press, 1986), xii, ii.

5. For Neusner's discussion of socialism and Yiddishism, see his *Death and Birth of Judaism: The Impact of Christianity, Secularism, and the Holocaust on Jewish Faith* (New York: Basic Books, 1987), 198–224.

6. Ibid., 341–42.

7. Ibid., 340.

8. Ibid., 19–20.

9. See Walter Benjamin's essay "Thesis of a Philosophy of History," in Walter Benjamin, *Illuminations*, ed. Hannah Arendt (New York: Schocken Books, 1969), 253–64. For my discussion of this tradition historically and in the present, see Marc H. Ellis, *Beyond Innocence and Redemption: Confronting the Holocaust and Israeli Power* (San Francisco: HarperCollins, 1990), 157–90.

10. For a recent and typical discussion of the prophets without the critique that follows in my analysis, see Daniel Maguire, *The Moral Core of Judaism and Christianity: Reclaiming the Revolution* (Minneapolis: Fortress Press, 1993), 166–93. My own sense is that we need to move beyond the recovery of the prophets and the moral core of Judaism and Christianity as innocent and revolutionary.

11. Susan Ackerman, *Under Every Green Tree: Popular Religion in Sixth-Century Judah* (Atlanta: Scholars Press, 1992), 37–100.

12. Ibid., 93–100, 99.

13. Ibid., 215, 213.

14. Ibid., 217, 215.

15. Ibid., 2.

16. Paula Fredriksen, *From Jesus to Christ: The Origins of the New Testament Images of Jesus* (New Haven: Yale University Press, 1988), 14.

17. Daniel Jeremy Silver, *Images of Moses* (New York: Basic Books, 1983), 53.

18. Ibid., 104–105, 116.

19. Fredriksen, *Jesus*, 16. Also see Wayne Meeks, *The First Urban Christians: The Social World of the Apostle Paul* (New Haven: Yale University Press, 1983), 37.

20. Daniel Silver comments in relation to the use of Chanukkah by the rabbis that with the Temple destroyed and the nation in exile "conventional rabbinic wisdom blamed the worldly way of the Hellenized generations for having earned for the whole community God's severe judgment. The nation had sinned when it had taken up worldly ways, with disastrous results. . . . The sermons routinely urged the faithful to reject the world of appearances, the world of passion and indulgence, including the world of art, theater and literature, in favor of God's world, the world of Torah." See Silver, *Moses*, 93–94.

21. Erwin R. Goodenough, *Jewish Symbols in the Greco-Roman Period*, ed. Jacob Neusner (Princeton: Princeton University Press, 1988), 254–255.

22. Ibid., 258.

23. Ibid., 259–60.

24. Ibid., 22. For Goodenough's analysis of the menorah and the shofar, see ibid., 79–82, 88–91.

25. Warren G. Moon, "Nudity and Narrative: Observations on the Frescoes from the Dura Synagogue," *Journal of the American Academy of Religion* LX (Winter 1992): 590–591; Goodenough, *Jewish Symbols*, xiii. For a collection of essays that deals in depth with Goodenough and the Dura-Europos synagogue, see Joseph Gutman, ed., *The Dura-Europos Synagogue: A Reevaluation, 1932–1992* (Atlanta: Scholars Press, 1992).

26. Goodenough, *Jewish Symbols*. For a detailed study of Christianity and paganism, see Robin Lane Fox, *Pagans and Christians* (San Francisco: HarperSanFrancisco, 1988).

27. Elisabeth Schüssler Fiorenza, *In Memory of Her: A Feminist Theological Reconstruction of Christian Origins* (New York: Crossroad, 1983), 41.

28. Ibid., 107, 133, 135, 138, 136.

29. For a Holocaust theologian's admonition to the rabbis for not realizing that the rabbinic framework has been overwhelmed, see Irving Greenberg, "The Third Great Cycle in Jewish History" (New York: National Jewish Resource Center, 1981), 19.

30. I have always argued that the Holocaust and Israel are the central realities of post-Auschwitz Jewish life. However, the understanding of this in relation to popular religiosity is crucial: legitimate concerns of Jews in relation to suffering and empowerment have too often been co-opted and thematised in connection with imperial power. Though the issue is, to say the least, difficult, this has been my main criticism of the work of Irving Greenberg. For an earlier critique of Greenberg, see Marc H. Ellis, *Beyond Innocence and Redemption:*

Confronting the Holocaust and Israeli Power (San Francisco: HarperCollins, 1990), 15–31.

31. Irving Greenberg, "Cloud of Smoke, Pillar of Fire: Judaism, Christianity and Modernity After the Holocaust," in Eva Fleischner, ed., *Auschwitz: Beginning of a New Era?* (New York: KTAV, 1977), 26, 27.

32. Ibid., 42–43.

Chapter 7: A Postcard from Auschwitz

1. Richard Rubenstein, *Power Struggle: An Autobiographical Confession* (New York: Charles Scribner & Sons, 1974), 162; idem, "Journey to Poland," *Judaism* 15 (Fall 1966): 480.

2. Elie Wiesel, *Night*, foreword by François Mauriac (New York: Hill & Wang, 1960); John Murray Cuddihy, *No Offense: Civil Religion and Protestant Taste* (New York: Seabury Press, 1978), 36.

3. Richard Fox, *Reinhold Niebuhr: A Biography* (San Francisco: HarperSanFrancisco, 1985), 293.

4. Harold Bloom and David Rosenberg, *The Book of J* (New York: Grove Weidenfeld, 1990), 319; Robin Morgan, *The Anatomy of Freedom: Feminism, Physics and Global Politics* (Garden City, N.Y.: Doubleday & Co., 1982), xvi. For an analysis of Leonard Cohen's work, see Leon Wieseltier, "The Prince of Bummers," *New Yorker* 69 (July 26, 1993): 40–45.

5. Irving Greenberg, "The Ethics of Jewish Power," *Perspectives* (New York: National Jewish Center for Learning and Leadership, 1988), 1–42. Nor can we hand on the anger of David Roskies when he writes sarcastically in relation to the use of Jesus on the cross by Jewish artists to symbolize Jewish suffering: "Not until the first decade of the twentieth century was the ancient taboo against portraying the Man on the Cross finally lifted—a real breakthrough." See David Roskies, *Against the Apocalypse: Responses to Catastrophe in Modern Jewish Culture* (Cambridge: Harvard University Press, 1984), 263.

6. Eliezer Berkovits, *Faith After the Holocaust* (New York: KTAV, 1973), 83, 84.

7. Roskies, *Apocalypse*, 212; Etty Hillesum, *Letters from Westerbork* (New York: Pantheon Books, 1986), 77.

8. Berkovits, *Faith*, 84, 85.

9. Gustavo Gutiérrez, *On Job: God-Talk and the Suffering of the Innocent* (Maryknoll, N.Y.: Orbis Books, 1987), 93.

10. James Cone, *Martin, Malcolm and America: A Dream or a Nightmare* (Maryknoll, N.Y.: Orbis Books, 1991), 316–17.

11. Rosemary Radford Ruether, *Gaia and God: An Ecofeminist Theology of Earth Healing* (San Francisco: HarperCollins, 1992), 273.

12. Richard Rubenstein, *After Auschwitz: History, Theology and Contemporary Judaism*, 2nd ed. (Baltimore: Johns Hopkins University Press, 1992), 266–80.

13. Richard Rubenstein, *The Cunning of History: Mass Death and the American Future* (New York: Harper & Row, 1975), 95.

Index